known.

What people are saying about...

known.

"There is nothing more important in the Christian life than building our sense of identity on the truth of who God says we are. Everything else flows from there. *Known* is a bit like a map that takes it's readers on a one year journey into embracing our identity in Christ more fully and more deeply. What an essential resource for any women wanting to walk more freely and more faithfully into knowing who we are in Him! A brilliantly helpful book..."

Rachel Hughes, Lead Pastor, Gas Street Church

"I found these readings were like a conversation with a friend, but at the same time like a springboard for a deep dive into scripture and into building my identity with God. If you're anything like me, becoming confident in my God-given identity is a lifelong process, and I can't think of any stage of my discipleship journey when this book wouldn't have been useful - in fact I wish it had accompanied me in many seasons that have past!"

Kath Johnson, New Wine national leadership team, Church and Community Mobilisation Lead, IJM UK, church leader.

We all long to be known. Our identity is the foundation for our beliefs and decisions and ultimately how we live our lives. Hils gives us such a beautiful, practical and challenging devotional to help us get closer to the ultimate source of knowing our identity in God. I have been, and you too, will be blessed by this book!

Julia Strachan, Author, World Record Atlantic rower and Anti-Slavery campaigner.

'It has been life-changing for me. If only I'd known about this years ago...'

Janice

This is the first book that's a devotional that I've read and I love it!

Marthina

I have found this a really transformational journey.

Judy

Hils explains Bible verses in a simple way revealing profound truths.

Amanda

This book is such a joy, challenge and encouragement. Exceptional wisdom.

Caroline

I'm finding this devotional incredibly powerful.

Jo

The words, encouragements and challenges have literally saved my life and guided me onto a new path. All the knowledge I had of God was in my head not in my heart.

Lyn

I cannot thank Hils enough for her amazing words and the difference it's making to me spiritually.

Rachel

It's truly inspiring. One theme spread out through a whole week gives an opportunity to be thorough. But then there is also breathing space again.

Annalise

Can I just say how perfect this book has been. I don't want it to end.

Jen

kn●wn.

BECOMING CONFIDENT IN THE TRUTH ABOUT YOU

a 365 day journey into identity

HILS GREW

KNOWN
Copyright © 2020 Hils Grew

Biddles Books, King's Lynn
Norfolk, PE32 1SF

Unless otherwise indicated, all Scripture quotations are taken from the Holy Bible, New
International Version®, NIV® Copyright © 1973, 1978, 1984, 2011 by Biblica, Inc.®
Used by permission. All rights reserved worldwide.
Scripture quotations marked NLT are taken from the New Living Translation. Copyright
© 1996, 2004, 2015 by Tyndale House Foundation. Used by permission of Tyndale
House Publishers, Inc., Carol Stream, Illinois 60188. All rights reserved.
Scripture quotations marked MSG are taken from THE MESSAGE, copyright © 1993,
2002, 2018 by Eugene H. Peterson. Used by permission of NavPress. All rights
reserved. Represented by Tyndale House Publishers Inc.
Scripture quotations marked NCV are taken from the New Century Version ®.
Copyright © 2005 by Thomas Nelson. Used by permission. All rights reserved.
Scripture quotations marked NKJV are taken from the New King James Version®.
Copyright © 1982 by Thomas Nelson. Used by permission. All rights reserved.
Scripture quotations marked TPT are taken from The Passion Translation®. Copyright ©
2017, 2018 by Passion & Fire Ministries, Inc. Used by permission. All rights reserved.
ThePassionTranslation.com
Scripture quotations marked TLB are taken from The Living Bible copyright © 1971 by
Tyndale House Foundation. Used by permission of Tyndale House Publishers, Inc.,
Carol Stream, Illinois 60188. All rights reserved.
Scripture quotations marked CEV are taken from the Contemporary English Version®
Copyright © 1995 American Bible Society. All rights reserved.
Scripture quotations marked GNT are taken from the Good News Translation® (Today's
English Version, Second Edition) Copyright © 1992 American Bible Society. All rights
reserved.

Cover design: ellasbooks.co.uk
Cover Image: iStock

ISBN 978-1-913663-39-1
Printed in the United Kingdom
First Edition
456789

*Dedicated to Harriet, Louisa, Linda and Steff, precious
daughters of the Living God who don't yet know
who they really are, and to the many more like them...*

CONTENTS

CONTENTS

Now I know in part; then I shall know fully, even as I am fully known.
(1 Cor 13:13)

The story is told of a chicken farmer who once stumbled across an eagle's egg as he was out walking. He picked it up, put it in with his chickens and left the egg to hatch. The young eagle grew up with the other chicks, doing whatever they did, because she thought she was one of them. She spent her life poking in the dirt, looking for worms and insects to eat, and only ever flew a few feet into the air.

One day, the eagle saw a bird flying high above her. She was so impressed, she asked the other chickens what it was. 'That's an eagle', they replied, 'queen of the birds. She belongs to the sky, but we belong to the earth because we're just chickens.' So the eagle lived and died as a chicken, believing that's who she was.

You and I were made to fly. We belong to the sky. We belong to Heaven. But in an age that seeks to define us by our achievements, our political views, our skin colour, our income stream, our possessions, our personality type, our life experiences, our successes and failures, our relationship status and more, we're continually being told we belong to the earth. Trying to find our identity in the things of this world distances us from what we were made for.

Jesus doesn't want us looking for worms and insects when He's invited us into life in all its fullness. He didn't call us into a behaviour modification programme but to follow Him; to live out of our true identity as His daughters. Friend, He has so much more for you. Who you are really matters. But it's who you think you are that matters more. It shapes your life. As it did the eagle's.

Key to becoming the women God made us to be and living this life He's called us to is knowing who we are and being confident in it. Confidence is a game-changer and it comes from knowing. Knowing how He's designed us, knowing what He's called us to, and knowing who He says

He is. Knowing our true identity connects us to ourselves, but it also connects us to Him and to our purpose in this world. And it really rattles the enemy. Yet so many of us settle for so much less.

So I want to invite you on a journey. A journey of discovering (or remembering) who you truly are. At the end of it, you'll find yourself in a different place to where you are today. You won't have finished the journey, because it's a lifetime one, but you will be more sure of your true identity, and you will know Him better. Not because this book is something special but because God's word is. And this book will help you engage with His word and hear His voice. Only He can tell you who you are, as only He fully knows you. The reason I've written it as a devotional, not as a book with chapters in, is because I believe little and often will take you further than lots to read all in one go!

I never intended to write a book, but I've always been passionate about identity. For many years now, I've had the privilege of leading, speaking to and working with women of all ages, both here and overseas, from big platforms to small front rooms. Over and over again, I've realised this need to know our God-given identity is something we all share (despite our different languages, experiences, dreams, abilities, and wounds) because it releases us to fly. As you dig into His living word over you and your identity, and as you meditate on it and apply it, I know you'll hear Him speak to you. And as you do, I pray you'll become more confident in the truth of who He says you are, and that you'll know Him better, just as you are fully known.

With my love
Hils

I'm so glad you decided to pick up this book and let it play a part in your journey of becoming who God made you to be.

OVERVIEW

Much as we might like to, we can't choose to be anyone we want to be. Since knowing *who* we are is the result of knowing *whose* we are, this devotional looks at different aspects of both our own God-given identity and His.

Confidence in who He's created us to be isn't something we can work up; it flows from our confidence in Him and what He's said. So the book is divided up into 52 weeks, each week looking alternately at one dimension of 'who I am', and one dimension of 'who He is'. As you sit with a dimension of your identity for a few days, you'll find yourself meditating on it, and as Psalm 1 says, life-giving change will follow.

You may be someone who likes to do things in order, you may be someone who likes to jump around (like me). You can use this book either way. If you put it down for a week or two, you won't get left behind because there are no dates in it!

EACH WEEK

In every week, there's a reading, an activation and a suggestion for prayer for each of the first 5 days. Days 6 and 7 are a little different. If you're behind with the other days, it's a chance to catch up. If you're not, it's an opportunity to do something else. These two days are designed as springboards for a slightly deeper connection with Jesus and a chance to reflect on the week and what God's been saying to you. And if you want to write things down, there is space to do that too.

EACH DAY

To get the most out of your time with God, I encourage you to sit down with a mug of coffee (or tea, if you're like me)! The verses won't take long to read (you'll get more out of it if you read the passage, not just the verse highlighted) and neither will the devotional reading. But every day there's a suggested response, as well as an encouragement for your connection with Jesus. To meet with Him and to hear His voice needs a few moments of downtime so He has your attention – it won't take longer than drinking a cup of something hot but I find having one with me always helps!

FIRST 3 WEEKS

The first three weeks are in the same format as the rest of the book but are intended to lay a foundation for what follows. They're devotionals designed to get you thinking about identity, its importance and how we move forward embracing all that God says about us.

Enjoy!

READ: Proverbs 4:23

Guard your heart above all else, for it determines the course of your life. (NLT)

'How's your heart?' That's the question a friend's father lovingly asked her on a regular basis. He was a godly man who understood the truth of this beautiful verse; that the life we live is directly connected to the condition of our heart. Your heart is the most important part of you, do you believe that? It's the place Jesus picked to make His home, so it's super precious to God. He knows your heart and cares about it.

We humans tend to look at externals. How someone looks, how they live, how they behave, what they 'do' in life. But God looks at the heart (1 Sam 16:7) because it's the truest part of who we are. It's where our most authentic worship, our fiercest love, our greatest generosity and our most courageous commitments come from. Today, the word 'heart' is often associated with feelings or emotions. 'She's a heart person' can mean she lives by her feelings, or she's very emotional. But when the Bible uses the word 'heart', it's talking about so much more than how we feel.

The word 'heart' is used as a metaphor for our inner world. It includes our mind and will, as well as our emotions. It describes the place where we feel, but also where we think, hope, remember, dream, suffer, trust, imagine, and choose. And it's the place where we connect with God. Sadly, following Jesus can be reduced to buying in to a code of behaviour, or believing in a slot machine, but He's called us to so much more. At its heart, the Christian faith is a love relationship of the heart. That's why your heart matters so much. It's the key to everything else in your life.

Friend, my prayer for you as you walk through this book with God, is that He'll help you get in touch - with what's in your heart and what's on your heart. And I pray you'll experience His touch in fresh ways as you respond to Him from that most true and precious place within you.

PRAY
Put your hand on your heart. Thank God that He cares about your heart and that it's your heart that matters to Him. Thank Jesus that He's made your heart His home.
Offer Him your heart again and ask Him to come and bless it; invite Him to breathe on you afresh and give Him permission to minister to your heart today in whatever way He wants.

READ: Proverbs 4:23

Guard your heart above all else, for it determines the course of your life. (NLT)

When my kids were younger, they loved watching the changing of the guard outside Buckingham Palace. I'm sure it was the smart red uniforms and funny big black hats that appealed so much. Those guards, along with the big iron fences that surround the palace, have an important duty to fulfil. They protect the royal residence and the royal family that lives in it. No one can just 'drop in' because they want to.

God says to 'guard your heart' like that palace. Take your inside world seriously. Look after it. Why? Because your inside world shapes your outside world. We give serious amounts of time and energy to many other things in life; from relationships to reputations, careers to pets, homes to wardrobes, looks and health to online identities. But what about your heart? Do you look after it with the same effort? Do you give as much attention to your inside world as you do to your outside world? Everything depends on the health of your heart. Including the direction of your life. When we know who we are and are confident in who God has promised to be for us, taking care of our hearts becomes easier. Knowing our identity connects us with how we were made.

Like any living thing, your heart can thrive, or it can struggle to survive. If you neglect it or lose touch with it, what's going on in your life will soon reflect that reality. The capacity you have to make your mark on the world, to give to others, to love others and receive from them, all flows from the health of your heart. So does your capacity to love Jesus and receive His love. He wants you to look after it.

PONDER
Would you say you're in touch with your heart? How much attention do you give your inside world compared to the other things in your life that matter to you? Do you need to pay more attention to your heart and if so, how could you do that?

PRAY
Talk to God. If you're not in touch with your heart, ask Him to help you reconnect with this most important part of you. If you've neglected it, ask Him to forgive you. Invite Him to teach you how to look after it more effectively. And ask Him to grow your love for Him as you go.

READ: Proverbs 4:23

Guard your heart above all else, for it determines the course of your life. (NLT)

Do you realise whatever's in your heart will flow out of it? When I squeeze my sun cream tube, sun cream comes out, not chocolate spread! If my heart is full of bitterness, bitterness ends up shaping my relationships and life choices. If my heart is full of shame, shame influences my decisions no matter what else I've got going for me. If my heart is full of fear, fear controls my life whatever gifts I've got. You get the picture.

Jesus wants your heart full of confidence. Confidence in His power, confidence in His blood, and confidence in His love for you. He wants that confidence to be what comes out of you in every situation, defining the way you live. You can't change your heart, only He can. But you can take care of it.

You may have had people in your life who put great value on your heart. You may not have been so fortunate. Perhaps you grew up believing how you feel or what you think is unimportant. Maybe your needs, or dreams and desires were treated as insignificant. Whatever your experience, God is passionate about you. That's why He's given you, and no one else, the mandate to 'guard your heart'. You might want your employer, your spouse, your parents, your boyfriend, your best friend or your church leader to look after your heart. But no one else will take care of it for you. God's not given them the job. It's not His job either. Note to self!

If you're like me, you haven't always done a good job of looking after your heart. We've allowed in some damaging influences and beliefs that still continue to harm us because we've let them stay. Along the way, we've also built up walls of self protection from wounds we've suffered. Let's recognise friend, those walls have the power to keep out what could actually help us. And that can include God. Jesus wants an 'Access All Areas' pass to your heart. The only person who can give Him one is you.

PAUSE

Do you believe it's your responsibility to guard your heart? Have you expected anyone else to look after it for you? Talk to Jesus about it. Does He have an 'Access *All* Areas' pass, into your fears, your dreams, your pain etc. or do you need to give Him one? Do that now.

READ: Proverbs 4:23

Guard your heart above all else, for it determines the course of your life. (NLT)

A couple of years ago I got a new laptop. I was excited to get it up and running as quick as possible. I personalised my desktop, made sure my internet connection was working, and was good to go when a message encouraged me to install some security software. Of course that was a no brainer. I wasn't going to risk losing everything on my new machine by ignoring that advice.

I can't tell you often enough – your heart matters. It's the operating system of your life. God says take care of it because:

1. It's valuable. Nobody bothers trying to protect something that isn't worth much. I put my rubbish out on the street on a Sunday night and I don't mind what happens to it (as long as it doesn't come back to me)! I don't bother looking after it. But can you imagine me doing the same with my laptop?

2. It's vulnerable. Your heart is continually under attack just like a computer. The fact that Jesus urges us to guard it is a reminder that we live on a battlefield, although I often forget this reality. The enemy hates everything that Jesus loves and that includes your heart. He knows full well the truth of this verse – that your heart is key to your life.

Remember the enemy assaults your heart in different ways. My own experiences have included rejection, lies, betrayal, false accusations, and a load of circumstances that have led to deep pain, doubt, disappointment, fear and discouragement. I could go on but I won't! All of them are designed to act like viruses that contaminate, compromise and disable my inner world. How do they affect me? I start to lose heart; my joy, my peace, my hope, my confidence in God's goodness and my sense of His nearness. Pretty quickly my outer world gets affected too. I've learned I have to guard my heart to guard my life. So do you.

PONDER
Your heart is valuable and vulnerable. Do you believe that? Do you believe you have to guard it to guard your life? What one thing can you do today that will upgrade your security software?

PRAY
Thank God for all the different ways He's defended your heart when you've been unaware of it.

READ: Psalm 46:10
Be still, and know that I am God. (NLT)

A friend came round once in a real mess. She couldn't think straight; she had so much going on in her life and her head. Her heart was hurting too. As I listened, I realised I wasn't what she needed. She needed Jesus and hadn't made room for Him in a while. I made her a coffee, led her to the only quiet room in my home and left her there with Him and the Bible for a while. When she emerged, her life hadn't changed, but her heart had. Because Jesus had touched her.

To stay connected to our heart and to know Jesus, we need time and space; with our heart and with Him. He wants to be close to the real you, but you have to be real with Him. And it's time and space that let your thoughts surface and your heart make a noise. We encounter Jesus when we're real, which means bringing our pain, our questions, our shame, our fears, our guilt, our longings, our dreams and more. The Hebrew word used here for 'know' is yada, which means to know through experience. The Bible says, 'Adam knew (yada) Eve and she conceived' (Gen 4:1). Yada describes intimacy. God wants an intimate relationship with you, with nothing coming between you.

Finding space. Being still. For a period of time each day. Our hearts stay soft and connected to their Source when we withdraw from the noise and busyness of life (and the digital world) to be with Jesus. He doesn't say 'be busy and know Me', but 'be still and know Me'. Faith grows, intimacy deepens and our hearts heal when we're with Him. That's why *everything* tries to stop you. The diary and the distractions. And even sometimes the discomfort – of facing your own heart and of facing God, because of how you feel. God can handle your heart. Have you made it a priority to find time to be still with Him? Have you decided on a place to pray and drawn up a plan to pray? If not, why not do it now?

PAUSE
Decide on a place to pray and a plan to pray, if you haven't already. Then, set a timer on your phone or your watch for five minutes (have your phone on silent). Invite Jesus to come close and sit in silence with Him for that time. Be still. Don't worry about what comes into your mind or what comes up in your heart. When the time is up – tell Him about those things, how you feel and how you'd like Him to help.

READ: Psalm 62:8

O my people, trust in Him at all times. Pour out your heart to Him, for God is our refuge. (NLT)

If ever there was a man who knew how to guard his heart, it was David. He had an authentic and intimate relationship with God. He was in touch with his heart and could freely express what was in it, as this psalm shows. He looked after it and gave himself to God whole-heart-edly. This is his encouragement to us to do the same.

PUSH IN

Read this verse two or three times. Hear God's invitation to you to trust Him at all times. He's a refuge and a safe place, and He cares deeply about your heart.

Find a piece of paper (or use the space below) and write a letter to God. 'Pour out your heart to Him.' Tell Him what's on your heart today. Be as honest as you can. What you're grateful for, what you long for, what you struggle with, what you'd love Him to do in you, etc. Put it somewhere safe!

20/09/24

Dear God,

I am struggling to know my self worth. What I am here for. I don't know who I am or why I am here. Please show me my purpose - I feel like I am just waiting for things to go wrong. I have so little support. Please help me feel fulfilled. Please sort the children's future's - education, friends, happiness. Thank you for all you do and have done + will do. Danny

PUSH IN

If you had to describe in three sentences what Jesus has been saying to you this week, what would you say? Long sentences allowed!

READ: Proverbs 4:23
Be careful what you think, because your thoughts run your life. (NCV)

I love this translation of the verse we've been looking at. It's such a pointed and powerful way of saying the same thing a bit differently. It reminds us God designed us to live from the inside out. What we think in our head (or heart) shapes everything else in our life.

Not long ago, a man was clearing out the small house of some elderly relatives who had recently died. He sent the contents to an auction house in Middlesex. Auction day arrived and a larger than expected crowd turned up. News had got out that among the contents was a very unusual vase. No one was more surprised than the man himself when the vase finally sold for, wait for it, £56 million! Turned out it was a precious Chinese heirloom, but the relatives who'd owned it had no idea. No idea of its history, no idea of its value and therefore no idea of what was in their hands. As a result, they'd kept it in the attic, thinking it was a worthless piece of junk.

Imagine how they'd have lived if they'd known they owned something so valuable. Would they have taken different holidays, worried less, moved to a different house, and given more to good causes if they knew what kind of fortune they were sitting on? Probably. But they didn't *think* they were millionaires, so they didn't *live* like millionaires.

It's not our decisions or our past experiences, or our mistakes or our circumstances that run our lives. Neither do the abilities or the gifts we have. Other peoples opinions of us, the opportunities we get, who we know or don't know, they don't make the difference either. Nor do the resources (or vases) we have. Not even God runs our life. This verse says your thoughts run your life. How seriously do you take them?

PONDER
What do you believe controls your life? What difference would believing this verse make to you? Memorise it and speak it back to yourself during the day today, as if you were encouraging a friend.

PRAY
Talk to Jesus about what this raises for you.

READ: Proverbs 23:7
For as (s)he thinks in his/her heart, so is (s)he. (NKJV)

In 1983, the first Sydney to Melbourne ultramarathon took place over a distance of 544 miles. That's one long race. A 61-year-old farmer called Cliff Young turned up to compete, much to the amusement of the crowds. He'd come to race against professional athletes dressed in wellie boots and dungarees. He'd also come without his dentures because they would've rattled as he ran! Despite being greeted with scorn as he stood on the starting line, 5½ days later he crossed the finishing line first, 10 hours ahead of the next competitor. He shot to fame overnight.

How did it happen? He didn't think like everyone else. He didn't have a trainer, telling him how to run properly, so he ran with a shuffle (which is how he ran after his sheep). It proved to be more energy efficient. He didn't believe he needed to stop and rest like the others were told, so he ran through the nights as they slept. He hadn't had a coach tell him he couldn't run in wellies, so he turned up in what he ran in on his farm. And he didn't think his age mattered. It wasn't the fittest or the best prepared person who won the race but the one with the best mindset. Cliff Young had one set of beliefs and expectations about the race and about himself, everyone else had another.

When you decided to follow Jesus and you received His forgiveness, everything changed for you, as it did for me. Jesus gave us a new identity and a new destiny right then. A whole load of things became true for us and possible for us in that moment that weren't true before. But it only becomes our experience as our beliefs and expectations line up with what Jesus says. As this story shows, one set of beliefs and expectations leads to a very different outcome than another. That's why the enemy is set on keeping us thinking the way we always have. No wonder the Holy Spirit is determined to get us to change the way we think.

PONDER
How have your expectations changed since you met Jesus? Are they still changing? In what way?

PRAY
Invite the Holy Spirit to move in you today to bring your thinking and your expectations more in line with His.

READ: Proverbs 4:23
Be careful what you think, because your thoughts run your life. (NCV)

'Who do you think you are?' The answer to that question matters. If our thoughts run our lives, then what *we think* about ourselves is much more important than what anyone else thinks about us. Sadly, what *we* believe about ourselves so often differs to what is really true.

Someone once said, 'Know who you are or someone else will tell you'. For most of us, that's already happened. Different voices have told us who they think we are, and it's not always been good news. Many of us still live with those voices ringing in our heads. Other things contribute to our sense of who we are too. I can believe I'm a success one day and a failure the next, just by how well I manage life that day. I can think I'm valuable one moment and insignificant the next, just by how those around me treat me. Have you noticed how easily we can let our roles, or our responsibilities, or our experiences define us? Let's nail this together. Who we are has nothing to do with what happens to us, what we do, how we do it or what others think of us.

Friend, don't let what you do or what happens to you, define you. Don't let others define you. Let the One who made you tell you who you are. He defines your identity. He knows you. But remember this: it's *your thoughts* that control your life. So what *you* believe about who He says you are matters most. You're deeply loved, but if you think you're not, you'll live as if you're not. You're a powerful person because He is in you, but if you think you're not, you won't live like that. Jesus cares more about changing the way we think (about ourselves and about Him) than about changing our circumstances (although He cares about those too). Because lasting change only happens when our thoughts change.

PONDER
Can you identify something that's happened to you, or something you've done or are currently doing, that defines how you think about yourself? How does it do that?

PRAY
Thank God that He defines you. Ask Him to reveal something to you today about who He says you really are.

READ: Numbers 13:1-2, 25-33
We seemed like grasshoppers in our own eyes, and we looked the same to them.

What you believe about yourself. What you believe about God. They both shape your experience of life and your life experiences. Here it is played out.

Moses chose 12 spies (the Israelite version of the SAS) to go and explore the land God had promised them as their new home. They had a checklist of questions to answer. What were the cities like, what was the land like, what was the food like (always important) and what were the people like? In other words, 'Would we want to live there, and could we live there?' Good questions! 12 went out, 12 came back. All of them saw the same things, but they didn't come back with the same answers.

All 12 agreed that they wanted to live there. Controversially, 10 believed the answer to the 'could they' part of the question was 'no'. They didn't think it was possible because the opposition was too great (v31). They believed they were 'like grasshoppers' and would never succeed. Only two, Joshua and Caleb thought differently. Yes, they were smaller and less powerful, but they saw themselves as the favoured children of a big God. So they were convinced their efforts to take the land would be successful (v30).

Who was right? Ironically, they both were. Joshua and Caleb got to live in the promised land, the rest never made it. Each lot of spies experienced what they expected. I find that both challenging and encouraging. God always has to enlarge our thinking before He can enlarge our territory. Are you up for it?

PONDER
Why do you think there was such a difference in the way these spies thought? Is there an area of your life that God wants to give you ground in? What change needs to happen in your thinking first?

PRAY
Talk to God about it and invite Him to shape the way you think in this area.

READ: Judges 6:7-16
...he said, 'The Lord is with you, mighty warrior.'

To live the life God made us for, we have to keep letting His thoughts about us replace our own. Changing our minds is a non-negotiable.

Nobody was more surprised at God's 'Hello' to Gideon than Gideon himself. Imagine God turning up at my door and saying, 'Hello Olympic-marathon-gold-medallist' (you'd laugh if you knew me). Gideon protested as he choked on his coffee; God had got the wrong chap. He was hiding away, terrified of the Midianites along with the rest of Israel. He was a winepress wimp, not a mighty warrior. Add in two facts: his family were 'the most insignificant in Manasseh' and he was 'the least important, least gifted member of that family'. Was this a classic case of mistaken identity? Was God at the wrong door?

Obviously not! God just sees us differently to how we see ourselves. He sees our potential, not our present scenario. He sees our worth, not our weakness. He sees what we can do with Him, not what we can't do without Him. It was actually Gideon who'd got the wrong guy.

Gideon became a hero and left a huge footprint on Israel's history as one of its mighty warriors. How did his story begin to change? With an interruption to the story he was telling himself – about who he was. He discovered his true identity by listening to God. Then he replaced his thoughts with God's thoughts. It's not always easy to agree with what God says when it doesn't match our reality. It was a struggle for Gideon because it didn't feel true. But the point is, he changed his mind. And unless we're willing to do the same, friend, we'll miss much of the life He's made us for, and our stories won't change.

PONDER
What story are you currently telling yourself? Decide today not to settle for a life in the winepress. Where do you need to agree with what God says about you and your future? Resolve to make agreeing with Him your priority, even if it involves a struggle.

PRAY
Thank God for His patience with you and His desire to show you who you really are. Ask Him to help you hear His voice, see as He sees, and be quick to agree with Him when you do.

READ: John 11:38-44

Jesus can speak to us powerfully through our imaginations. He gave you your imagination and it's part of the language of your heart. Invite Him to speak to you through it now.

PLAY the PART

Close your eyes and imagine yourself standing outside a tomb, like Lazarus. Hear Jesus say your name. You're alive because of Him.

– THANK HIM that He's called your name, and called you out of darkness into His kingdom of light. Thank Him you're no longer in the tomb. Thank Him that He's come for you and He uses His power for your good. Thank Him He's the One who defines you.

– FEEL and smell the strips of cloth all around you, covering you. They've been there for a while; the lies you've been fed, your old mindsets, and the worldly ways of defining you. Notice how they hide who you really are. Notice how they restrict your ability to move freely. How do they make you feel? What can't you do?

– ASK Jesus if there are any lies or ways of thinking that He wants to draw your attention to in this moment. Note what He says.

– NOTICE what it feels like as the grave clothes begin to be taken off you. How do you feel as they are being removed? What can you see? What can you hear? What else changes?

As we allow Jesus to change us by changing the way we think about ourselves and about Him, it's like grave clothes being taken off.

Thank Him that His desire is to release you into greater freedom.

RE-READ: Numbers 13:1-2, 25-33

**We seemed like grasshoppers in our own eyes, and we looked
the same to them.**

PUSH IN

– Is there a big or seemingly hopeless situation you're facing right now? Do you have a dream to see something impossible happen?

– What do you think the 'ten' would say about it and what do you think the 'two' would say?

– Make a note to self that those who bring a negative perspective about what can't be done, or what won't work out, or what God won't do, are always in the majority (even amongst God's people), just as they were here.

– Ask Jesus to show you one thing you need to do to set yourself up for success in becoming or remaining one of the two, not one of the ten.

Write it down and ask Him to help you do it.

READ: Romans 12:2

Stop imitating the ideals and opinions of the culture around you, but be inwardly transformed by the Holy Spirit through a total reformation of how you think. This will empower you to discern God's will as you live a beautiful life, satisfying and perfect in His eyes. (TPT)

I love this translation because I love the idea of a total reformation of how I think. My thought life can get me into trouble. It's my anxious thoughts that wake me up at night, my insecure thoughts that make me draw back rather than step forward, my hopeless thoughts that drain the life out of me and my condemning thoughts that beat me up. No matter what their origin, it's what goes on in my head that messes with my life.

A 'total reformation' of how we think is what Jesus is after. He doesn't offer an upgrade on our thought life but an upload of totally different software. He's more concerned about our thinking than our behaviour because it's our thinking that runs our lives. That's how He designed us. We tend to beat ourselves up about the things we do or don't do and the things we've done or haven't done, but ignore how we think. Jesus wants us to think His thoughts about us and others, and about God. It's the upload of His software that empowers us to live a big life and enables us to discern His purposes for us. Joshua and Caleb had had that software installed before their spy trip; Gideon got his upload too.

Do you believe you have a choice about what you think? The answer to this question is key. If we don't believe we can choose what we think, we won't believe we can change our minds. So we won't. But Paul says we can. We have a choice. We *can* take control of our thoughts because we have the Holy Spirit with us to help us think differently. We wouldn't stand by and let a crazy toddler cause chaos in our homes, but we stand by and let crazy thoughts mess with our minds. How crazy is that?

PONDER

Do you believe you have a choice over what goes on in your head? What does your answer mean for you?

PRAY

Thank Jesus that a total reformation of how you think is not only possible, but His plan for you.

READ: Matthew 26:33-35, 69-75
With a shattered heart, Peter went out of the courtyard, sobbing with bitter tears. (TPT)

Who you are has little to do with how you feel. Our culture says if it feels good then do it. If it feels true, then it must be. Feelings have been rightly recognised as being important, but wrongly elevated as being what defines us. How you feel matters to God because He cares about your heart. But you are not what you feel. You may feel a failure but you are not failure. Jesus defines us. But He can only bring our thinking into line with His if we're willing to break up with our feelings and refuse to let them have the final say about who we are.

Jesus gave Simon a new identity, as He does to all of us when we become His. Jesus told Simon he would be the 'rock' on which He'd build His church (Matt 16:18). Why a rock? Because, according to Jesus, Simon had a solid, strong soul that could take tons of pressure. Jesus saw that in Peter. Peter means rock, which is how we know him. Here, we find 'the rock' sobbing with bitter tears and a shattered heart; he'd crumbled in weakness and fear, and lied about not knowing Jesus in front of a young girl. Not very rock-like if you ask me (sorry Peter)!

How do you think Peter *felt*? Devastated? Like a failure? Ashamed? He was so broken by what he'd done, he didn't believe what Jesus said about him. So he went back to what he had been: a fisherman. Were his feelings telling him the truth about who he was? No. Only about what he'd done. Did what he felt in that moment change who he was? No. Only in his head. Had Jesus got it wrong? Did it prove Peter was a failure, a hopeless friend, and a loser? No, even if the onlookers thought it did. After He rose again, Jesus reminded Peter he was *still* who He said he was; the rock, who was going to launch His church. And Peter did so, a few weeks later, with the Holy Spirit. To walk in freedom and in your true identity, Jesus, not your feelings, must have the final word.

PAUSE
What's the difference between failing at a task, feeling like a failure and being a failure? Does Jesus have the last word over who you are, or do your feelings? What would breaking up with your feelings look like for you? Talk to Him about what's on your mind today.

READ: Hebrews 11:1-6
Faith means being sure of the things we hope for and knowing that something is real even if we do not see it. (NCV)

The thing I like least about flying is going through cloud. Travelling at hundreds of miles an hour and not being able to see anything in any direction isn't good for my heart rate! What if there's another plane close by and we just can't see it? The pilots can only see cloud too. But fortunately, they have devices in the cockpit to tell them about what they can't see and which direction of travel is safe. They've decided to trust those devices and rely on them completely.

The Holy Spirit is set on changing our thinking so He can enlarge our living. He wants us to know who we are, so we can live the life we've been made for. Changing the way we think about who we are requires believing we can choose what we think, and letting Jesus have the final word. It also requires us to have faith. Faith is trusting something is real and true when we don't see it or feel it. It's not wishful thinking, or making something up and clinging to it. It's not something some people have and others don't. Faith is a choice to agree with what Jesus says (about anything) and to trust His words. To trust them more than our own thoughts, what we understand or how we feel.

Like the pilots, we can rely on what we can see, which is super limited, or on something else. Someone else. Letting Jesus have the last word and *acting* on it releases His power to move us forwards. How different would your life look if you had more confidence in the fact that you're a daughter of the King, a co-heir with Jesus, a masterpiece, an overcomer, a difference maker and part of a royal priesthood? That you're chosen and cherished by the God in Heaven who's on your side and ready to provide for your every need? Jesus wants to give you a greater revelation of your identity – trust what He says more than what you can see.

PONDER
What's your biggest obstacle when it comes to trusting what Jesus says?

PRAY
Ask Him to give you a fresh revelation of your identity in Him. Ask Him for a new determination to believe and act on what He tells you even if you can only see cloud out of your window!

READ: Luke 3:21-22, Luke 4:1-13
If you are the Son of God...

There's a battle going on over your identity, as there is for all God's women. It's not a battle to decide who you are; that was decided at creation and confirmed at the cross. It's a battle to prevent you *knowing* who you are and being so sure about it that it shapes your life.

Jesus fought this same battle in the desert so we're in good company. The battle was over His identity. Not who He was, but who He *thought* He was. What was the enemy's tactic? To undermine His confidence in His identity as God's son. 'If you are the Son of God...' That statement has only one aim doesn't it? To introduce a question mark. To open the door to doubt. 'Jesus, how can you possibly think you are *His* son? Joseph and Mary are your parents. Nobody's seen you do anything yet – go on, *prove* you're God's son by turning these stones into bread.'

Friend, how many of your actions and decisions are driven by a need to prove who you are? To prove you're worth loving, to prove you're successful, to prove you have something to offer, to prove you're a good mother, to prove you don't need help, to prove you're worth promoting... At Jesus' first public appearance a few verses earlier, God only said one thing to Him. It wasn't a pep talk for the mission ahead, but a powerful reminder of who He was. 'You're My precious Son.' The battle was over whether He'd believe it when the pressure was on. Or would He need to prove it; to Himself, to the enemy, to the world? By doing something?

Jesus slammed the door on doubt and the rest is history. God wants to empower you to do the same; to be so sure about who He says you are that you don't need to prove yourself to anyone by what you do. You need your energy for much bigger things. Don't be surprised by the battle. You need to know who you are for your sake and the sake of the world around you.

PRAY
Talk to God. Ask Him to highlight a scenario in your life where you're trying to prove something about yourself by what you're doing or by the way you're doing it. It may be at home, online, at work... Ask Him to show you what you're trying to prove. Own it with Him and ask Him to show you what you'd do differently if there was no 'proving' attached to it. Ask Him to give you strength to do it that way.

READ: James 1:22-25
...two minutes later, they have no idea who they are, what they look like. (MSG)

I have a love-hate relationship with my mirror! Some days I like it, some days I don't. Sometimes I'm OK with what it tells me, often I'm not. But whether I like it or not, what it does reliably (and unfortunately) is give me feedback on what I look like. Like the camera, it doesn't lie.

Are you aware that you've stood in front of virtual mirrors all your life? They've given you feedback on what you look like on the inside; on who you are, how valuable you are, how significant you are, and how you're doing in life. These mirrors take the form of parents, classmates, teachers, church leaders, friends, boyfriends, siblings, social media, employers, even experiences. Gideon spoke out feedback that different mirrors had given him; who they'd said he was. 'Weak', 'unimportant', 'insignificant'. Sometimes the mirrors give their feedback through things that are said. Often it's more subtle. But we get the message all the same.

Unfortunately, these mirrors regularly lie because they can't see into our hearts. There's only one mirror that'll tell you the truth about who you really are and what you look like on the inside. James says that reading God's word is like looking into a mirror. Because He's the only One who truly knows who you are. But James points out an unlikely danger; it's possible to look into it, discover who we are, and then walk away forgetting what we've just seen!

Friend, you're called to a life of great faith which flows from a close relationship with a great God. But you have to know who you are and believe it for your confidence and faith to prosper. I pray that over these coming weeks, this book will help you look into the stunning mirror of God's word. I pray it'll help you discover more of who you are and Whose you are (they're connected). And I pray it'll help you *remember* who you are so when you walk away from it, what you've seen shapes your life.

PONDER
Which mirrors have been significant in your life? What kind of feedback have they given you?

PRAY
Thank God for His mirror and its truth. Tell Him you want His mirror to be the most important mirror in your life and ask Him to help you run to it when you've forgotten what you look like.

RE-VISIT: Day 5

Let's pick up from yesterday and think about the mirrors that have been significant in your life.

PUSH IN

Ask God to help you forgive the people who have given you false feedback and not reflected His truth about you. (Remember, they were probably unaware they were giving you false feedback).

Ask Jesus to help you identify one mirror now (trust whichever one comes to mind).

– Tell Him what feedback this mirror gave you. What did it say about you?

– Admit how the feedback made you feel at the time and what impact it still has on you.

– Invite Jesus to come and comfort you.

– Declare that this was a false mirror (even if it felt true at the time or still feels true).

– Forgive the 'mirror' and let it go.

– Choose to turn your back on the feedback it gave you (it might help to imagine yourself doing this).

– Ask Jesus to show you how He sees you as you stand before Him.

– Speak His truth over yourself. Declare it again when you remember, during the day today.

Thank Him that He helps you to change the way you think about yourself.

READ: Psalm 46:10
Be still, and know that I am God. (NLT)

Spend some time being still with Jesus. Invite Him to come and be with you.

PUSH IN

– Put any agenda you may have to one side for a bit, get comfortable, close your eyes, take a few deep breaths and relax. Invite Jesus to touch your heart and make you aware of His presence. Trust He is with you and loves you deeply. Thank Him that He is with you. Sit in silence for a while, however hard that might be for you, and think about Him. Hear Jesus speaking this verse to you a few times, and let it still your thoughts. Listen for anything He wants to say or what rises in your heart. Take note of what comes to mind – don't push it away.

– After a few moments, turn what is in your heart or any whisper you've heard into prayer. Talk to Him about how hard you find it to be still, or how much you long for His peace, or where you need His help, or what you want Him to do in you or for you...

Then, thank Him for His love for you and His commitment to you. Thank Him that He is God, that you are not, and that you can rest in this truth today.

READ: 2 Corinthians 5:16-17

Therefore, if anyone is in Christ, that person is a new creation.

New. I love that word and all it promises, don't you? I love the idea of a new coffee shop opening, new shoes, a new day dawning, new mercy every morning (Lam 3:23), a new baby, a new job, a new start. If the blogs and books are anything to go by, many of us are looking for a 'new' life, or ways of becoming 'new' ourselves. We seem dissatisfied that we're not who we want to be, or living the life we think we should be.

Jesus does new. Only He can make us new and only He can deal with what stops us living the life we were made for. And He has. On the cross. The moment you faced Him, received His forgiveness and trusted His death was enough to deal with your sin, you became new and got a new life. Immediately! You may not have felt like a new person, you probably didn't look new; you may not even have realised what happened in that moment. But the Father says *everything* changed. You literally became 'a new creation'. You got a brand new nature because Jesus moved in to your heart. The old has gone, the new is here!' (v 17).

What's the big deal with this? It means you have a new identity. He's given you a new heart, a new purpose, new assignments and a new destiny. You're not who you were before you started following Him. But one of the biggest lies the enemy tells us is that nothing has really changed. That's what he wants us to believe. If we fall for it friend, we won't *experience* the truth of what's happened to us, and we'll miss the life He's saved us for. God says you *are* a new creation. Ugly caterpillars (sorry caterpillar lovers) become beautiful butterflies virtually overnight. There's no going back, so the butterfly has to learn to live differently. It has to learn to fly. So do we. We have to learn to be human, differently. Listen to Him, keep trusting Him and He'll keep teaching you how.

PONDER
Do you feel like a new creation? How do you need to change the way you think about yourself?

PRAY
Thank Jesus you're no longer a caterpillar but a beautiful butterfly. Imagine your old mindsets and your old identity hanging on the cross. Thank Him that 'the old has gone' and you have a new nature. Thank Him that He's teaching you to fly.

READ: Ezekiel 36:25-27

And I will give you a new heart, and I will put a new spirit in you. (NLT)

I'm a sucker for makeover programmes. I often need to watch them with tissues! Whether it's a house, a garden, a woman, or her wardrobe, I love a good transformation story. I love watching an expert at work, turning something old or neglected into something new and beautiful. And of course, all the reactions that go with it.

Jesus says it's the human heart that needs a makeover. Left to its own devices, the human heart is an unhappy, unhealthy place, full of pride and prejudice and with no desire to love Him or be led by Him. Unlike the programmes I watch, it's the inside not the outside that needs attention. Religious types put a priority on outward stuff like behaviour. God says the priority is our heart. Jesus said (Mt 15:8) that we can do and say the right things, but it doesn't count if our hearts aren't right with the Father. The makeover our hearts need is so radical, that in this verse, God promises a radical solution. He promises to give a heart transplant to everyone who asks. A brand new heart and spirit. A brand new nature. The old one is too broken to fix.

You're a new creation, a new person because Jesus has given you a new heart and a new start. He's put a new spirit in you. His Spirit. You now have a radically new nature. It's amazing. We've been made over. How do we know? Well it's not to do with whether we still sin or how much faith we have, let's get that clear. First, we know because of this promise. God promised to make us new when we began to trust Jesus. Second, we know because of the proof. He says the evidence of our new heart and spirit would be desire (v 27). A desire for Him, a desire to hear His voice and a desire to do things His way, even when we mess up.

Do you have that desire? It's because you're no longer a caterpillar but a butterfly. You have a new identity and a new life. You *are* a new you.

PRAY

Put your hand on your heart and thank Jesus He's put His Spirit in you making you new, giving you a new identity and destiny. Declare: 'I am a new creation and I have a new heart and a new spirit in me.' Ask Him to help you be aware of His presence in you throughout the day today.

READ: Song of Songs 2:14-15
Show me your face, let me hear your voice; for your voice is sweet and your face is lovely.

Do you remember playing hide and seek when you were smaller? I wasn't very good at it as I used to find it too hard to keep still and silent once I was hiding. Do you know many of us still play it now? We've just changed the hiding places. Gone are the big full-length curtains or under stairs cupboards. Instead, it's amazing what we can hide behind a smile, a social media image, or a phrase like, 'I'm fine'. Things like achievement, activity, perfectionism, blame-shifting and criticism have all become effective places to make sure our true selves aren't discovered.

Jesus has given us a new identity and freed us to come out of hiding. We aren't who we think we are. We are now His and that changes everything. Get real with Him and share your heart with Him. Be honest with Him. Show Him your face and let Him hear your voice with the confidence of a girl who knows she's been made over and made new. As you do, He'll teach you how to live as that new you. That happens in the context of a close relationship, which is only possible when we don't hide.

Shame makes us hide. From others and from God. Shame says, 'There's something wrong with you and no one will love you or rate you or fight for you when they know the full story about you.' It keeps us hidden and it keeps us shackled to the past. Friend, Jesus has unlocked your shackles, but it's as we come out of hiding into His love that we discover it. Hear Him calling you: 'I long to see your face and I want to hear your voice.' You see the old you, He sees who He's made you. You're forgiven. He sees your new heart and your new spirit. He sees your new desire – to know Him, love Him and please Him. However weak that desire it is. And you delight Him.

PONDER
Can you identify what kind of attitudes or actions you hide behind? Who do you hide from?

PRAY
Thank Jesus that He wants to hear *your* voice and see *your* face, not just other people's. Repent of the times you've held back from being honest with Him because of fear. Talk to Him about any of your hiding places and ask Him to grow your courage to leave them behind.

READ: Genesis 17:3-7
No longer will you be called Abram; your name will be Abraham...

You may be a new creation, but what do you do when you wonder if anything's changed? Last summer we had a breakthrough. Even without green fingers, the token gesture of planting some raspberries finally paid off, and we filled a whole bowl. This year we filled a few more (with some cream) but the first year there were no raspberries; only green leaves in the summer, and brown sticks in the winter. Despite the sad lack of fruit that year, we still called them raspberry plants. Because they were!

Sometimes, it's hard to believe we are who God says we are when we can't see fruit connected with the truth we're trying to trust. God changed Abram's name to Abraham (meaning father of many) long before his son Isaac was born. Was God joking? As an old man with *no* children, how do you think Abraham felt every time he introduced himself? 'Hi, I'm Abraham, father of many.' What did people think of him? But God made him say it before he saw it. That's how faith works.

Everything changed for Abram when He met God. God made him a new. He gave him a new name which contained his new identity, and He gave him a new purpose. As a father of nations. But in the kingdom, God says things *before* we see them. Abraham's new name came first, his experience of it came second. It's so important we remember this, as it's the opposite to how the world works. In between God saying it and us seeing it, He makes us do the same. He waits for us to show our trust in what He's said by speaking it out too! Remember, you may well be the only voice doing that. In making you new, God has given you a load of new names. Many of them are in this book. They're new badges and labels that replace the old ones which got stuck to the old you. But like Abraham, you've got to let the new ones stick to you first. You wear them by speaking them out, (however unlikely they may sound) *before* your experience catches up.

PRAY

Thank God that you're a new creation and have a new identity. Thank Him in faith for all the new names He's given you even if you don't know what they all are. Thank Him that He nailed all your old names and labels to the cross. Resolve to thank Him regularly throughout the day that He's made you new. Let that badge stick. Keep saying it out loud like Abraham did!

READ: Romans 4:18-21
**Without weakening in his faith, he faced the fact that his body
was as good as dead...**

You're a new woman! You're a new you. You have a new identity because you belong to God. You were lost, now you're found. You had a heart of stone, now you have a heart of flesh. You were an orphan, now you're His child. You were disconnected from God, now you're His friend. You were dead, now you're alive. You had a past, now you have a future. You were under judgement, now you're forgiven. You have a new name, and even a new wardrobe (Col 3:12).

How many of these things did you make happen? Not one! Jesus has done all the work. They're all gifts of His grace to you. The challenge is that what Jesus says about us and what we see or feel on a daily basis don't always stack up. The answer is not to *try* harder but to *trust* harder. Look at Abraham again. God gave him his new identity as a father of many when he was a father of none (don't forget that he and Sarah were no spring chickens either!). Romans tells us that Abraham was real about what he saw with his eyes (two clapped out bodies) *without* letting go of what God had said to him. He held his experience in one hand and God's word in the other. Not easy, but he did it and Heaven applauded him for letting God's word speak louder.

The way we walk forward in God's truth over who we are, until we experience it more fully in our daily life, is how Abraham did it:
Receive it – listen to what He says and thank Him for what He says
Believe it – agree with God, rather than with what your situation says
Say it – declare it out loud (like Abraham had to when he said his name)
See it – in the meantime, God will do His part and finish what He began.

PONDER
Which of these first 3 steps do you find hardest? What could you do differently to move forward?

PRAY
Be real with God about where something He has said about you and your current experience don't stack up. Ask Him to grow your confidence in what He's said. Choose to agree with Him where you need to and thank Him again that what He has said about you is true no matter how you feel.

READ: 2 Corinthians 5:17
The old has gone, the new is here. (NLT)

PUSH IN

Gather some small bits of paper together.

– Ask God to show you any names or labels that you wear that are connected to your old identity. They often sound like this: *'I am _____'*; *'I am not _____'.*
  e.g. I am a failure, I am guilty, I am not good enough.

(At this stage, you may still believe they're true, but if you've prayed and asked God to show you first, then *trust* that what pops into your head is the whisper of the Holy Spirit.)

– Write each one down on a separate bit of paper. One by one, screw up the pieces of paper and throw them in a bin. For each one, thank Jesus out loud that you are no longer defined by that label as it belongs to your old identity – you are now a new creation.

– Declare: 'I am who God says I am, not who my experiences say I am.'

Thank Him the old has gone, the new is here, because of what He has done for you. Ask Him if there is anything else He wants to say to you about your new identity today.

PUSH IN

If we were sitting chatting in a coffee shop and I asked you, 'Who are you?', how would you answer that question? Write down some of the first things that come to mind.

_____

_____

_____

_____

_____

_____

_____

Does what you've written describe more about what you do, your past experiences, or who God's word says you are?

Talk to God about what you've written and what's on your heart.

READ: John 14:1-10
Anyone who has seen Me has seen the Father.

God wants to be a father to you. It's one of the deepest longings of His heart. That may not sound like good news to you, depending on the experience you had with your earthly father. For many of us, that relationship has been so challenging that the thought of God as Father may seem too much to take on. For others of us, that relationship may not have been so difficult; but it will still have been deficient as no human father is perfect, however hard they tried.

Since Adam and Eve had to leave the Garden, we humans have had a tricky time knowing what God is really like. There are more misconceptions about Him than I've had chocolate bars! You and I have plenty of misconceptions about Him too, whether or not we realise it. The people that hung around Jesus (including the religious know-it-alls and the disciples) found it hard to recognise God in their midst. How was that possible? Because Jesus didn't fit their idea of what God was like. After spending three years with Jesus, Philip said to Him, 'Jesus, please, just show us the Father!' Crazy.

Jesus didn't just come to teach us how to be human, but to show us what the Father is like. He was God in human skin. He was God's plan to help us get God. Instead of showing us a grandfather or a judge, a policeman or a killjoy, a headmaster or a taskmaster, He shows us a father. A father who loves His kids and who wants them to know Him as a dad. Every time you wonder, 'Father, what are You really like?', look at Jesus.

Your life with God is about relationship. He's a personal God who made you for a personal relationship with Him. He wants to be a father to you.

PAUSE
Ask the Holy Spirit to show you what word(s) come(s) to mind when you think of God as Father. Note them down. We'll come back to them on Day 6.

PRAY
Have an honest moment with Jesus about how you feel about the thought of God as your Father. He can handle it! Ask the Holy Spirit to help you better know your Heavenly Father as He really is, not as you think He is.

READ: Luke 15:11-24
So he divided his property between them.

Everyone loves a good story, and Jesus was a supreme storyteller. My favourite is this one of the prodigal son, although I'd argue it should be called the story of the phenomenal father. In telling it, Jesus is holding up a photo of the Father and saying, 'Hey everyone, this is Him, this is what He's really like. This is My Father, and He's your Father too.'

What does Jesus want us to know about God? He describes three stages (we'll cover one each day) of a strained relationship between a dad and his son to show us what the Father is like. The first stage is rejection; the young man turned his back on his dad. He says, 'I want your money, not you.' What advice would you have given the dad at this point?

The culture of the day screamed, 'Make him pay; punish him for insulting you like that'. The father could have been less harsh but still refused to give his son the money. He could have forced him to stay. But not this dad. He does the unthinkable (some would say idiotic) thing; he takes it on the chin, gives his money to the selfish boy and lets him leave. Why?

The shocking thing Jesus wants us to know is that God's highest goal is connection with us, not respect or obedience. He may be the God of the universe, but He's after loving relationship. No amount of respect or obedience will make up for a lack of love. So he let his son go. The son's heart wasn't in it, and it was his heart the father wanted. Never fall for the lie that respect and obedience or even doing great things for God are what He's after. If you do, it will kill your love for Him. Friend, what He wants most is an affectionate relationship with you. He wants your heart.

PONDER

In letting his son go with a pile of his own money, what risk was the father taking? Do you ever feel God wants to control your choices? How so?

PRAY

The Father loves you. Even when you reject His love or ignore Him, the Father longs for your love more than anything else. Talk to Him about how this makes you feel and ask Him to help you grasp the truth of this more fully. Give Him your heart again today.

READ: Luke 15:11-24
And while he was still a long way off, his father saw him coming. (NLT)

How do you like playing the waiting game? Waiting for responses to messages, test results, answers to prayer and the like? Personally, I'm not a fan. I enjoy waiting as much as I enjoy rolling in mud! I prefer certainty, closure and being in control. The father had two easy options in this story: write off his son and get on with his own life, or go after him and try and get him back. He did neither. But he's no ordinary dad.

Stage two is about the remoteness of the son. Jesus wants us to see a father who never closes His heart to us, or writes us off; who never gives up on us in impatience or forgets about us in frustration. He wants us to see a father whose heart for us is never shaped by disapproval or disappointment. Is that how you see God?

The son was miles away both physically and emotionally and didn't give his father a second thought as he partied his life away. The father, however, never stopped thinking about his boy. He spotted him in the distance because he was looking out for him, wondering if today was the day he'd come home. I wonder how many times he'd gone to bed at night, hoping the next day would bring news of the son he missed.

If you think God is disappointed in you or disapproves of you, it's in your imagination. If you think the Father is frustrated with you or irritated with you, it's the enemy's whispers you're listening to, not the Holy Spirit's. No matter how far away from God you may feel, no matter what you've done or not done, none of it changes how He feels about you. There may be distance between you, but He didn't put it there. He's longing for you to come close. That's His desire for you. Draw near to Him today and He will draw near to you.

PONDER
Spend a moment thinking about the incredible patience of this father. In what ways was he patient with his son?

PRAY
Thank God for His patience with you. Ask Him if there's anything you need to do to let Him get closer to you today. Keep asking Him to reveal more of the depths of His love to you.

READ: Luke 15:11-24
Filled with love and compassion, he ran to his son, embraced him, and kissed him... (NLT)

What kind of response would you have expected coming home to face a dad whose love you'd snubbed, whose money you'd blown, and whose honour you'd trashed? Probably not this one, which was why Jesus' story was so shocking to those who were listening.

The last stage of it paints a picture of a radical father who's beyond his son's wildest dreams. Jesus wants us to see God as a dad who runs. He can't wait to get to us when we move towards Him. He's an affectionate father who kisses us and gives big bear hugs if we'll get close enough (no matter how bad we smell!). He's a compassionate father whose heart is moved, not maddened, by the reckless choices we make. And He's an extravagant father who cares more about giving gifts and throwing parties than about receiving explanations and promises of reformed behaviour. How well do you know the Father?

The son wasn't expecting this response; it's not what most of us expect from the Father either. Like the son, we can assume we've blown it and somehow written off our chances of being treated like a daughter again. Like him, we can assume an apology and a resolution to do better and try harder is the answer. Isn't that how we feel we should make things up to God?

The Father's heart for us never changes. Nor does His desire for an affectionate, intimate relationship with us. He is better than we think. What needs to change is the way we see Him and our openness to His love. The answer is always turning round; the answer is always coming back to Him. The answer is always ditching the resolutions and letting Him welcome us home with open arms.

PONDER
Think about these words for a moment: 'running', 'affectionate', 'compassionate', 'extravagant'. Which of them do you find hardest to associate with the Father? Ask Him to show you why that is.

PRAY
Sit quietly and ask God if there's anything He wants to say to you as your Dad. Be still for a moment or two and listen for His whisper. Write down what you sense Him saying.

READ: Luke 15:25-32
So his father went out and begged him to come in... (NCV)

I'm a big fan of happy-ever-after stories but this isn't one of them. Jesus adds on this sad epilogue about the older brother but doesn't tell us how the family saga pans out. It's like a film that's been switched off too soon. Does the other son decide to go to the party or not?

Much is made of this guy's resentment and jealousy of his little brother and the over-the-top fuss made of him as he comes home. He's seriously cheesed off by the welcome this selfish man gets, especially given how he left and lived once he'd ridden off into the sunset. Who can blame this responsible, older brother who just tried to do the right thing?

But there's a deeper problem. His resentment and jealousy are merely signs this son doesn't know his dad either. All this time he'd worked hard for him, believing that's what would earn him his father's favour and generosity. But he didn't love his dad any more than his brother did. He'd slaved away, hoping for blessing to be the reward, only to discover it was a free gift all along. Ouch.

Reckless living can't destroy the Father's love, and right living can't deserve it. No amount of activity for His causes will impress Him into loving and blessing us. We can't buy His love with our good choices or great achievements and we can't blow it up with our bad ones either. Jesus is desperate for us to get this because it changes everything. Friend, you can't make the Father love you and you can't make Him stop loving you. Whoever you are, whatever kind of life you're living, whatever your past, He loves you with this same deep, compassionate, affectionate love. He wants to be a father to you and He wants you confident of His never-changing love.

PONDER
What are some of the ways the Father has shown His love for you, when you knew you'd done nothing to deserve it? Do you relate to the older brother in any way?

PRAY
Talk to the Father about whatever is on your heart today.

READThe: Matthew 23:9

**And don't address anyone here on earth as 'Father,' for only God
in Heaven is your Father.** (NLT)

Much of how we relate to God as Father is influenced by our relationship with our own father or significant authority figures in our life. We tend to look at God through the broken lenses of our past experiences as much as anything else. That's why He needs to *reveal* Himself as Father to us.

Part of this process of discovering more of His heart for us is allowing Him to identify for us the broken lenses we look through. Those broken lenses are shaped by lies we believe about His love for us, partly due to past or painful experiences. Asking Him to expose and identify them is never about finger-pointing, only ever about freedom.

PUSH IN

– Pray and ask the Father to come and speak to you now.

– Look at the list of words you made on Day 1 this week, when you thought of God as Father. Add any more that you have thought of since.

– Ask Jesus to show you the truth, and then write down alongside each one, the word(s) that this story would use to describe Him.

– Notice where the words are different. Ask Jesus to show you any lie you've believed about the Father's nature, or His love for you personally. Ask Him to show you how it's affected your relationship with Him.

– Decide to stop agreeing with any lies. e.g. 'I refuse to believe the lie that You are impatient with me'. Choose to start agreeing with Him by thanking Him for the truth He's shown you. e.g. 'Thank You that You're a Father who waits and that You're so patient with me.' Ask Him to help that truth become more real to you as you walk with Him.

Pray about each word on your list.

READ: 1 John 3:1

See what great love the Father has lavished on us, that we should be called children of God! And that is what we are!

In the story of the phenomenal father, he gave his son three gifts as the young man arrived home:

1. He gave him the best robe in the house to cover the smelly rags he was wearing. This symbolised restoration to the family even though he'd always been a son.

2. He gave him a ring which enabled him to exercise the authority of a son. He would have used it to put the family seal on documents.

3. He gave him some sandals which only family members were allowed to wear. The servants all had bare feet.

Each gift reinforced to the son that his identity hadn't changed; he was still a son and would still be treated as one. Every time we do something to wound the Father and to undermine our relationship with Him, His response to us is the same. Our choices may have consequences, but they never change either the fact that we're a daughter, or His love for us.

PUSH IN

Close your eyes and draw near to the Father. Picture a place you love to be in, perhaps somewhere that is special to you. Imagine yourself meeting Him there.

– Is there anything you currently regret that you want to tell Him about? Is there anything you've done that has wounded His heart or affected your relationship with Him? Be honest with Him.

– Imagine Him giving you a gift like the father did his son. Notice what He gives you. Receive it by thanking Him for it. Ask Him what is significant about it or what He wants you to do with it.

Thank Him for the truth of this verse. Thank Him that He has lavished His great love on you. Be specific about some of the ways He has done that.

READ: Ephesians 1:3-8

Long, long ago He decided to adopt us into His family through Jesus. (MSG)

The most important truth about your new identity is that you're a daughter. Not just any old daughter, but the daughter of the King. We were all born to human fathers, but the most significant truth about us is we have a heavenly Father. He's the most phenomenal father to us every day and will be forever. But we didn't start life like this.

Paul says here we've been adopted. Adoption involves a choice. I have some friends who want to adopt a child. They're currently going through a long process which will result in them choosing a child to become their own. Whichever little person is lucky enough to join their family, he or she will end up enjoying the same legal rights, the same love and the same privileges as their biological child.

God is your Father. He's adopted you to be His very own daughter. You belong to Him. He wanted you. What's more, verse 5 says it gave Him great pleasure to adopt you. Isn't that incredible? He loves you intimately and personally. His arms are open to embrace you not as a sinner or a stranger or even a servant, but as His daughter. Jesus says something extraordinary – that the Father loves us as much as He loves Jesus (Jn 17:23). Think about that for a moment; your picture is up there on His wall right next to His picture of Jesus.

We're all looking for love through friendship and relationship. But human love never fully delivers what we're longing for *because* it is human love. Stop expecting it to, if you need to. The reason Jesus was free from anxiety and insecurity, and full of peace and confidence, was because He was so sure of His Dad's love for Him. Our heavenly Father is committed to making that our experience too.

PONDER

Hear God saying, 'My daughter'. Hear Him tell you it gave Him great pleasure to adopt *you*.

PRAY

Thank Him that you're His girl and that He wanted you in His family. Thank Him that He loves you as much He loves Jesus and tell Him how that makes you feel.

READ: John 14:18-20
I will not leave you as orphans.

I don't always agree with Chinese philosophers, but it's hard to disagree with this one! Lao Tzu said, '*The journey of a thousand miles begins with one step.*' Learning to live like a daughter and learning to be loved as a daughter is a journey which happens one step at a time.

Do you ever wonder whether the Father really approves of you and will come through for you? Do you ever act as if He's not really your Father? Do you ever wonder if He knows where you are and cares about your needs? Do you ever wonder whether He's turned His back on you or changed His mind about you? These are questions from our old orphan nature reflecting our uncertainty about the Father's goodness and His heart for us. No one is born into God's family (even if we were born into a family of believers). We're adopted into it. So God has to delete our 'orphan' thinking and teach us how to live as a royal daughter and how to relate to Him as a loving Father.

Friend, this is the bottom line of the journey of transformation we're on. It's a journey of many steps that takes a lifetime. It's all about learning to love Him as Father, turn to Him as Father, depend on Him as Father, listen to Him as Father and obey Him as Father. It's all about learning to live out of our identity as a royal daughter. And all the implications of that identity. Don't let this journey become about anything else. And don't lose touch with it. Whatever else we wrestle with in life, the more personal our experience of His love and the more He reveals Himself to us, the more our hearts and lives change. Is that what you're after?

PONDER
Think about your journey with God so far. How far have you travelled in learning to live like a precious daughter? What has changed along the way? Do you need to reset what you think the journey of transformation is about?

PRAY
Commit your day to Him. Ask Him to draw your attention to the moments during today when you act/react like someone who isn't confident about her Dad's love. When He prompts you, thank Him that you're no longer an orphan and that He is your Dad.

READ: Luke 11:1-4
When you pray, say 'Father'... (NLT)

The journey of learning to live as a daughter is shaped, amongst other things, by our personal encounters with God's love for us as His child. He wants you to experience His love, not just know about it in theory.

Several years ago, I asked God to show me how to let Him love me as a Father. I wanted to learn how to live as His daughter, not an orphan. He's still teaching me, but He began by starting to remove some of the obstacles that prevented me from trusting His love. My sound track was that I wasn't good enough for Him to love me, so He couldn't love me in the way He loved Jesus. I didn't see it at the time, but I was actually rejecting His love. It was a vicious circle, because my lack of experience of His love just reinforced my suspicion that there was something about me that disqualified me!

One of the many things I struggled to believe was that God wanted to bless me just because I'm His daughter. No other reason. I could get my head around rewards for good people doing good things, but not random blessings just because I'm me and I'm His. So I asked Him for a birthday present. He'd been speaking about being Father so I prayed a bit of an audacious prayer with no idea how He would answer it.

Fast forward to the day. That evening, someone (who didn't know it was my birthday) popped round with a gift. She was buying something for herself that week but got to the till to pay and sensed God say, 'Please give that to Hils'. So she did! On my birthday. And guess what? She'd bought a framed print of the Luke 15 moment - the Father embracing His child. His love for me as my Father sank in a whole lot deeper that day.

God's love isn't a theory. It's a reality to be enjoyed and experienced by His daughters. Is it more theory, or more reality for you?

PRAY
Call God 'Father'. Say it, slowly, a few times, just as Jesus suggests. Then ask Him to show you, if you were a jewel, which jewel you would be. Ask the Father what He loves about that jewel and what is significant about it. Pray any audacious prayers that are on your heart.

READ: Matthew 18:1-5
**...unless you turn and become like children, you will never enter
the kingdom of heaven...** (ESV)

Do you remember the classmate who asked the questions that everyone else was too afraid to ask in case they looked bad? I love the fact that Jesus' disciples asked Him all kinds of questions, confident nothing would offend Him and nothing would change how He felt about them. This time they ask Him, 'Who gets to be the greatest in the kingdom of God?' Bit cocky?

His answer wasn't what they expected, but what's new? He says to these grown men, probably with a twinkle in His eye, 'If you want to fly high in My kingdom, you've got to go low and live like children'. What's the deal with young children? They're usually fun-loving, playful, unafraid to ask for stuff, carefree (it's the parents who worry), uninhibited, trusting and brilliant at receiving things, including love. They're also honest about their needs and happy to depend on others for life. What about us?

Sadly, we can lose so many of these characteristics as we grow up. Independence is highly prized in our individualistic age. We become less trusting of others, especially if we've been let down in the past. Then we bring these mindsets to our relationship with God. But Jesus says to live the kingdom life we were made for, we can only find it by living like small children. His life is only accessible through trust and dependence.

Let's not underestimate the challenge of what Jesus is saying; it's radical, but it leads to radical freedom. Instead of relying on ourselves, we must learn to rely more on the Father. Instead of needing to be in control, we must learn to let Him be in control. Instead of acting independently from Him, we must grow in dependence on Him. I find it challenging! How are you doing?

PONDER
Which of the characteristics of small children is true of you? Which do you find most challenging?

PRAY
Thank the Father that He invites you to come to Him with the simplicity of a child. Picture yourself on His lap. Ask Him to show you what you could do differently to grow in childlikeness.

READ: Matthew 3:13-17

And a voice from Heaven said, 'This is My dearly loved Son, who brings Me great joy.' (NLT)

Wouldn't you love to hear a voice from Heaven? As Jesus made his debut 2,000 years ago, the Father proudly declared, 'Hey everyone, look! Here's My incredible Son who I adore. He makes Me so proud and brings Me so much joy'. Jesus was no longer a little boy, but a fully grown, well-built carpenter. And yet His Father wanted Him, and everyone else around, to know just how much He adored Him.

The same voice from heaven speaks those same words over you today. 'You're My dearly loved daughter and you bring Me great joy.' The Father loves you the same way He loves Jesus, remember? Sadly, many of us find it difficult to recognise the Father's tender voice and can't get our heads round the fact He'd say this about us. Why is that?

It's partly because of our human father experiences. Let's be aware that we tend to make many assumptions about God based on them (e.g. my father wasn't interested in me so God won't be either). God wants to correct these assumptions and let the truth about who He is change our thinking and our living. It's a journey, as we've said. Learning to live like a treasured daughter rather than a troubled orphan means letting Him work in us as we go. But it involves being willing to:

1. Recognise: that our earthly father and any other father figures don't/didn't reflect God accurately, no matter how hard they tried. They are/were not perfect.

2. Revise: our view of the Father where necessary. We need God to help us separate our human experiences from the truth of who He is and let Him teach us about His heart.

3. Release: our father or other father figures from any unforgiveness we hold against them for the ways they may have wounded us.

It's 'daughter' thinking, not 'orphan' thinking that releases us to live more freely and fully in His love. Let Him help you take a step forward today.

PAUSE

Take a few moments to hear the Father tell you, '*You* are my dearly loved daughter...' Don't reject His words, thank Him. Instead go back to them as many times as you remember today.

PUSH IN

God is a perfect Father and has all the characteristics on the right-hand side of these two columns. Ask Him to highlight the word on the right-hand side that you most struggle to associate with Him today.

Critical	*Affirming*	Unforgiving	*Forgiving*
Cold	*Affectionate*	Distant	*Close*
Disinterested	*Involved*	Abusive	*Kind*
Indifferent	*Passionate*	Stingy	*Generous*
Passive	*Proactive*	Controlling	*Releasing*
Demanding	*Patient*	Moody	*Joyful*
Unpredictable	*Consistent*	Unreliable	*Trustworthy*
Inaccessible	*Available*	Judgemental	*Merciful*
Negligent	*Protective*	Absent	*Present*

If your own father failed to model that characteristic to you, choose to forgive him for misrepresenting God to you in that specific way. Here are some helpful steps to do that:

1. Ask the Holy Spirit whether you're still carrying in your heart any anger, bitterness, resentment, disappointment, disillusionment, or hurt from it. Pause until He shows you. Ask Him to show you what it would look like if what's in your heart was an object.

2. Tell God how you feel. Be honest. Receive His comfort. He cares about your heart.

3. Make a decision to forgive your father for his weakness in that area and how it affected you. Forgiving means acknowledging he didn't do things the way God would have done them. It means refusing to blame him for the way you feel. It means letting go of any desire to pay him back, and it means letting go of any expectations that he might change or put things right if he's still alive. Give God the object.

4. Ask God to bless your father if he's still alive. Thank God that He is different, and ask Him to reveal to you the particular aspect of His heart that is currently so difficult for you to connect with. Ask Him to show you how your relationship with Him would change if you believed this truth about Him. Ask Him what He wants to give you in place of the object and ask Him to help you begin to trust that He is really like He says He is.

READ: 1 John 3:1

How great is the love that the Father has lavished on us, that we should be called children of God. And that is what we are!

PUSH IN

Read this verse a couple of times and then grab a bit of paper, your phone, or use the space below. Write down what you believe the Father has been saying to you this week. Talk to Him about it, and about what's on your heart today.

Thank Him for the truth of this verse. Memorise it, and make 'us' and 'we' personal as 'me' and 'I'. Declare it over yourself now, and keep doing so during the day today.

READ: Psalm 34:8-14
Oh, taste and see that the Lord is good... (NKJV)

God is good. We read it, we say it and we sing it. But one of the biggest and deepest questions we wrestle with is this: 'Is God really good?' I'm sure you don't have to try too hard to fill in the blank with your own version of, 'If God is really good then why _____ ?' Eve's version might have gone like this: 'If God is so good, then why tell us we couldn't eat a yummy-looking apple that would make us more like Him?'

Whether it's staring at an appetising apple that's out of bounds, standing by a graveside, struggling with a diagnosis, waiting for a prayer to be answered, stepping in to the unknown, or a quick study of the headlines, life provides plenty of opportunities to ask the question, 'Is God really good?' If the answer is 'yes', then it means He's incapable of doing or causing anything bad. You're not truly good unless you're always good. To everyone. The challenge is, how do we answer this question?

God doesn't say we can understand His goodness with our minds. It's not surprising, given what life throws at us. Beware: a trap awaits us if try. If we could explain everything, we wouldn't need to trust Him. We can explain a lot, but being able to say, 'I don't understand, but I trust He is good', matters. Easier said than done, I know. Instead of offering us an explanation, God offers us an invitation; to 'taste and see' that He is good. They are experience words. He wants us to experience His goodness even when we can't explain it. God wants His daughters to step forward and step up, particularly in tough times, to partner with Him to destroy the works of the enemy in this world. The more confident we are that He is always good, the more effective we will be. The Father invites you again today into a deeper experience of His radical goodness.

PONDER

How have you tasted and seen that God is good? Have you got stuck in trying to reconcile God's goodness with an experience in your life? Do you need to surrender your need for an explanation and lay down your right to understand?

PRAY

Ask the Holy Spirit to awaken your spiritual senses and lead you into a deeper experience of the Father's goodness. Ask to know His heart for you better, so you can represent Him better.

READ: Acts 10:34-43
...He went around doing good and healing all who were under the power of the devil, because God was with Him.

I was with someone this morning who isn't sure yet about God. She thinks He may be real, but doesn't understand 'why He causes so much trouble'. I get it – it's a common stumbling block when we imagine God would run the world by remote control. He seems to get the blame for so much, and the credit for so little. How do we grow our confidence about what He's really like and whether He is truly good when so many things complicate the matter? God's answer to us is this: 'Look at Jesus.'

Hebrews 1:3 says Jesus 'perfectly mirrors God.' In other words, God is saying, 'The way to be sure about what I'm like is to look at Jesus, not your circumstances.' And this verse above sums Jesus up. He went around doing good. Only good. Pause for a moment. When did He refuse to heal someone? When did He bless someone in their pain? When did He initiate suffering? When did He refuse to help someone who asked? When did He show He doesn't care? When did He refuse to give someone a second chance? When did He refuse to sacrifice Himself for others? You're on dangerous ground if you draw conclusions about what the Father's like that you can't back up from the life of Jesus.

There are many reasons for the trouble in our world and in our lives. Some we can explain, some we can't. But one explanation that makes little sense, because of Jesus, is that God isn't good and wants to harm us. Faith trusts. When there aren't explanations. Reason draws wrong conclusions about Him. Friend, know that when you're in pain, He feels it with you. He gave His Son to heal you and free you. Because He's good. Because He delights to do good to you. Day in. Day out. Forever.

PONDER
Do you believe something about God that you can't find in the life of Jesus?

PRAY
Spend some time thanking God that He is good, whether or not it feels true for you today. Thank Jesus for showing you what the Father is like. Thank Him that the cross proves just how good He is to you and thank Him that He's working for your good today.

READ: Genesis 50:15-21
Don't you see, you planned evil against me but God used those same plans for my good... (MSG)

Not everything that happens in life is the Father's plan A. It stretches our minds to accept He's in charge as God, without controlling everything that happens. But let's admit it, if we could understand it all and fit His big ways into our little brains, He wouldn't be any bigger than us!

Joseph's brothers devised a cruel plan. They plotted to kill him because they wanted rid of him. Then they downgraded the plan and sold him. This wasn't the Father's intention for Joseph. He's a good Father, but He didn't stop it, because He refuses to control us like robots. By the time Joseph and his brothers met and made up many years later, Joseph had discovered this and discovered the heart and power of his God. He tells them, 'Yes, you plotted to hurt me, but God had other plans. He turned your evil plan into an opportunity for my good.' He says God also turned it into an opportunity for the good of tons of others too. He is so good.

God isn't the author of the bad stuff in your life. We live in a broken world, full of people who make bad choices (like Joseph's brothers), and we do too. We also have an enemy. But God is good, and because He is, He takes the evil that comes our way and uses it as a chance to do something really good for us. Joseph confidently declared that God didn't plan his trouble; instead, He turned it into a plan for Joseph's good. When we end up somewhere we didn't intend or don't want to be, sat navs are great at rerouting us to our destination. But they have nothing on the Father. He takes ruined plan A and somehow turns it into plan A*. God is better than you know and He's working for your good today. Trust Him, whatever your circumstances.

PONDER
How does the Father want to change your perspective on the bad stuff that happens in your life? How does He want to change your response to it?

PRAY
Ask Him to increase your confidence in His ability *and* desire to turn bad stuff into good. Ask Him to help you confront every difficulty in your life with this perspective and this confidence, so that how you pray and what you say about your difficulties changes.

READ: Matthew 7:7-12
Or when asked for a piece of fish, what parent would offer his child a snake instead? (TPT)

Jesus knows us so well because the Father knows us so well. Why else would He say what He says here, unless He was trying to reassure us that God is truly good? I think He's speaking to the deep uncertainty within us, that God can't be trusted not to pull a fast one on us. I think He's speaking to the deep fear that God might give us something, or do something to us, that's unkind at best or cruel at worst.

When my sons were small, they didn't ask for fish for supper because they hated fish! But they did ask for sausages. And when they did, I didn't serve up sushi. Why would I? I have many faults as a mum, but that would've been mean. I love my kids and wouldn't give them what they couldn't swallow! Jesus says, 'Well, your heavenly Dad is a better parent than you. He's so good. Why would you think He'd give you a snake when you asked for a fish finger?' Why would we? But we do.

When someone painfully tells me the Father 'took their baby away', they're saying they asked for a piece of fish and got a snake. When I question if God caused the situation that's causing me to suffer, I'm asking the same thing. I imagine it breaks Jesus' heart that we would question His heart like that. But if He needed to say what He said, it's because we need to hear it. Over and over again. Because all kinds of things, including prayers that haven't been answered in the way we wanted, can feed our suspicion that He's not truly good. Jesus is desperate for you to be sure about God's heart for you. Let Him grow your confidence in God's goodness a little more today.

PAUSE
Memorise: 'So if you sinful people know how to give good gifts to your children, how much more will your heavenly Father give good gifts to those who ask Him.'
As you do, ask the Holy Spirit to show you anything that's preventing you from trusting this promise more fully. Repeat this verse to yourself during the day today, and each time you do, ask the Father to help you become more confident that He is always good to you.

READ: Psalm 27:7-14

I would have lost heart, unless I had believed that I would see the goodness of the Lord in the land of the living. (NKJV)

The Father spoke to me through this verse in a season of real turmoil and trouble. He showed me that the condition of my heart was connected to what I focused on – and specifically whether I expected Him to be good to me in my tomorrows. I couldn't join David in saying, 'I would've lost heart if I didn't expect to see God's goodness break through in my life'. God said to me, 'Daughter, you *are* losing heart. You're not convinced I'm always good so you're not expecting Me to come through for you.'

When we lose sight of the Father's goodness and that His plans for us are good (Jer 29:11), we start to lose heart. The problem is, the truth that God is good tends to get buried under a pile of endless disappointments and defeats. If we believe He's behind our hurt and pain, or our trouble today, how can we trust He won't bring more tomorrow? How can we trust He intends to help us today? And how can we carry a confidence of breakthrough for ourselves and others? Trouble gives us the opportunity to look under the bonnet of our hearts and check our level of confidence in the Father's goodness.

Friend, do you need to fight for your heart today? We must fight the disappointment, the cynicism and the resignation that try and take hold so we lose heart. We need our hearts to live this life we've been called to. How do we take heart when we're losing heart? We have to decide to switch our focus. We have to choose, moment by moment if we need to, to focus on His promises, on His word, on the things He's said to us, and to focus on the things He's *already* done for us. Not the things that haven't happened for us. Hope rises when we do. Let's let the cross, not our experiences, have the final say on God's heart for us.

PONDER

Ask the Holy Spirit to show you if you're losing heart over any situation in your life.

PRAY

Confess any disappointment or resignation that's settled in your heart. Tell the Father you don't want it anymore. Ask Him to remind you of a promise He wants you to focus on today.

READ: Psalm 103:8-17

Ask the Holy Spirit to speak to you about His goodness as you read these verses. Read them through slowly.

PUSH IN

– Go back over the passage and stop and write down the aspect of God's goodness that stands out to you most today.

– Spend a few moments thinking about this expression of His goodness.

– What does it mean for you?

– If you believed it with all your heart, how would your life look different?

– Is there any lie about the Father that the Holy Spirit wants to replace with this truth today?

If you were going to describe this dimension of His goodness to a friend who doesn't know Him, how would you do it in your own words?

READ: Matthew 4:23

Jesus traveled throughout the region of Galilee, teaching in the synagogues and announcing the Good News about the Kingdom. And He healed every kind of disease and illness. (NLT)

PUSH IN

God is good, and Jesus brought good news. In what ways is the kingdom good news to you? Be as specific as you can and note them down.

Turn your answers into thanks and praise to your King.

READ: Isaiah 41:8-10
I have chosen you and have not rejected you.

Do you know what it's like to feel rejected? To be overlooked, dismissed, left out, cast aside, or pushed away? Of course you do! I've been there, you've been there, we've all been there, even Jesus has been there. Depending on who's rejected you, it will have been more painful or less painful. But I know you'll agree it's not an experience to recommend.

God doesn't reject you, He never has, and He wasn't behind your experiences of rejection. He wants you sure that He's chosen *you*. You might want to re-read that. He's singled you out, died for you and called your name. He wants to draw you closer and deeper into His love and He wants to lead you further into His purposes for you. The reason you know Him is not because you chose Him, but because Jesus chose you.

The enemy wants you to believe, through your experiences of rejection, that there's something wrong with you; that you wouldn't have been rejected 'if you were...' or 'if you hadn't...' Friend, you must stand against those lies. The truth is, the Father in Heaven has picked you. Nothing you can ever do will make Him change His mind about you. In fact, He saw you and chose you before you even knew He existed. Before you could try and impress Him, He saw all there was to see about you, your flaws and faults included. He knows you fully, and He still chose you.

God says a loud 'yes' over your life every day. You are chosen. He shouted 'yes' over you the day you were born, 'yes' over you yesterday, and He'll shout 'yes' again tomorrow. Let His 'yes' get hold of you now. Hear it in your heart and let it be your soundtrack throughout the day today.

PONDER
Ask God to show you if there is someone who has rejected you that He wants you to forgive today from your heart.

PRAY
Be honest with Him about how their rejection of you made you feel. Release them to God and thank Him that He's different, that He's chosen you and that He will never reject you. Re-read the verse above. Spend a moment silently listening to His 'yes' over you.

READ: Colossians 3:12-15
So, chosen by God for this new life of love... (MSG)

Are you a bath or a shower girl? God intended (from the start) to shower you with His love and soak you in His kindness, not just for a short time but for a lifetime. The Father has chosen you for a life of love. Have you ever wondered why you long to be loved? Why you are able to love other people but the flies on your window can't? Maybe not, but let me tell you, it's because you're made in His image and your Father is a God of love. He's chosen you to love you. How much do you believe that?

It's easy to think God made us and chose us to do something. So much of life seems to be about what we do or how we do it. 'What do you do with your time?' 'What do you do for a living?' 'What did you do today?' It's not that these are bad questions, they're just not the most important questions. The world overemphasises performance and underemphasises love. Jesus does the opposite. He hasn't chosen you primarily to do something for Him, but to receive something from Him. His love.

Paul prays in chapter 3 of Ephesians for God to help us become 'rooted and established' in His love. His love, and a real experience of it, is meant to be the bedrock and the soundtrack to our lives. It's what everything else is meant to be built on; including our relationships, our speech, our studies, our decisions, our dreams and our work.

God has chosen you to love you. He's chosen you for a life that's meant to be defined by and driven by His love for you. If you're tempted to think you can influence His heart for you by the way you live or the choices you make, then decide again today to let that mindset go. You can't! You can only get better at receiving His love and walking in it.

PONDER
How good are you at receiving things (e.g. gifts, compliments, help etc)? Do you need to practise receiving? How easy do you find it to receive God's love?

PRAY
The last phrase in today's reading gives us a big clue how to receive something: being thankful. Spend some time thanking God that He's chosen you to love you. Practise being thankful today – thank Him that He loves you whenever you remember, even if you don't feel His love.

READ: Ephesians 1:3-8
Even before He made the world, God loved us and chose us... (NLT)

This verse (v4) is mind-blowing (in my humble opinion!). Whatever the circumstances of your physical beginnings in this life, whether or not your parents were together, whether or not you were planned, God chose you before He made the world. Pause and let that sink in for a moment.

Imagine the scene. Darkness is covering the earth. The Spirit is hovering over the waters. There is no sea, no sun, no trees, no birds, no animals, and the Father is thinking, 'I want a Sarah', 'I want an Abi', I want a '*your name*'. That's when He made His decision about you; before He'd said, 'Let there be light.' Long ago, before your ancestors even existed, you were a dream in the Father's heart. You were His idea. He wanted you. And as verse 5 says, He didn't want to love you from a distance, but to welcome you into His family as His daughter. He chose you because He wanted a close relationship with you.

Unfortunately, some Christian teaching leaves us feeling that God needs us; that He needs our worship, our work, our money, for us to be good people, or for us to change the world for Him. I hate to break this to you friend, but God doesn't need anything from you. I know you have some outstanding qualities and some amazing gifts – He made you after all – but He managed to make the universe without your help. I didn't have kids to help me with my housework and neither did the Father.

He doesn't need you but He longs for you. There's one thing you can offer Him that no one else can – your heart. No one else can offer God a relationship with you. There's only one you, with your personality, your heart, your history and your DNA. No one else can be the daughter you can, and no one else can have the Father/daughter partnership with Him that He longs to have with you.

PAUSE
Think about how God chose you for relationship with Him before He'd even made the stars. How does that make you feel? Do you prioritise your relationship with Him over what you do for Him? Declare out loud: 'I am loved and chosen by God and He chose me before I was even born.'

READ: Romans 8:26-30
For God knew His people in advance, and He chose them to become like His Son... (NLT)

How do you fancy being full of joy? How do you fancy being free from the need to seek the approval of others? How do you fancy never worrying, always hearing the voice of God, being full of courage and power and able to love anyone who crosses your path? Jesus was all of the above and much more, and God has chosen us to become like Him. He's more concerned about how like Jesus we are than how many likes we get!

When we talk about change, and becoming more like Him, there are two potential traps to fall into. The first is to think we have to change for God to fully love us; that the more we do, the more He'll love us. Nothing could be further from the truth. He's chosen you to love you and to enjoy a relationship with you as His own daughter. You don't have to persuade Him by trying to impress Him. There isn't a love-upgrade on offer. He loves you now as much as He loves Jesus, make sure you remember that.

The second trap is to think we're supposed to change ourselves. Let me tell you a secret – you'll never succeed! Trying hard to do good or follow some rules, or beating yourself up into becoming someone different doesn't work. I've tried it – it's a dead-end street. All that stuff is outside stuff and we're designed to live from the inside out, not the outside in.

God has chosen you and is making you like Jesus. But that doesn't happen through you trying hard but through you trusting and walking with Him. It's a heart thing. The more we experience His love and the more we trust Him, the more we become like His Son. And the more we become like Jesus, the more fully we become who we were made to be.

PONDER
Which of the characteristics of Jesus would you most like to see more of in your life?

PRAY
Thank the Father that He's chosen you to become like Jesus, but that you don't have to make this happen yourself. Lay that down if that's something you try and do. Invite Him to grow in you the characteristics you've identified and ask Him to reassure you of His heart for you today.

READ: John 15:5-16
**You didn't choose Me, remember; I chose you, and put you in the world
to bear fruit...** (MSG)

Have you ever felt ordinary or insignificant, like you're nothing special, or is that a no-brainer? This is one of those verses (v16) we should put in our pocket and pull out when we do. Jesus wants to remind you, 'Precious daughter, you didn't choose Me, remember? You didn't find Me, I came and found you. I chose you. And I chose you to be fruitful.'

The reason you have a desire to make a difference in this world and make your life count for Him is because that longing is in your new heart. It's part of Jesus' DNA and it's a core part of who you are. He's chosen you to be a difference maker. How amazing is that? He has a purpose for you and a plan for your life which will fulfil your deep longing for significance. It will also leave a lasting impact on the lives of others.

But here's the thing about fruit: it grows effortlessly. There's no man-made manufacturing process involved but a God-made supernatural one. The Father has chosen you to bear fruit and live a life of significance. He's chosen to use you even if you think it's impossible. But you don't have to strive to make it happen or fight for it. Lasting, life-changing fruit doesn't come from our best efforts and plans. It isn't produced by sussing the seven steps to success or knowing the right people. We know Him. It comes from hanging out with Him, enjoying His love, listening to what He says and living it out. Jesus is describing that here.

The Father has a purpose and a plan for your life that are bigger than your dreams. If they weren't, you wouldn't need Him. Jesus has chosen you, not just to bear fruit, but to bear *much* fruit. Focus on sticking and staying close to Him and you'll be amazed what He grows in your life.

PONDER
What evidence is there that you're making an impact for Him in some way? Ask the Holy Spirit to show you. Do you believe He's chosen you for more?

PRAY
Hear Jesus speaking His words again as you re-read the verse above. Let His words sink in and ask Him to give you His vision for your life. Is there anything else He wants to say to you today?

RE-READ: Isaiah 41:8-10

PUSH IN

As you look at these three verses, replace the names 'Israel' and 'Jacob' with your own name. Take your time to read and re-read them a few times, out loud, and listen to the Father speaking His words to you. Let them soak into your heart and over any situations you're currently facing.

Note anything that comes up in your heart and anything He impresses on you, as you listen to Him. Be real with Him and talk to Him about whatever that is.

Write down anything else you think He might be saying to you.

PUSH IN

Remind yourself today of what the Father has chosen you for. Write the different things down.

– Ask the Holy Spirit to show you any lie you've believed about being chosen that He wants you to let go of today.

– Ask Him to show you how it's affected the way you've been living and relating to God.

– Choose to refuse to partner with that lie anymore. What truth do you need to take hold of in its place? How does that truth affect your relationship with God? Write it down.

Go back and pick a verse from this week. Plant it in your heart by committing it to memory. Declare it over yourself now.

READ: Numbers 23:16-20
Does He speak and not do what He says? Does He promise and not come through? (MSG)

Do you expect God to keep His promises to you? We live in a world of broken promises. Advertisers, politicians, friends, loved ones and others make all kinds of promises (big and small) that they don't deliver on. Many of their promises are empty. I'm guilty too. I make promises to myself that I'll eat less, or exercise more. I make promises to others to pray for them or call them and then forget. And worse. Broken promises can leave us from disappointed or disillusioned to devastated. Let's be honest, sometimes we expect the same from the Father.

Human promises made to us can be empty at the outset. Or they can be broken; because someone changes their mind or because in their weakness, they fail to deliver. God says, 'I'm not like other people; I don't lie and I don't change My mind. I do what I say and I keep My word.' It's easy to make promises, less easy to keep them but the Father says He's a promise keeper not a promise breaker. Do you need to remember that today? Let's admit it can be tough to hold on to – we're not used to someone *always* keeping their promises.

Others have let you down, He won't. Maybe you're feeling let down by God at the moment. Be real with Him about that, but ask yourself this question: when your experience and His word seem to contradict each other, which one do you believe? Others break their word to you, He promises He won't. Others will be unfaithful, He promises He won't. We often have high expectations of others and low expectations of God. It should be the other way round. The more we believe He'll keep His promises to us, the more our hearts will be full of peace. Are you expecting Him to keep His word to you today?

PONDER
Re-read the verse above twice and let the truth of it impact you again. Ask the Holy Spirit to show you if you've believed any lies about God's commitment to fulfil His promises to you. Is there anyone you need to forgive who has broken a promise to you?

PRAY
Thank the Father in faith that He never breaks His promises. Confess your doubts where you have them. Ask Him to grow your confidence in His ability and desire to come through for you.

READ: 2 Samuel 7:25-30

Now, Lord God, keep the promise forever that You made about my family and me, Your servant. Do what You have said. (NCV)

How boldly do you pray? How confident are you when you talk to God? David, who God describes as a man after His own heart, acknowledges (v27) that he's praying boldly and daringly. He's basically saying, 'Lord, You've made a promise, so now keep it.' That could sound cheeky depending on how you hear it. Or it could sound like a child, coming to a loving parent who'd promised to take them to the park at 3pm, saying, 'You said we could go, so let's go!'

The Father wants us to pray boldly and live boldly. Boldness never comes from thinking we deserve something or we've earned something. It comes from believing He's serious about what He's promised. God's promises reveal His intentions. When we find or receive a promise that relates to our situation, we've found God's desire for us. David was so convinced God was a promise keeper, he took the promise God made him and prayed it straight back to Him. David assumed He'd keep it. Is that what we do? How many times do you bring a promise to God that would make a difference to your life, or to someone else's, or to your nation's future, and say, 'Lord, You promised it, so now do what You've said.' I find it's easier to pray over problems than pray God's promises over them. But praying about our problems doesn't release boldness in us. The Father's looking for His girls to take Him seriously. He's honoured when we do, and we get bolder when we do.

You'll never pray a more powerful prayer than, 'Lord, You said it, You do it.' The more we know what He's promised in His word, the more effective our prayers will be. We may need to pray the same promise for a while before we see it for real, but that tests our confidence in it and in Him. Those who take Him at His word, and expect Him to deliver on His word, are those who see Him do so. Like David. He wants that for you.

PAUSE

How familiar are you with God's promises? Think of a situation you're asking God to intervene in. Can you pray, 'Lord, You said (promise), now do it'? If not, find some time today to look up a promise for your situation that will help you pray and keep praying more boldly.

READ: Luke 1:35-45
The Lord has blessed you because you believed that He will keep His promise. (CEV)

Today, like every day, you get to decide what to do with your trust. Who or what will you trust to keep you safe, make life work, provide for your needs, and give you purpose? Will you trust your money, your influence, your abilities, your contacts or your experience? We all trust something.

Mary was a woman who lived an extraordinary life and left a great legacy. She gave birth to a Miracle who changed the destiny of the world. God chose Mary to fulfil His purposes, and He richly blessed her. This verse tells us why; because she believed the Father would keep His impossible promise. She simply trusted Him to keep His word. Imagine what else this verse could have said: 'The Lord has blessed you because – you've worked so hard / you've done so many good things / you're so gifted / you have so much going for you / you've got the right experience / you know the right people / you deserve it because of all you've been through / you were born in the right place / you're so reliable / you never messed up. This is such good news, friend! Take a deep breath and let out a sigh of relief. You don't have to tick any of these boxes for God to bless you like Mary.

Trusting God to keep His promises, no matter how impossible they seem, will take us further than our own resources ever could. Mary put her effort into trusting and was rewarded for it. Simple. And yet not always easy. The Father moves and works because He's promised to. It's our trust in His word that opens the door for Him to do so. Let's be real about the wrestle to trust some of those promises, but let's also keep wrestling to live as daughters who trust Him to keep them.

PONDER
Read the above verse out loud, replacing the first 'you' with 'me' and replacing the second 'you' with 'I'. Read it again.

PRAY
Thank Jesus that He's freed you from needing to qualify in some way for His blessing. Thank Him that His promises contain His blessings, and that 'all' you need to do is believe them. Ask Him to help you trust that He is faithful to every one of them.

READ: Luke 1:8-20
How can I be sure this will happen? I'm an old man now... (NLT)

This sounds like a perfectly reasonable question. God has just told old man Zechariah that his wife is going to have a baby, even though it's not physically possible. He's got some doubts and understandably, he wants reassuring before he gets his hopes up. He and Elizabeth have prayed for this for years (v13) and faced years of disappointment. The last thing he wants is to be disappointed again if it doesn't happen.

We long for God to leave us no room for doubt. Trusting He will keep His promises and waiting to see them fulfilled is a risk, especially when we haven't had our miracles. We risk looking stupid, if He doesn't deliver, and we risk being disappointed. Again. Zechariah was visited by a strapping great angel like Mary was, but for him, it wasn't enough to convince him that God would keep His promise. Fear – of being let down again had taken root. Too many years of hoping alongside negative pregnancy tests. Years of reflecting on what God hadn't done for them prevented him from embracing what the Father was going to do. So he lost out in another way and lost his voice.

God won't persuade us He's going to do what He's promised. He requires us to bring our trust to the table. That means He leaves room for questions and doubts. But faith is what He's after. Trusting is a journey – we trust more on some days than on others. But if our trust isn't growing over time, it's shrinking. Remember; disappointment in what God hasn't done has the power to stop us trusting what He's promised to do, however sensible our questions or doubts sound. Don't give it a chance, friend. Deal with your disappointment instead, by admitting it to yourself and to the Father and asking Him to show you what to do with it.

PAUSE

Have you received a promise from God that feels dormant at the moment? That you've stopped crying out for? Confess any struggle you're having in believing He'll keep it. Confess your doubts and fears to Him. Ask Him if there's disappointment in your heart. Acknowledge it and give it to Him, telling Him you don't want it anymore. Ask Him to show you what He wants you to do next. Ask Him to give you the strength to trust Him to do what He's said, and to keep praying about the promise until you see it.

READ: Hebrews 6:13-18
Then Abraham waited patiently, and he received what God had promised... (NLT)

Do you ever wonder if God hears your prayers? Patiently waiting for God to fulfil a promise He's made can be super challenging. I bet it was for Abraham. God promised him a son, even though he and Sarah were seriously old. Physically it was impossible. And it didn't happen. For more than 20 years. An old couple getting older. I imagine the phrase, 'Abraham waited patiently' hides a lot of questions that he struggled with over this time: 'Did I hear God? Can He really do it? Did I take a wrong turn somewhere? Has He forgotten us or changed His mind?'

God's timing stretches our trust in Him as a promise keeper. We live in a world where we can get instant deliveries from Amazon and instant answers from Google. But we know God doesn't always do instant. Often there's a big delay between receiving or discovering a promise (and starting to pray it back to Him) and seeing it fulfilled. If it was better for us to have an immediate answer, He'd give it, which He does sometimes. But other times, He works in the delay. That's where we discover if we're still confident He'll keep His promises. Waiting is always a workout for our faith.

Abraham wrestled with doubt, but wasn't won over by it. His confidence that God would keep His promise grew, rather than shrank, through his long wait. Abraham moved between, 'I doubt' and 'I hope', to eventually, 'I know'. If you're holding on to a promise that God has yet to fulfil, you're in good company. If you're fighting to believe that God will keep a promise to you, you're not alone. Be encouraged; God is growing your faith by testing it. Don't give up. Decide again today, to turn down the volume on your doubts and turn it up on His nature as the Promise Keeper. Trust His timing, keep praying and you'll get wiser while you wait.

PONDER

Ask the Holy Spirit who needs encouraging with this verse today, and then message them with it.

PRAY

Thank the Father that He doesn't change His mind, and He hasn't forgotten you. Ask Him to strengthen and grow your faith as you wait for Him to do what He has promised. Then pray for anyone you know who is waiting for God to deliver on a promise to them.

PUSH IN

From this short list of promises, pick one out. Write it on a Post-it Note *and* on a bigger piece of paper. (If you're up for a challenge, try doing two!) Stick the Post-it Note on a mirror or cupboard and each time you see it over the next few days, test yourself to see if you can remember the promise. Take the other, bigger piece of paper that you've written the promise on, and stand on it now. As you do, see it as a prophetic declaration that you are going to stand on God's word to you until He fulfils it. Pray about it, ask God to do what He's said, and thank Him that He is going to.

(Alternatively, find a different promise from the Bible that is relevant to you at the moment and do the same with it.)

I will never leave you or abandon you. (Heb 13:5)

But my God shall supply your every need according to His riches in glory by Christ Jesus. (Phil 4:19)

I will repay you for the years the locusts have eaten. (Joel 2:25)

If we confess our sins, He is faithful and just and will forgive us our sins and purify us from all unrighteousness. (1 Jn 1:9)

When you walk through the fire, you will not be burned. (Is 43:2)

The Lord will fight for you; you need only to be still. (Ex 14:14)

Keep on asking and you will receive what you ask for. Keep on seeking and you will find. Keep on knocking and the door will be opened to you. (Lk 11:9 NLT)

I will pour out My Spirit on all people. (Joel 2:28)

His mercies begin afresh each morning. (Lam 3:23 NLT)

Nothing can get between me and God's love. (Rom 8:38 MSG)

I tell you the truth, anyone who believes in Me will do the same works I have done, and even greater works... (Jn 14:12 NLT)

READ: Psalm 77:1-15
But then I recall all You have done, O Lord; I remember Your wonderful deeds of long ago. (NLT)

'Remember...'. The Father frequently tells us to remember what He's done, because we have such short memories! Often, the writers of the psalms put this command into practice to encourage themselves.

The person writing this psalm is struggling. He's still waiting for the breakthrough he's been crying out for, that God promised. His struggles with hopelessness and unbelief are tangible in his words. I am so reassured by his gut-wrenching honesty. His openness reveals an inner battle to keep trusting. In verse 11 however, he introduces a 'but'. It's a strategic decision because 'but' is a powerful word. 'But' is a word that shifts gears. It shifts our focus from the reality of our experience to the reality of Heaven. 'But' shifts us from the flesh into the spirit. 'But' shifts us from walking by feelings to walking by faith. 'But' shifts us from discouragement to encouragement. He says, 'But, I recall....' We need to master the 'but' word too.

PUSH IN
Get some paper and a pen, your phone, or use the space below. Make a list of the promises that God has kept to you this far. Remember what He's *already* done for you. Spend some time thanking Him that He's been faithful and kind to you. Let faith and praise rise as you remember that you're the daughter of a promise keeper. Thank Him in faith for the promises He's going to fulfil in the future because you're praying, 'You said it. Now do it.'

READ: Ephesians 2:4-10
For we are God's masterpiece. (NLT)

Whether it's comparing hairstyles or homes, bank balances or body shapes, families or friends, social media followers or success stories, we give in so easily to the toxic temptation of comparison. But it's so ridiculous when we remember that God says we are each a masterpiece.

The original word used here implies a work of art. A handmade masterpiece not a factory-made one. That means one thing: you're unique. You're uniquely designed and uniquely shaped for a unique purpose that only you can fulfil. The Father doesn't do repeats. Every snowflake has a different structure, every zebra has a different set of stripes, and each of His daughters is just as unique. Once God made you, He threw away the mould. You're an original. There is only one of you.

Since you're His masterpiece and an original, you're also uniquely valuable. Anything painted by Van Gogh sells for millions. The copies don't. Anyone designed and created by God, no matter how their life has panned out, is worth infinitely more – the life of His Son. When we try and copy others, whether it's their gifts or their way of doing things, what they have or where they're going, we undermine our own value. God has made each one of us different to everyone else.

Friend, comparison compromises. It compromises our calling and our confidence. No one else can fill your shoes or run your race and you can't run anyone else's either. It's one thing to be inspired by others, it's another to think you need to imitate them to fulfil His plans and purposes for you. The Father loves to grow your confidence in who you are and wants to free you to be your beautiful self. He says you are a masterpiece. You're made for a unique purpose.

PONDER
Who are the people you are most likely to compare yourself with? What do you compare?

PRAY
Ask the Father to forgive you for comparing yourself. Thank Him you're an original and that there is no one else like you. Thank Him that He has a unique role for you to play on earth. Ask Him to help you enjoy being the one-of-a-kind that is you and move away from comparison.

READ: Psalm 139:13-16

Thank you for making me so wonderfully complex! Your workmanship is marvellous - how well I know it. (NLT)

Do you know how unique you are? David wrote Psalm 139 thousands of years ago saying we're 'wonderfully complex.' Here's a bit of science from the internet to elaborate. In the natural realm, your physical parents created you. One cell (a very exhausted cell) from your biological father met one cell from your biological mother. Each cell carried 23 chromosomes, and the two cells merged into one. This new cell then formed a new DNA code for you (it functions a bit like a guidebook). It had 3 billion characters on it describing who God designed you to be. If you typed at 200 characters a minute, it would take 29 years to type out this description of you!

That one cell set about building 'you' from that guidebook blueprint. You ended up with about 37 trillion cells in your body (give or take a few). If you took out the DNA in each one and stretched it out, it would cover 42 billion miles. That's going to the moon and back almost 85,000 times.

You are incredible and you are unique. The Father says so. You truly are a masterpiece. No wonder David says to God, 'Your workmanship is marvellous.' No one will ever totally get you (which might be a bit disappointing) because you're 'wonderfully complex'. Don't expect them to. But God does. He's the One who understands you as you're His work of art. He wrote your DNA and He knows you. Completely. Psalm 33:15 says, 'He made their hearts, so He understands everything they do.' Isn't that reassuring?

You have a unique set of stripes! A unique combination of capacity, gifts, passions, personality, dreams, abilities, experiences and limitations (yes limitations). When we become confident in our uniqueness, no one can make us feel inferior and comparison becomes pointless. Why not commit to celebrating your differences in future rather than getting sucked into the comparison thing?

PAUSE

Spend a few moments reflecting on the fact that God has made you both unique, and 'wonderfully complex.' Let this verse sink in, declare it over yourself, and thank Him that you're *His* masterpiece. Ask Him to show you what He's celebrating in you today.

READ: Romans 9:20

Clay doesn't talk back to the fingers that mould it, saying, 'Why did you shape me like this?' (MSG)

God has given you some things to do in this life that only you can do. He's given you a unique set of attributes and abilities, and made you for a unique set of assignments. You can accept them and ask Jesus to lead you into them (it's not automatic), or you can reject them and do life your way. But to play your part, you have to be you. And part of being you is accepting your limitations.

This verse tells us we can resent who we are or aren't and wish we were like someone else. We might not actually say to God, 'Why did you make me like this?' but our dissatisfaction and our efforts to be like others – to do it how they do it, or have what they have – amount to the same thing. Our efforts to change or redefine ourselves are no different. In the Chronicles of Narnia, there's a powerful moment when Lucy wishes she was like her beautiful big sister. This wish comes true and she morphs into Susan. She's catapulted into Susan's life but quickly discovers there's no Narnia. She can't understand why not until Aslan appears and reminds her it was Lucy who discovered Narnia, not Susan. No Lucy, no Narnia. She immediately regrets her wish, realising she's got a different but equally valuable part to play in the world. But she has to play it as Lucy.

You're needed in this world as you. The Father formed you as you are for a reason, friend, and that includes your limitations. He knows all about them. They're designed to keep you in your lane, close to Him and doing what you've been assigned to do. When you reject them and try and be someone you're not, it eventually leads to burn out. So accept who God has made you to be and accept your limitations. And accept others as God has made them to be too. Limitations and all.

PONDER

Which of your limitations do you find the most frustrating, or would you change if you could?

PRAY

Acknowledge your frustrations with the Father. Ask Him to help you accept yourself. Thank Him that your limitations don't limit Him and what He wants to accomplish through you.

READ: Jeremiah 18:6
As the clay is in the potter's hand, so are you in My hand. (TLB)

Are you still breathing? I hope so! Since you are, God is still at work. He's still working on your heart and in your life. He's still working through you to impact the lives of others. You're not damaged goods, or broken beyond repair whatever you think. He says you're His masterpiece. But a masterpiece-in-the-making rather than the finished article.

I love this beautiful image of clay in a potter's hand. God paints this picture to help us understand what's going on in our lives. Imagine a potter sitting in his workshop, bending over his wheel, hands covered in muck. Imagine him working with his clay. Carefully and creatively moulding and shaping it into something beautiful and useful. It's what God does with us, through our relationship with Him. It's a very intimate process.

Do you know what He's doing? Can you point to where He's working in you? There are gifts He wants to grow in you and traps He wants to free you from. Wounds He wants to heal and weaknesses He wants to strengthen. Mindsets He wants to change and secrets He wants to reveal to you. He's still at work. The Bible calls this work of His, sanctification.

Since God is still at work on His masterpiece, it means you're not yet perfect. He's never surprised by our limits and our weaknesses. He doesn't expect us to be perfect. We're His work, not our own. Let that take any pressure off you today. The great news about grace is that it's not our job to make ourselves into the final work of art, it's His. It's not about what we do for Him, but about what He does for us. So friend, cut yourself some slack, enjoy the journey more, and trust that the potter knows exactly what He's doing with His masterpiece. With you.

PONDER
Do you wrestle with perfectionism? How would embracing the fact that you're an unfinished work in God's hands make a difference to you?

PRAY
Ask the Father what He's doing in your life at the moment. Ask Him what He's asking you to do in response. Note down anything He says to you and talk to Him about it.

READ: Isaiah 64:8

Yet You, Lord, are our Father. We are the clay, You are the potter; we are all the work of Your hand.

I'm a bad-news-first girl, are you? I always want to hear it before I hear the good news – maybe it's the romantic in me that likes a happy ending. Well, there's good news and bad news about being a masterpiece-in-the-making, but I'm giving you the bad news first!

As clay in His hands, the moulding and the shaping process can be an uncomfortable one. Sometimes the pressure is on, and it feels like the potter is squeezing pretty hard. God uses all kinds of things as tools in this shaping process, including the everyday circumstances that make us afraid or angry, desperate or doubtful, unsettled or upset. He lets the tough stuff challenge and stretch us, but only because He needs to work in our hearts to prepare us for what lies ahead of us. The more we become dependent on Him rather than distant from Him when the squeeze is on, the more He's able to shape and mould us to be like Him. Resist the urge to escape the potters wheel.

Now the good news. As Isaiah says, the potter is your Father. The One who formed you, knows you, understands you, and adores you. There is no safer pair of hands. Give me a canvas, some oils and a paintbrush and the result wouldn't be much to write home about. My family would crack the jokes. Put the same things in Van Gogh's hands and you'd get the opposite result that would fetch millions at auction. The hands we're in are what counts.

You're God's daughter, and your life is His concern. Each time you're struggling but you choose to stick close to Him, putting your troubles into His hands, He uses them to grow you and has His way in you.

PONDER

What tough challenge are you facing at the moment? What feelings does it stir up in you? How is the potter wanting to shape you through it?

PRAY

Imagine yourself in the Father's hands. Feel His hands on the clay. Feel Him shaping and moulding your heart. Spend some time thanking God that He's your Father as well as the potter. Thank Him that His hands are safe and skilful, and He knows exactly what He's doing.

PUSH IN

Grab a piece of paper or use the space below and jot down some of the things that make you you. You may want to think about what stirs your heart, what you're passionate about, what abilities and gifts you have (be as honest as you can), what experiences you've had that are significant, what personality traits you have, what opportunities you have at the moment, what dreams you have and any prophetic words you've received.

Ask the Father to show you something unique about you today that He particularly enjoys. Write that down too.

Talk to God. Thank Him again that He's made you an original, that what you've written represents a small part of the picture of the uniqueness of you. Ask Him to speak to you about how He wants to use you further for His purposes.

RE-READ: Isaiah 64:8
Yet you, Lord, are our Father. We are the clay, You are the potter; we are all the work of Your hand.

PUSH IN

Re-read this verse a few times out loud, replacing 'our' with 'my', and 'we are' with 'I am.'   Let the truth of this verse touch your heart as you do so. Memorise it.

Then, clench your fists. Ask God to show you if there is anything you're holding on to, carrying, or trying to fix, that He wants you to put into His hands. Give whatever He shows you to Him. Open your fists. Ask Him what He wants to put into your hands. Thank Him for it. If it's relevant, ask Him what He wants you to do with it.

READ: Psalm 23:1-6
The Lord is my Shepherd... (GNT)

I don't know any shepherds, do you? There aren't many in my part of the industrialised world, so what they do doesn't feature in my everyday conversation! But this is the most common metaphor God uses to describe Himself in the Bible. It speaks loudly about His heart for us and what He's like. David calls Him, '*My* Shepherd.' He's not describing a concept He knows about God, but his personal experience of Him.

Shepherd's do virtually all the work in their relationship with their sheep, so they work incredibly long hours. It's a picture of our relationship with God. The shepherd knows where the food and water are, he heals his sheep, he leads them and protects them, he calms their fears and rescues them when they get stuck or wander off. As we read the gospels, we see the wonderful Shepherd in action, doing all of this and more.

The words in this psalm paint an incredible picture of peace. Peace is the result of knowing you have a shepherd. 'Lacking nothing' shows contentment. 'Lying down' speaks of rest. 'Green pastures' suggests a satisfying environment. 'Quiet waters' paints a picture of refreshment and calm. 'Restores' promises broken things get fixed. Yes please! We may live in peacetime conditions, but true peace of mind and heart seem rare today. Yet Jesus promises us this if we call Him, '*My* Shepherd.'

The amazing thing about this peace is that it doesn't depend on our circumstances, only on the Shepherd's presence. But to experience it, we have to let Him *be* a shepherd to us. We follow Him, He doesn't follow us. We let Him have control instead of trying to hold on to it ourselves. The more I lean in to the truth in these verses, the more peace I have. All along, we were made to be loved and taken care of by a Father with a shepherd's heart. David says, 'Look who my Shepherd is, look who's in control of my life.' To what extent can you say this too?

PAUSE

'You're MY Shepherd.' Declare this out loud to Jesus, a number of times, and slowly. Let your heart be stirred and strengthened by it. Receive His peace as you do and let it fill your heart. Does anything make it difficult to say? Add your thanks and turn it into prayer. Talk to Him about how hard you find it to let Him be in control and look after you.

READ: Psalm 23:1
The Lord is my Shepherd; I have all that I need. (NLT)

One of the causes of stress is anxiety, and much anxiety is caused by worry or fear – they're sisters! The question beneath most of our worries and fears is, 'Will I be OK?' or, 'Will those I love be OK?' Then there are other questions like, 'Will I have what I need when I need it?' or 'How will I get what I need?' or 'How will I cope?' David is effectively saying, 'If you're with the Shepherd and He's with you, you'll be fine.' Can you hear his confidence?

Who are you expecting to take care of your needs? If the answer to that question is any combination of, 'Myself, my friends, my family, my spouse, my boyfriend, the politicians, my doctor, my church, or anyone else', you're on shaky ground, friend. None of those people can ultimately deliver what we need, which is why we worry. If they could, we wouldn't worry! It's also why we get angry, frustrated or disappointed when they don't deliver. Peace and freedom don't come from relying on others to meet our needs, or being in control ourselves, but from knowing and relying on Jesus to be our Shepherd.

The Father wants you to expect more of Him, and less of yourself and others. Jesus doesn't want us relying on other people, or ourselves, to sort our lives out, make us feel better, safer, or more valuable. When you next start worrying, instead of forgetting He's the good Shepherd, worship Him as the good Shepherd. Be quick to declare the truth of who He is over your heart and the thing you're worrying about. Start thanking Him, and start expecting Him to be who He has said He is for you. We say it before we see it, remember? If you want to be someone who worries less, worship Jesus as your Shepherd.

PONDER
What need do you have today? Do you trust God to meet it? Have you asked Him? How easy do you find it to ask for what you need on a regular basis?

PRAY
Ask the Father to reassure you of His desire to meet your needs and His power to do so. Are there any other needs you can tell Him about now? What about the needs of others?

READ: Psalm 23:3
He guides me along right paths, bringing honour to His name. (NLT)

Do you trust God to lead you? Are you relying on Him to guide you, wherever you are today? When we set off on a journey, we know where we want to go but not necessarily how to get there. We don't need to work out the best route, we just need a sat nav. We trust it to get us there as we follow its directions. In the same way, the Holy Spirit knows how to lead us and guide us through life. He knows our needs, and the desires of our hearts and He leads us like a shepherd leads his sheep.

If we want Jesus to guide us into His purposes and His peace, we must listen to His voice and obey it. It's only when we stop listening or obeying that we get lost. Jesus says in John 10 that His sheep follow Him because they recognise His voice. In parts of the Middle East, when a man is driving sheep from behind, it's usually a butcher, taking them to you-know-where! God leads us, most often by speaking to us. Which means, if we feel pushed to live to a certain standard, it's not the Shepherd's voice we're hearing. If we feel under pressure to achieve or perform in a certain way, it's not the Shepherd we're following. He doesn't use fear or guilt or shame to guide us. And He doesn't confuse us.

Jesus promises to lead us in the decisions we make and the steps we take. If we ask and if we listen! No matter what life throws our way and what roadblocks appear out of nowhere, He knows how to get us where He wants us, even when the curveball is a pandemic. He knows the way. And when we're not sure what He's saying, which we often aren't, but we step forward *in faith*, He promises not to let our feet slip (Ps 121:3). Phew! Trust Him to know the 'right paths' for you. Put your confidence in *His* ability to lead you rather than *your* ability to follow. You don't need to know the way, you just need to trust Him as your Shepherd.

PONDER
How has Jesus spoken to you and led you in the past? Do you believe He can guide you into His will for your life or are you tempted to think He's forgotten you at times?

PRAY
Thank Him that He speaks to you. Ask Him about something on your heart. Ask Him to speak to you today through whatever He chooses. Ask Him to direct your steps and then trust that He will.

READ: Psalm 23:4

Lord, even when your path takes me through the valley of deepest darkness, fear will never conquer me, for You already have! (TPT)

I have walked through a long valley of deep darkness; so long, in fact, I wondered if it would ever end. On my worst days, when the darkness seemed so dark, I questioned all kinds of things, including whether I'd taken a wrong turn somewhere or done something bad. Remembering this verse brought reassurance. The Shepherd sometimes leads His sheep through a dark valley because, for some reason, it's the best route to get where they're going.

If you're walking through a valley at the moment, it doesn't mean you're in the wrong place. Valleys are part of the landscape. There are no mountains and no mountain tops without valleys, and sheep don't get to bypass them in cable cars! Jesus doesn't keep us from the valleys, but leads us through them and stays with us. Remember, when it's dark you can't see much, so sometimes we can't see or sense His presence. It can feel like He's abandoned us. But He hasn't. He wouldn't dream of leaving His sheep to walk such a dangerous path alone.

The path is dangerous because it's dark, and in the dark, we get fearful. We can't see what's coming. When the path will end, when the circumstances will change and how they'll change. In the dark, it's tempting to pull away from Jesus and do our own thing, but remember, He's taking you somewhere. The key word here is 'through'. The valley is never the destination. If you're going 'through' something, the thing to do is to keep going. Don't set up camp and make your home there. Keep putting one foot in front of the other, do what you know to do, and stay *close* to the Shepherd. And have people around you who'll encourage you to keep doing that too. He's promised to look after you, and He *is* the One who knows the best way out of the valley.

PONDER

Do you know anyone going through a dark valley at the moment? What could you do for them today to make their journey a little easier?

PRAY

Ask the Father to help them know His nearness today and ask Him to encourage them forwards.

READ: Psalm 23:5
You anoint my head with oil...

Have you ever seen some of the thoughts in your head as annoying flies that you can't get rid of or that won't go away? Especially at night? The sound track that you can't switch off, the conversation that goes on and on, the voice that keeps accusing, the finger that keeps pointing, the 'what ifs' and the 'if onlys', the shouldas and the couldas? If so, let this verse encourage you.

A shepherd anoints his sheep with oil for an important reason. They are vulnerable to flies landing on their noses and then laying eggs inside them (disgusting, I know!). The eggs hatch into worms which then try and burrow into the brain of the poor sheep. To try and find relief from the uncontrollable itching which drives them crazy, the sheep run round endlessly or bang their heads against a wall. Obviously, they can die from this, so the shepherd rubs oil on the sheep's nose every day to prevent the flies from laying their eggs. It's another beautiful picture of his tender care for his sheep.

If this scene describes your life sometimes (as it does mine), be encouraged. What you need is for Jesus to anoint your head with oil every day. Why every day? Because there are (f)lies trying to land every day. Lies from the world, lies from the enemy and lies from our flesh all trying to steal our joy and our peace. Jesus wants to anoint our heads to protect us or to bring relief where those flies have already landed. What is the oil? It's His word. The truth has the power to heal us and protect us. And to set us free and keep us free. We can't avoid the flies, and we don't need to defeat them. We just need anointed heads! Keep your head in His word, friend. Reach for it, read it, repeat it, rely on it and remember it. As you do, He will anoint and protect your mind.

PAUSE
Name any flies that have been buzzing round your head this week. Come to Jesus as your Shepherd, put your hands on your head and ask Him to anoint your head with oil again today. As you do, picture His hands over yours. Thank Him that His word is powerful, and able to heal and protect your mind. Ask Him to give you a verse to cling to today.

RE-READ: Psalm 23

Read the psalm through slowly.

PUSH IN

Get some paper and a pen or use the space below. Invite Jesus to draw near to you and speak to you as you spend this time with Him.

– Make a list of everything in this psalm that David says the Shepherd does (i.e. He leads me...).

– Look at your list. What do these actions say about His heart for you?

– Which one stands out to you the most today?

– What difference would it make to your life if you trusted this statement more?

– Ask the Holy Spirit to reveal whether you have believed any lie about the Shepherd that He wants to free you from today. Whatever He shows you, acknowledge it as a lie and stop agreeing with it. Speak the truth out loud, and then ask Him to lead you into an experience of that truth. Ask Him what He wants you to do differently going forwards.

READ: John 10:11-14

I am the Good Shepherd; I know My own sheep and they know Me. (NLT)

PUSH IN

– Spend some time thanking Jesus that He's a *good* Shepherd and that He is *your* Shepherd. Thank Him for the times when He's rescued you when you've wandered off. Thank Him for the times He's led you and fed you, and for the way He speaks to you.

– Spend a few moments reflecting on the fact He knows you. What does that mean to you? Turn it into prayer. Ask Him if there is anything He wants to show you about His shepherd heart for you today.

READ: Psalm 100
He made us, and we are His; we are His people, the sheep of His pasture. (NLT)

As far as I can see, nobody wants to be a sheep. I haven't met a child yet who gunned for the sheep part in the school nativity play. I came across a motivational article last week which encouraged its readers to be sheepdogs, not sheep! You can be inspired or insulted, but Jesus says we are sheep. You're a precious, dearly loved daughter of the King but you've also got to get your head around why He calls you a sheep!

Picture for a moment one of those funny-looking animals (that looks like a cloud on sticks), grazing on a hillside. Why did Jesus say we're like sheep? Well, it's not because they're strong. Sheep are vulnerable to attack from other creatures because they can't defend themselves. It's not because they're intelligent. They're actually quite stupid (sorry sheep lovers) and can't even find green grass to graze on, on their own. It's not because they're brave. They're easily scared, as you'll know if you've ever been near one. They run away from most things that move. (Oh, how well He knows me). And I'm sure it's not because they taste good!

The thing about sheep is this: they need a shepherd if they're going to survive. Independence, for sheep, is a death sentence! Jesus uses all kinds of relational pictures like this one to help us grasp what having a relationship with Him looks like. He's painting a picture here of 100% dependence. We need a shepherd. To guide and provide for us. To protect and correct us. To rescue us when we go astray or get stuck. Just like sheep. There's no room for pride or self sufficiency in this relationship with Jesus. Other animals focus on surviving. Not sheep. They just focus on the shepherd. Friend, the more we get this, the freer we become. Whatever's in your diary this week, Jesus wants your focus to be on Him, so He can make life happen for you and take care of you.

PONDER

Have you ever thought of yourself as a sheep before? What do you associate with sheep?

PRAY

Ask God to show you an area of your life or your thinking where you're doing it without Him. Ask Him to show you what it would be like for you if you trusted Him as your Shepherd in this area. Invite Him to teach you how to live dependently on Him.

READ: Psalm 23:1-2
He makes me lie down in green pastures...

Do you ever feel overwhelmed by life, overwhelmed by the challenges on your plate or the decisions you face? Remember you're a sheep, and let it comfort you. In a world which continually offers me advice on how to do it all, have it all, change it all, and even make myself all I want to be, letting the Father remind me I'm His sheep takes the pressure off. Off me. It's one of His kind ways of reminding me that He doesn't expect as much of me as I expect of myself, or as the world expects of me.

Sheep don't do pressure. They don't strive, trying to make their lives work. Jesus gives us this identity to remind us we weren't designed to either. Sheep need rest, and the shepherd 'makes' them rest if they don't take rest themselves. You need rest. Rest for your mind, rest for your soul and rest for your body. Rest re-creates us. Rest re-charges us. Adam and Eve were created last in the order of creation. That means the first thing they did was rest as God made the Sabbath the next day. Perhaps they were like a new phone needing charge! The Father then built rest into the 10 commandments and into the rhythm of life. Have you built it into the rhythm of yours?

When we resist the need for rest, (and I don't mean sleep) however we explain it to ourselves or others, we're resisting both our design and our identity. We're living as if Jesus hasn't given us enough time, or can't meet our needs or fulfil our desires without our help! Eventually, that way of living takes its toll. Friend, the Shepherd 'makes' us lie down by telling us to. It's a matter of obedience. If we don't, we end up lying down another way; through burnout, sickness, stress or another kind of crisis. Your body, your mind and your soul can't function well without re-creative rest. We live in age where rest needs to be contended for. David said, 'The Lord is my Shepherd, so I have all I need. And He makes me rest.' Why not join him, say it, and keep saying it until you really believe it.

PAUSE

Spend a few moments thinking about the fact you're a sheep. What encourages you about this aspect of your identity? Where do you need to raise your expectations of your Shepherd and lower your expectations of yourself? What implications does it have on the pattern of rest in your life? Let His commitment to love you and look after you as His precious sheep, encourage you.

READ: John 10:1-14
My sheep hear My voice, and I know them, and they follow Me. (NKJV)

Do you expect to hear God speaking to you on a regular basis? Since sheep are prone to wandering off and getting lost, the key to their protection and their prospering, is hearing their shepherd's voice. It's a beautiful picture of the simplicity of the relationship the Father's invited us into. The key to living in His love and living out your purpose is listening to His voice and obeying it.

Jesus says, 'My sheep hear My voice'. That means two things. First, He has a voice and uses it. He's a God who speaks. Can you imagine going out for coffee with a friend and neither of you saying anything? (They're more likely to discover a calorie-free chocolate!) It's no different with Jesus. He loves to talk to you. He speaks to His sheep and does so much of the time. Second, since you're His sheep, it means you hear His voice.

Notice what Jesus isn't saying. He isn't saying that hearing His voice is a reward for super-spiritual people or a gift for selected individuals. He isn't saying you'd hear it if you found the right method or if you lived a better life. Hearing His voice isn't complicated. The only condition is to be an unspectacular, unintelligent sheep That's meant to encourage us and excite us. It's not Him who makes it complicated, it's us.

It's this central and this simple; your life with God hinges on hearing. Do you expect Him to speak to you? To know His heart, be given His direction, hear His encouragement, receive His healing, and be led into the full life He's planned for you, you have to hear from Heaven. Sheep don't follow rules, or other voices. They only follow their shepherd's voice. That's it.

PONDER
Do you expect to hear Jesus speaking to you? If not, can you identify why not? What needs to change today in your thinking about hearing His voice?

PRAY
Put your hands on your ears and thank God that He speaks to you. Confess any fear about what you may hear or any unbelief you may have. Thank Him in faith that whatever He says, it's always loving and always for your good. Ask Him to speak to you today and tell Him you're listening.

READ: John 10:1-21
He goes on ahead of them, and His sheep follow Him because they know His voice.

Each time my mobile goes, I can see who's calling before I pick up. Not so with my landline; there are no clues until the person speaks. If it's someone I know well, one little word like 'Hi' is enough for me to recognise who it is because I know their voice. I have a crazy friend who loves trying to fool me by disguising his voice, but it doesn't work. I know him too well!

Jesus talks about His sheep hearing His voice and knowing His voice. There's a difference. You can hear a voice but not know whose it is. You can even hear God's voice and not know it's Him speaking. That's what happened to Samuel when he was a boy (you can find his story in 1 Sam 3). He thought it was a priest talking to him when actually, it was God. How crazy is that? Samuel became a great prophet, but even he had to learn to recognise God's voice. So do His sheep. It's a process.

How do we grow in knowing His voice? It involves a few things. It involves practise which means being OK with making mistakes. Nobody becomes an expert at anything overnight. But remember friend, if you're learning to recognise the Shepherd's voice, He'll lead you and protect you even when you think you may be hearing His voice and you're not. It also involves acting on what you think He's saying to you. Disobedience tends to make us deaf. And most importantly, it involves making and taking time to listen. You can't hear others talking to you if you have earphones in, and you can't hear Jesus speaking if your heart is full of other noise. Do you give Him a chance? He has much to say to you about Himself, your heart, your struggles, your relationships, your future, and His kingdom. He knows what you need to hear. Are you listening?

PONDER
Is there anything you think God has been saying to you that you may not have believed was Him? Does it contradict what's in the Bible? If not, what do you need to do today to act on it?

PRAY
Talk to the Father about what's on your heart and ask Him to speak to you and give you a promise for now. Note down what He says. Keep your heart open to what else He may say to you today.

READ: John 10:3
The sheep hear His voice as He calls His own sheep by name... (GNT)

Many people talk to God, and about God. Not as many hear His voice. The sheep bleat, particularly when they're in distress, but they also hear their shepherd's voice each day. Jesus calls His sheep by name. He knows us and He speaks personally and intimately to each of us. The question is never, 'Is God speaking?' but, 'Are we listening?'

Closeness and connection in any relationship requires conversation, and conversation is for two, not one! And yet we can pray and tell God what's on our hearts or what we need, without ever stopping to hear what He wants to say back to us. It's like leaving messages on an answer machine – information gets passed on, but it does nothing for intimate friendship. Let's give Him a chance to speak to us. He opens His mouth when we open His word. And we're better positioned to hear Him speak when we ask Him to, and when we ask Him questions.

I regularly pray, 'Lord, please speak to me.' If I sit next to someone and want to talk to them, I ask them a question and then listen when they reply. I do the same with Jesus. We can ask Him all kinds of questions; the more specific, the easier it is to identify His reply. When you read the Bible (the more you read it, the more you'll recognise His voice), ask Him questions about what you've read; 'Lord, how do You want me to apply this?' When you're facing a situation you're unsure about, ask Him, 'Lord, what should I do?' When you're praying for someone, ask Him, 'How do You want me to pray for this person?' When you're beginning your day, ask Him, 'Lord, what do You want me to do today?' I could carry on! He doesn't always answer bigger questions immediately, but asking helps us to listen, and to expect Him to speak.

Jesus is so kind and merciful that He guides us, cares for us and speaks to us through different situations and circumstances. But He longs for us to become more familiar with His voice. Make practising listening a priority.

PAUSE
Ask the Father to show you one person He wants you to pray for now. Trust that the first person who pops into your mind is Him speaking to you. Ask Him to show you what He wants to do in their life. Then go for it, and pray that for them.

READ: Luke 10:38-42

Jesus wasn't saying what Martha was doing was wrong. He was saying her priorities were wrong. The effect of having got her priorities wrong showed up in her heart and then her attitude, as it always does! He was telling her, 'If there's only time for one thing, Martha, then spend it with Me and listen to Me.'

PUSH IN

– Ask Jesus to speak to you as you read through these four verses again.

– Ask Him things like:
- 'What do You want to draw my attention to in this story?'
- 'Is there a wrong belief, attitude or distraction stopping me from hanging out with You, like there was for Martha?'
- 'What do You want to say to me from this story about Your heart for me?'
- 'What do You want me to do differently that will help me grow closer to You?'

– Ask Him anything else that's on your heart.

Note down what He says and then pray about it. Note down anything you need to do.

READ: Matthew 10:16
I am sending you out as sheep among wolves.

This is Jesus' rather unnerving comment to His disciples as He sent them off on a road trip to tell others about Him. Nothing has changed. It's with the same mandate and into the same conditions that He sends us out. We're to live and work in the world He's placed us in – as sheep.

PUSH IN

– What's the biggest implication for you of being sent as a sheep into a world full of wolves?

– Why do you think Jesus is confident about sending us out like this?

Talk to Him. Ask Him if there's anything He wants to say to you right now. Ask Him any questions you have and trust He'll tell you what you need to hear.

READ: Psalm 139:7-10

If I climb to the sky, You're there! If I go underground, You're there! (MSG)

Recently my husband went on a long trip overseas. I love that connection is so easy with Facebook and Facetime and we could stay in contact. But a phone in my hand, and all I know about him in my head didn't make up for him not being here. I missed his physical presence with me. I missed things like the shared, spontaneous moments of the day, enjoying a meal with him and the comfort of knowing he was near.

The Father is present with us 24/7. Wherever we go. He's an always-present God. There's no place too distant, too dark or too dirty to put Him off. David sums it up in this psalm: 'Wherever I go, You got there first!' This isn't an encouraging theory to make us feel better. It has many implications. A key one is that we can experience the Father's touch anywhere because He is with us. The adventure of following Jesus is meant to include genuine encounters with Him. Otherwise, we end up in a relationship where we know about Him, without experiences of Him.

Friend, we can't know anyone just by studying them. I once bumped into a celebrity in a shop and went up to say 'Hi' because in a mindless moment, I thought I knew her. Actually, I knew a lot about her, which isn't the same thing. She looked at me as if I was from Mars! We are going to look at a couple of ways to help us be more open to experiencing His presence over the next two days. But let's remember, expectation precedes experience in the kingdom. Do you expect to experience Him with you in the doctor's surgery, in the boardroom, on the train, at the party, at your desk, in the middle of the night, in your loneliness, or in your pain? If we expect to experience Him, we are more likely to. We will listen for His voice, become more sensitive to His touch and look for what He is doing. Everywhere we go. God wants you to know Him through experience. Do you need to upgrade your expectations today?

PRAY

Get comfortable and spend a few moments being still in God's presence. Close your eyes, take a few deep breaths, and thank Him that He's with you right now. Ask Him to help you become aware of Him and ask Him to make His presence more real to you. Receive His love for you and ask if there's anything He wants to say to you. Enjoy just being with Him.

READ: Psalm 100:1-5
Enter with the password: Thank you! (MSG)

I learned an important lesson about experiencing the nearness of God some years ago. I was struggling with a load of stuff in my life, and at the same time, struggling to believe God was with me. He felt about as present as a snowstorm on a sunny day. One dark day (confession time), I was complaining to Him about what wasn't happening and wasn't changing. And the fact He felt distant. I invited Jesus to my pity party, but He declined.

I had to catch my breath in the middle of my lecture to God about why He should feel bad for me, so I paused briefly. He seized the opportunity and whispered something to my heart: 'Start thanking Me, Hils.' That wasn't the response I was after! I was blinded by my earthly perspective, so I could only see problems. I couldn't think of anything to be truly thankful for (I'm ashamed to say). I whispered back, 'Please help me.' Something popped into my head and I turned it into a 'thank You' prayer. As I did, another blessing came to mind, so I thanked Him for that too. It kept happening, and I kept turning them into 'thank You's'. The trickle of thanks became a steady flow of praise. As it did, the Father's tangible presence began to fill my heart and mind like sunlight fills a room as you open the curtains.

The Father is always with us. He's the always-present One. But Psalm 100 reminds us there's a password to *experiencing* His presence. It's one we often forget, particularly when we don't understand what's going on or why things turn out the way they do. What can you thank Him for? The prayers He has answered? The things He's done for you? The blessings you take for granted? The promises He's made to you? How much He loves you? The future He's prepared for you? We can thank Him with facts for what He's already done, and with faith for what He's promised to do. 'Thank You' is the password. How often do you use it?

PAUSE
Being honest with God about our struggles is not incompatible with gratitude; but self pity is. Spend some time using the password 'thank You.' Thank Him for what He's done and what He has promised to do for you. Be specific and be persistent. Let gratitude rise in your heart. Why not decide to turn aside and use the password regularly throughout today, whatever it holds?

READ: 2 Corinthians 12:9
My grace is enough; it's all you need. (MSG)

How easy do you find it to live in the present moment? Not looking back to yesterday and not running ahead to tomorrow? Regret about the past and fear about the future both have the power to hijack our 'now'. To blind us to today's blessings and today's opportunities. And to distract us from God's presence with us. Jesus is with us in the present moment, offering us everything we need. But we miss Him when we miss the moment, which we do whenever our mind or emotions are in overdrive.

I am learning to replace my 'what ifs' with 'even if'. A notification from my phone distracts me from what I'm doing. In the same way, the 'what ifs' that ping in my mind disconnect me from His grace for my present moment. 'What if I had done things differently?' 'What if that hadn't happened?' 'What if this goes wrong?' 'What if the diagnosis is bad?' 'What if we don't have enough money?' It's like God is saying here, 'Hils, I've got you. And I've got what you need *now*. Stay focused.' But the 'what ifs' try and pull me back to yesterday or forwards to tomorrow, distracting me from what Jesus has for me today.

I need God's presence in these moments. I need His peace to suffocate the regret or the fear and reconnect me to what He's doing now. I'm learning to say 'even if' to my 'what ifs'! 'Even if I took a wrong turn, God works all things together for good.' 'Even if we run out of money, God is my Provider and He'll look after me.' 'Even if this goes wrong, He will rescue me.' We can't rewrite the past and we can't read the future. But we do have the power to preach to ourselves *today*. About our always-present Father who promises His grace is *more* than enough. More than enough to guide us, redeem our mistakes, empower us and look after us. Friend, a lifetime is made up of a life of present moments. Let's live as if this verse is true – that He is enough for each one.

PONDER
What kind of 'what ifs' are part of your mental soundtrack? List a few 'even ifs' you could learn to replace them with. How good are you at preaching to yourself?

PRAY
Thank Jesus for this promise and tell Him what it means to you. Ask Him to help you live it out.

READ: Luke 24:13-32

Jesus came up and walked along with them. But they were not able to recognise who He was. (MSG)

Have you ever seen one of those 'Where's Wally?' books? Each page is covered with hundreds of tiny cartoon characters, and somewhere in the mix is Wally in his stripey hat. Finding him can be so difficult, I sometimes think he's not there! God is always with us, but at times, it feels like He's not there. After Jesus was crucified, two of His friends were walking and weeping together. Jesus joined them, but they didn't realise. They were too upset and too confused by recent events. I don't get how the God of the universe could be with them and they not know it. But He was.

Friend, let this story encourage you. Let it remind you that it can feel like the Father's on another planet when He's right there by your side. Jesus had the same experience on the cross. The One who was always obedient and walked in the most intimate connection with God cried out, 'Father, why have You abandoned me?' God hadn't abandoned the Son He adored, but in the nightmare of what was happening, it felt to Jesus like He had. And that increased His agony.

The Father has never left you. He was with you in the abortion clinic, in the prison, in the operating theatre, in the injustice and by the graveside. Even if it felt like He wasn't. That was the experience of these guys. Maybe you've felt abandoned – perhaps that's how you feel now. Be honest with Him about it (like Jesus was (Matt 27:46)). He can take it. But don't put your faith in what your feelings say about Him. Don't believe them. Believe what He's said; that He's always with you and will never leave you. The last thing Jesus did was to pray (Lk 23:46). He died praying to the One who could *still* hear Him. Your feelings will trick you about what's true, but the Father never will. Keep trusting and keep talking to Him. That's faith. He's always listening because He's always with you.

PONDER

Can you identify a time when it felt like God had abandoned you?

PRAY

Thank Him that He's always walked with you even if it doesn't feel true. Talk to Him about that time. Ask Him to show you where He was, just like He did to these disciples.

READ: 1 Samuel 17:37:49
Saul said to David, 'Go, and the Lord be with you.'

The presence of problems in your life isn't evidence of the absence of God. It's the presence of God with you that enables you to live differently in the face of those problems. When my three boys were younger, they played in the park opposite our house. One day, two big teenage guys came over and started threatening them. My boys got scared. We were watching from home and decided it was time for Dad to join them. As my sons saw him approach, their attitude and posture changed. Their chests filled out, their voices got louder, and they started acting more confident. Dad was now around, and the teenagers legged it.

Life is full of giants, and those giants stand between us and what's next for us. They stand between where we are now and where God is taking us. He said, 'Follow Me', remember? Those giants aim to scare us, demoralise us and paralyse us. Whether it's a giant of unbelief, of fear of failure or pain, of hopelessness, or of impossibility, God expects us to take on our giants. Because He is with us. Our Heavenly Dad is for us, and His presence gives us the confidence and strength we need to stand up to those giants and step forwards.

David didn't have impressive weapons, he had an impressive Father who was with him. And he knew it. He stepped forwards and hurled something small as everyone else stood back. God did the rest. You may need to battle discouragement, deal with overwhelming grief or speak up instead of keeping quiet. You may need to take a radical risk, tell faith stories, confront darkness, believe for the impossible, or just keep going for one more day. The giant that's threatening to shut you down or keep you down, is one that God wants you to take down. Step forwards again today, friend. The giant *will* fall. The Father is with you in your pain, your fear, or your struggle. Keep going.

PONDER
Is there a giant threatening to bring you down or hold you back at the moment? Ask God what stepping towards it looks like, and what small thing He wants you to hurl at it today.

PRAY
Ask the Holy Spirit to increase your confidence in the Father's presence with you.

READ: Mark 4:35-41
'Teacher, don't You care that we're going to drown?'
'Why are you afraid?' (NLT)

PUSH IN
– Read the story, and imagine what it must have been like to be one of the disciples on the boat with Jesus. Why do you think His presence with them didn't seem to make any difference to their experience during the storm?

The disciples asked Jesus a question and He asked one back: 'Why are you afraid?'

– Think about any uncertainty in your life right now that is causing you anxiety. Allow Jesus to ask you the same question. How do you answer?

– Write down what you're afraid of and admit your fears to Him.

Invite Him to speak to your heart.

READ: Deuteronomy 31:8

The Lord Himself will go before you. He will be with you; He will not leave you or forget you. Don't be afraid and don't worry. (NCV)

Although this promise was given to Joshua as he prepared to lead God's people into the Promised Land, the writer to the Hebrews in the New Testament repeats this promise to all God's children (v5).

PUSH IN

Spend some time reflecting on this promise and thank the Father He is with you.

– Read it and re-read it a few times , slowly. Each time, put the emphasis on a different word.

– Ask the Holy Spirit to show you if there is a lie you have believed about God's presence with you. If one comes to mind, confess it as a lie and refuse to agree with it any more.

– Ask Jesus what truth He's inviting you to believe from now on. Ask Him to show you what difference this will make to your life.

Write down any other things He's been speaking to you about this week, and how He wants your life to change as a result.

READ: Matthew 5:14-16
You are the light of the world.

Jesus makes all kinds of staggering statements. He makes great claims about Himself including, 'I am the bread of life, the light of the world, and the only way to God.' But He doesn't stop there. He also makes great claims about His daughters. He says we're the light of the world. You may be used to singing that He's the light of the world, but He says, 'You're the light of the world'. He's never had a minor role for you to play.

Whenever we have a power failure here, we make a dash for the candles or the torches, whichever we find first as we stumble about in the darkness. All we need to do to see again, is light one small candle. The amount of light it produces is phenomenal and suddenly, an entire room becomes visible. The flame may be small, but it's impact is seismic. You friend, are the light of the world, because you carry the Light within you. Be confident. He calls you to light up your world rather than keep your light hidden. You do that best when you live an open and honest life in Him, not by being perfect.

Every time you walk into a room or office, each time you go to the school gate or the nail bar, you're in that bit of the world as light. He's called you to let your light shine right there. You don't need to be discovered, He's already put you on display; to display Him. Those around you need the Light you carry. Wherever you are, He's given you influence. You don't need to go looking for it, you need to look for how He wants you to use it. It might mean talking to the person no one else is talking to, offering to pray for someone, or going the extra mile. It might mean refusing to criticise others, encouraging someone or putting another's need above your own. It might mean something else. Ask Him and He'll show you. The world needs light. Remember, you're that light, and you need to let your light shine. You have what the world around you needs.

PONDER
Do you see yourself as the light of the world? Think about the places you'll in be today. Imagine them being in darkness until you arrive. Declare this verse over yourself saying, 'I am the light ...'

PRAY
Ask Jesus to help you walk in this truth this week. Begin by asking Him to show you how to let your light shine today everywhere you go.

READ: Philippians 2:12-18
Then you will shine among them like stars in the sky.

One of the things I love doing when I'm on holiday is lying on a sunbed – wait for it – at night, looking up at the stars. They're stunning in every way, shining brightly and signposting me to my Maker. It's an obvious thing to say, but they don't look nearly as good during the day when I'm lying in the same place. Apparently they're still there, but it's the contrast to the night sky that makes them stand out.

Paul is saying here, 'You're the light of the world', but a bit differently. He's saying, 'Shine like a star in the dark night sky.' Shine like a star in your favourite coffee shop. Shine like a star at university. Shine like a star in the hospital. Shine like a star in the boardroom or on the shop floor. Shine like a star at work and shine like a star at home. A star doesn't work hard to shine and stand out. The contrasting night sky shows it off. The same is true for us. We're meant to look different to the world around us.

Paul zooms in on one unusual thing that makes us shine; no arguing and no complaining. Really? How is that going to change the world? Do everything without doing either, he says. When you're in the office and you refuse to complain about someone behind their back, or about how others do things, your light shines. When you refuse to argue with someone you disagree with, but still listen humbly and treat them with kindness, your light shines. When you get home and don't complain about what needs doing, or how much you've got on, your light shines. Jesus says we'll stand out against the night sky of this world when we stop complaining or arguing. Because that's not how most people live (just look at social media). God is serious about complaining and arguing (1 Cor 10:10). Friend, this doesn't feel like a world-changing choice, but Jesus uses small things, not big things, to make a significant impact. A picnic fed 5,000, remember? Shine like a star, and you *will* light up your world, giving others the chance to see Him.

PONDER
What do you find easier? Not arguing or not complaining? What do you argue/complain about?

PRAY
Thank Jesus for choosing you to light up a dark world. Ask Him to set a guard on your tongue today.

READ: Isaiah 60:1-2
Arise, shine, for your light has come, and the glory of the Lord rises upon you.

Light is a problem for darkness. Darkness is defeated the moment a light shines. So for darkness to prevail, light just has to stay away. That's why the enemy wants you to keep your light hidden. Let me tell you friend, your light is needed. The world is getting darker – trouble, difficulty and pain abound, but God's answer is in this verse. He's calling His daughters to 'arise' because His glory rises upon us. The spotlight of the Father's love and goodness is shining on you. You don't need to take on the darkness, you just need to rise up and shine *in* it. Show His love, goodness and power to others, whoever they are, and keep doing so.

Is anything keeping you down? Maybe it's your beliefs about yourself and what you can't do. Maybe others have put crushing expectations on you. He's calling you to rise above them. Perhaps you've fallen down. He encourages you to rise up again. Maybe you've been knocked over by one of life's curveballs. He says, 'Daughter, arise and shine.' The phrase, 'Arise and shine' was actually a Hebrew idiom encouraging God's people to stand up straight, rather than being bent over with difficulty. Rise up friend if you need to – stand up straight and go again.

Your purpose in life is to rise to each occasion and spread the love and light of Jesus in the unique way only you can. And you can do that even if you're walking through you're own valley of darkness. Even in the darkest moments of life, there's always someone we can give to or pray for, someone we can stand up for or bless because of His love and light shining on us. That's my experience. But it's a choice. Today if you need to, choose to rise up. Out of regret, out of despair, out of inadequacy, out of sin, out of shame, out of weariness, out of frustration or out of fear. Refuse to let your light be hidden, but stand up straight and walk closely with your God. Be a problem for the power of darkness in your world instead of being hidden by it.

PRAY
Read this verse over a few times, slowly. Hear the Father speaking this over your life. Ask Him to help you rise up today if you need to. Offer Him your life again, to be a bright light for Him.

READ: Nehemiah 1:1-10
When I heard this I sat down and wept. (NLT)

Do you have a divine discontent in your heart? Are you troubled by some kind of trouble others face? Do you have a heart to help people in a specific way? Do you see a need that needs meeting? Do you dream of making a difference? Nehemiah ticked the boxes. He'd heard news that the walls around Jerusalem had been destroyed, leaving the city and its people vulnerable and exposed. It got under his skin. As he thought about what he'd heard, a divine discontent got hold of him. It moved his heart, and his heart moved him to the Father. So he fasted and prayed.

You're the light of the world, and you bring light to others wherever you are. We're called to bring hope to the hopeless, help to the helpless, provision to the needy, healing to the sick, freedom to the captive, love to the unloved and the kingdom to the lost. We're called to let the light of Jesus in us shine into the dark places around us. But sometimes the Holy Spirit calls us to shine in a specific place in a specific way. For Nehemiah, he was to bring light to Jerusalem by following his dream; to see the walls rebuilt, the city fortified, and the people protected.

Nehemiah had to act to test out his dream. He had to take a risk, trust God to open a door and try moving into position. His light had been shining in the palace as he served the king, but the Father was calling him to light up a different darkness elsewhere. Is He calling you to do the same? In Nehemiah 2:11, he confirms that God put this dream in his heart. It was sown into the soil of his divine discontent. Human discontent leads to criticism about a problem, divine discontent leads to a cry to God for His kingdom solution. God's answer to Nehemiah was, 'You go, let your light shine there and I'll shine through you'. Everything changed because one small light began to shine. Pay attention, friend, to what's in your heart. Is a divine discontent about something disturbing you? *You* may be the solution Jesus wants to provide.

PAUSE
Spend a few moments being still with Jesus. Listen to what's in your heart. Is there a divine discontent there that you need to talk to Him about? Do you have a dream to be a light in the darkness in a specific way in a specific place? Pray about what this raises in you.

READ: Matthew 5:14-16
Shine! Keep open house; be generous with your lives. (MSG)

Jesus calls us to do hard things. Life is tough, but He doesn't say, 'Lovely one, sit back, hold on tight, try and survive and I'll help you.' Instead, He says (my summary), 'Life is tough so make it better for others, and I'll make it better for you. That's the way you'll thrive.' His command to 'shine', to be 'generous with our lives', wasn't spoken to those who had it all and had it all together, but to every one of His kids, everywhere. Jesus didn't add an 'except if you're...' condition to His mandate for living.

To be generous is to give, and to give more than is expected or necessary. You may be time-rich, or have a healthy bank balance or a lovely home. Or you may be sleep-deprived, battling an illness, rushed off your feet or struggling to make ends meet. Jesus doesn't measure our generosity against anyone else's, but against what we have. When we give away what we could keep, because we love Him, we shine brightly and make Him visible. And when we do it for Him, He somehow gives it back to us (Lk 6:38). Whether that's our time or energy, our resources or reputations. Trust Him friend; no one can out-give Jesus.

Since He doesn't measure you against others, don't measure yourself either. And don't measure them. Every star in the sky is different. You're in a unique position to express His heart and life as only you can. You're different to every other one of His girls. You have a unique story, a unique set of passions and abilities and a unique personality. Comparison will make you forget these. Measuring yourself against others will kill your light, whether you feel inferior or superior. Focus on being you. He's made you as you and He loves you as you. Be generous with what you have, however much or little. Be generous with who you are, wherever you're positioned. And be generous with your life as He's been generous to you with His.

PONDER
Can you think of an example in the recent past where you've been generous with your life?

PRAY
Thank Jesus that He was crazily generous with His life for you. Ask Him to grow His generosity in your heart and to open your eyes to the opportunities He gives you to be generous today.

READ: Matthew 5:14
You are the light of the world. (NLT)

PUSH IN

Think of one of the specific, dark sky places that you encounter on a regular basis, that needs your light.

– Spend some time praying for God's light to break into that place and into the lives of those you meet there. Use your imagination as you pray; what would it look like if His light was shining brightly there? Ask Him to move in power and bring it about.

– Finally, ask Him to show you if there's anything in particular you can do in that place to let your light shine more brightly. Spend a few moments in silence waiting for Him to speak. Take note of any thoughts that 'pop' into your mind.

READ: Psalm 34:1-6
Gaze upon Him, join your life with His, and joy will come.
Your faces will glisten with glory.
You'll never wear that shame-face again. (TPT)

There is a 'glistening', a radiance which comes from intimacy with Jesus. What this verse says is that a close connection from time spent with Him shows up in our faces. It's more powerful and effective than any beauty treatment (the verse doesn't say that!).

PUSH IN

– Spend a few moments reflecting on your connection with Jesus. How do you want it to grow? What would that involve from you?

– Spend some time being still and quiet in His presence. 'Join your life with His' again today. Invite Him to draw near to you. Turn the eyes of your heart to gaze upon Him. Think about how much He loves you and what He's done for you. Put on some quiet worship music if it would help you. Bring any concerns or anxieties that invade your peace, straight to Him, and trust Him with them. Rest in His love for you and His sovereignty over your life.

READ: Genesis 16:1-16
You are 'God who sees me.' (NCV)

Have you ever felt nobody really gets you, or knows how you're feeling or what you're wrestling with? Many thousands of years ago a young woman called Hagar was feeling like that. Plot summary: she was Sarah's (Abraham's wife) slave girl and Abraham had got her pregnant at Sarah's suggestion. Sarah was trying to help God keep His promise of giving them a son (big mistake!), but once Hagar got pregnant, Sarah got jealous. And then life got tricky, so Hagar got moving and ran away.

Enter the hero. God shows up in her desolation and introduces Himself. Hagar calls Him 'the God who sees me'. The God who notices. The God who cares. The God who knows. Her employers, her friends and anyone else who knew her may have known what was going on in her womb, but no one knew what was going on in her heart. No one except God as it turned out. And because He did, He came running after her.

God is a Father who sees; who notices when no one else does. He. Sees. You. He sees your dreams and your desires. He sees your pain and your shame. He sees your struggles and your fears. He sees your hopes and your efforts. He sees your heart. And He cares. The Bible says He knows each hair on your head. He even sees when you do your hair differently.

Hagar had been mistreated at the hands of people she trusted. God saw and came after her. He sees each time you're misunderstood and mistreated too. The fact that He saw her encouraged Hagar and helped her to obey Him. He wanted her to go back and face her troubles as He had more for her in the place she was running from. You are not hidden from God however it may feel today. He hasn't forgotten you. He sees what you care about and what's on your plate and He wants to help you with every big thing and every small thing today.

PONDER
Is there anything or anyone you're wanting to run away from? What difference does it make that God sees you, knows you and cares about you?

PRAY
Ask Him to speak to you, and ask Him what He wants you to do today. Thank God He sees you.

READ: Psalm 56:3-11
You have kept a list of my tears. Aren't they in Your records? (NCV)

I have active tear ducts! They go into action when I'm cutting onions, watching films, reading stories, at friend's weddings, (or any wedding), and on other occasions that are too embarrassing to mention. During a particular season when God was doing some surgery in my heart, a friend bought me some waterproof mascara. She felt sorry for me because she'd seen so much of the non-waterproof stuff decorating my cheeks!

God is a tender Father. Whether your tear ducts are more or less active, He notices every tear that has ever fallen from them. The tears you cried as a newborn baby, the tears you cried as a little girl, the tears you cried as a growing teenager, and the tears you cry as a woman. The tears you've shed in pain, the tears you've shed in joy and everything else in between. Every one of them is recorded in Heaven. Why? Because every one is precious to Him. You can't remember them all, but He noticed every one and noted them down. His heart for you is sooo big.

There was a woman called Mary who couldn't keep her tears from falling during a social event. We don't know if she had the mascara nightmare or not, but we do know that her tears flowed over Jesus' feet. As they did, He was so moved that He promised the story would be told forever. Her tears were literally recorded in His book (Lk 7:36-50). I believe that when we cry with Jesus, inviting Him into our vulnerability and pain, He sees it not as a sign of weakness but as an act of worship. It moves Him.

The Father knows and notices everything about you. The One who flung the stars into space treasures your tears because He treasures you. Do you know how tender His heart is for you? Go ahead and cry all you need to. Trust Him with your tears and let Him touch your heart.

PONDER
How easy do you find it to cry when you need to? Do you see 'tears' (yours or others') as weakness?

PRAY
Re-read this verse slowly, saying it back to the Father. Ask the Holy Spirit to deepen your experience of the Father's tender heart towards you. If you need to repent of refusing to let yourself cry when you've needed to, do so now. Talk to Him about anything that's come up.

READ: Genesis 3:6-10
The Lord God called to the man, 'Where are you?'

I used to love playing hide and seek with my kids when they were little. It was either the bits of their bodies sticking out of their hiding places, or the giggles and fidgeting that gave them away, but the fun part was that they were so convinced I couldn't see them. Of course, I played along.

The most ridiculous game of hide and seek ever played was in the Garden. Adam and Eve somehow thought they could hide from the Father, from the One who sees everything. What were they thinking? When God asked them, 'Where are you?', it wasn't because He'd given up and couldn't find them. He was inviting them to admit what was going on. But there's a difference between God seeing, and letting ourselves be seen and known by Him. That requires a calculated choice on our part to open up our heart, and invite Him in to the secret places in our life.

Sadly, many of God's daughters go through life knowing that He sees them without being fully known. They don't know His healing touch on their wounds, His comfort in their pain, His compassion in their weakness, and His deliverance from their darkness. Why? Because they hide their hearts. It's only when we allow Him to know us fully by inviting Him into those places we'd rather not acknowledge, that we discover the full riches of relationship with Him and His complete acceptance of us.

God doesn't just want to use you, or direct you, or shape you. He wants to know you, as you are, and to walk closely with you. He loves you today as much as He ever will, but you stop hiding when you refuse to be anything other than real and honest with Him about your life and your heart. No excuses, no denial, no pretence. Don't be what you're not when you're with Him. Be brave and be honest, and you'll discover the depths of His love in the way you long to.

PONDER
How open and honest are you with God and with yourself?

PRAY
Thank Him that He knows you and welcomes you as you are. Be honest with Him and tell Him about anything you've kept out of your relationship with Him. Tell Him why you've done so.

READ: Romans 4:7-8
Oh, what joy for those...whose sins are put out of sight. (NLT)

Do you remember those optical illusions? Those patterns and pictures that someone shows you and tells you to look for some random shape that's not obvious, like a rabbit? I would never see what's there unless I was told to look for it, as you have to look at the picture so differently.

The Father sees things differently to you and me and He wants to teach us to see what He sees and how He sees. But it doesn't come naturally to us as He has supernatural eyesight. Lazarus' friends saw a dying man, Jesus saw a chance to glorify God. Sarah saw a childless woman, God saw the mother of a nation. Gideon saw a fearful farmer, God saw a mighty warrior. The men with the stones saw an adulterous woman needing punishing, Jesus saw a precious daughter needing forgiveness. The disciples saw the cross as a terrible tragedy, God saw it as a total triumph. We could go on...

When God sees you, He doesn't see what you see. He doesn't see your sin. He doesn't see the things you wish you could delete but can't. Paul says in verse 7 that your sins are out of sight. Which means no one can see them because they've been erased by the blood of Jesus. So stop looking back at them! When your Father sees you, He sees the blood of His Son. He sees what He's done, not what you've done. He sees His efforts, not yours. We need to see as He sees.

He also sees what we struggle to see. When He sees your circumstances, He sees their potential. When He sees you, He sees your potential. Who you are, who you're becoming, how far you've come and what you can do each day with His Spirit inside you. He sees you as His chosen daughter, a masterpiece made to make an impact, and so much more. Are you learning to see yourself, your circumstances and others as He does?

PRAY

Bring yourself, a situation you're concerned about, or someone you want to love better, before the Father and ask Him to show you how He sees them/it. Be still for a moment and listen for His still small voice. Talk to Him about what He shows you and decide to trust His perspective. Ask Him to teach you to see supernaturally, as He sees, in all areas of life.

READ: Jeremiah 29:11-13
'For I know the plans I have for you' declares the Lord...

Hindsight is a wonderful thing, so they say. How many things would we go back and do differently, I wonder, if we knew then what we know now? There may be benefits of hindsight, but there are many more of foresight. As the One who sees, God not only sees you in your here and now, He sees your future. He sees what's ahead of you and what He's planned for you. And it's good, because all His purposes for you are good.

Jeremiah may have penned these words as God's spokesman to the Israelites while they were in captivity, but they're still true for all His daughters today. This is His promise to you too. You may be walking through a dark valley, or crawling through a dry desert. You may be braving it through a storm that's raging, or travelling through the fog of confusion or uncertainty. Or you may be running freely with the wind in your hair! Whatever the landscape of your life, the Father is with you now, but He also sees where He's taking you, and what He's got for you. He'll get you there if you stick close to Him and trust Him.

Friend, don't get discouraged when you can't see the way ahead. When Jesus called us to follow Him, He never said where He would take us, just what He would make us! When He called the disciples to follow Him, He said He'd make them fishers of men (Matt 4:19). That's giving them a new identity and destiny, not a new destination. He rarely tells us what will happen next, just how to take the next step. When you're discouraged about your future, resist any need you have to take control and do things your way. Instead, remember He sees the way ahead and makes a way even when there is no way. Do what you know to do, respond to each situation you face with His love and grace, and choose life by letting this promise encourage you.

PONDER
Commit this verse to memory now. Message it to someone else later on today.

PRAY
Spend some time thanking Him that He knows the plans He has for you and they are good. Thank Him in faith for where He's taking you and what He has planned for you.

READ: Psalm 139:1-16

Ask the Holy Spirit to come and speak to you now as you read through these verses.

PUSH IN

− Jot down what this psalm says He sees and knows about you.

− Spend a bit of time thinking about the importance of being seen and known by God. What difference would it make to you if He didn't see you or didn't know you?

Pick a verse from this psalm and memorise it. Set an alarm on your phone to go off three times during today. When it does, remind yourself of the verse and turn it into a short prayer.

READ: Matthew 6:3-8

Your Father who sees what is done in secret will reward you.

PUSH IN

Spend a few moments thinking about what these words of Jesus mean.

– Why do you think He said what He did here?

– What does He want us to know?

– Is there anything you need to start or stop doing, or do differently?

Hear Him speak to you...'I see what you do in secret, My precious daughter. I see what others don't see and the ways you help others that go unnoticed and unappreciated. But that doesn't mean what you do is worthless. The way you serve Me brings Me great joy and what is unseen here I will reward in Heaven where it is seen. You may not receive glory from what you do, but you bring Me glory every time you do something that others don't see. Nothing you lovingly do for Me will ever be wasted. Trust that I will reward you. Thank you for what you do in secret.'

READ: 1 Peter 1:15-19
...live out your time as foreigners here in reverent fear.

Do you like travelling overseas? I love it! I got the bug young and have had the privilege of visiting some incredible places and meeting some amazing people along the way. However, being a visitor in a foreign country for a brief time is one thing; being a resident in a foreign land is another. You may not have access to your favourite food in the local shops. You may have to speak another language. You may have to get used to a different climate and currency, and you have to learn a different set of national laws and customs. And that's just the start.

Faith in Jesus makes us foreigners here on earth. Whether we live in the nation of our birth or not, as God's daughter, we're foreigners here. God says we became citizens of His kingdom when Jesus made us new. Heaven became our new home, our new destiny, and our new nation. The kingdom of God and the kingdom of this world have little in common, so there are lots of implications of being a foreigner. I find one of the toughest is walking by faith, not by sight (2 Cor 5:7). Chasing and trusting the invisible, believing that what we can't see and Who we can't see is more real than what we can see is a crazy concept to this world.

I'm surrounded by people who only deal with the visible. Whether that's what they see with their own eyes, what they've experienced, or what they understand. As a foreigner, I'm trying to trust a Father I can't see and His ways I don't always get. But I'm often confronted by experiences, or perspectives and opinions about my choices and beliefs, that make trusting harder. Sometimes I've been called 'brave' by people who really meant 'stupid'! Walking by faith in a world that lives by feelings and facts can be a huge challenge. Friend, remember you're a foreigner and you're called to live out your time here as one. Don't be surprised when you have to battle to believe what you can't see when you're amongst a people who believe what they can see.

PONDER
Do you ever feel like a foreigner? If so, what makes you feel like one?

PRAY
What are you believing for that you can't see? Ask the Holy Spirit to strengthen your faith today.

READ: Isaiah 61:1-3

He has sent Me...to give them...the garment of praise instead of a spirit of heaviness. (NKJV)

The last time I was in Addis Ababa speaking at a women's conference, they gave me a national costume as a gift. It was such an honour to receive so I put it on for them. But I didn't look nearly as good in it, with my pasty white skin, as the beautiful Ethiopian women do! Many nations have a national costume or dress code, and Heaven is no exception. Jesus announced in these words in Isaiah, that He'd come to give His daughters a new item of clothing; a garment of praise. Are you wearing yours?

Praising God for who He is and what He's done is our privilege and our priority. This garment of praise belongs only to the people of Heaven. It's something that marks us out as foreigners here. You won't find other people wearing one (which is why it's tempting to take it off), but it's to be worn all the time, in every situation. It's easier to put it on for special occasions (such as when you feel like celebrating, or when you go to church) and to leave it in the wardrobe the rest of the time. But it's a powerful item of clothing, capable of preventing heaviness from settling in our heart and stealing our joy.

Keeping on my garment of praise is often the last thing I feel like doing, especially on a tough day or in tough times. Frankly, I'd prefer to leave it off and comfort myself with a bar of chocolate and a mug of self pity! But I've learnt that doing so opens the door to a place where my strength evaporates, my mood dips and my hope fades. My mind gets agitated and I lose my connection with the power and presence of my Father. While we're here on earth, we need to protect that connection. Keep your garment on all the time, friend, no matter how hard it may be.

PONDER

When do you wear your garment of praise? What stops you from wearing it?

PRAY

Thank Jesus for His kindness to you. Be specific. about ways He has blessed you. Set an alarm on your phone to go off at three different times today, and when it does, stop what you're doing to spend a couple of minutes praising Him for His love for you and what He's done for you.

READ: John 14:1-4
...I'll come back and get you so you can live where I live. (MSG)

Earth is not your home. Heaven is. And yet most people pay no attention to it. Just before Jesus died, He tells His friends He's returning to the Father. He promises there will be a place for them there. There are tons of rooms in God's house and He says He's off to get them ready. Does He mean there's decorating to do? Joking aside, He's saying Heaven is like a home. It's God's home. Is that how you think of Heaven?

There's a room waiting for you there if you belong to the Father. Think of the best things about home life on earth (even if it's not your experience) – delicious meals, family gatherings, fun games, great parties, and good laughs. A place where you're welcome, wanted, known, loved and celebrated, and where you can relax in your slippers. It's a tiny foretaste of what's coming. Heaven will be incredible and exhilarating. There'll be no pain or heartache, we'll be with Jesus, we'll feel more alive than ever, and it will be forever. Wow! But we're not there yet. So if you're wearing your slippers, you need to take them off.

Have you made this world your home? You weren't designed to spend your time, your money and your resources making life here either as comfortable as possible, as relaxing as possible, as safe as possible, as enjoyable as possible or even as long as possible. It's why we sometimes feel like we don't fit here and it's why we long for more. We're passing through. God intends for us to invest what we have here into our real home. How we've lived on earth will be rewarded in eternity, like getting interest on a deposit in a bank account. Make investing, not spending, your priority. Invest in knowing Him, growing in Him, loving Him and sowing into the lives and futures of others. Invest in living out His kingdom purposes while you're here as a foreigner.

PONDER
How does remembering life is short and here is not home, change how you think about your life?

PRAY
Thank God that Heaven is His home and there is a room for you there. Ask Him what step you could take today to invest in your true home.

READ: 1 Peter 2:9-12
...as 'temporary residents and foreigners' keep away from worldly desires that wage war against your very souls. (NLT)

This verse says we're at war. There's a battle on against your soul today. Maybe some days you're more aware of it than others, but it's ongoing. It's because this world is not our true home. Friend, let's remember that being a foreigner here means there will always be pressure on us from the world around us. Pressure to think like everyone else, act like them, and want what they want. We're easily influenced by what's around us. I'm wearing striped trousers today as stripes are currently in! Influence on my taste in fashion is one thing, but influence on my soul is another.

Think about how you speak, how you treat others, or what you hope for. The culture of the world wants us to do things its way. The Holy Spirit wants us to do things Heaven's way. Culture says cancel your enemies, Heaven says love them. Culture says you're powerful when you're strong, Heaven says you're powerful when you're weak. Culture says do what you like as long as no one gets hurt. Jesus says, 'Do what I say because I know what's best.' Culture says trust yourself, Heaven says trust Jesus. Paul says, 'Be aware of this pressure and don't give in to it.' Don't adopt the world's wants and ways. It's like he's saying, 'Hey foreigner, don't let the world influence you. Jesus wants you to influence it back' (v9).

How do we stop the world influencing our inner world? First, by recognising the battle, and that the pressure on us is real. Second, by making sure His word is a stronger influence on us than the world is. We can please God or people, but not both. Heaven's culture is contained in God's word, and we give it power over our lives when we read it, agree with it and act on it. Let Heaven be the greatest influence on your soul by putting God's word into practice. The battle is won, one choice at a time.

PONDER
Have you acknowledged there is a battle against your soul? Where are you under pressure to give in to the way the world does things? How much do you let the Bible influence your soul?

PRAY
Be honest with Jesus about any pressure you're facing right now, or any pressure you've given in to in the past. Ask Him for help, or for forgiveness, whichever you need.

READ: Daniel 1:8-17
But Daniel resolved not to defile himself...

I've lived in a couple of cities that have been significant tourist destinations. Many of the foreigners who visited were easy to spot. They stood out because they looked, acted and sounded different. That was Daniel. He was a foreigner in every sense. He was a young Jew living in a foreign land (Babylon), and a man of faith, living among a people who didn't believe in God. God gave him a position of influence working for the king. Daniel was easy to spot because he stood out.

God wants us to stand out, not blend in. Some people stand out because they love attention or they're weird, because they're rebellious or they have exceptional gifts. Most people blend in by living how everyone else lives; same values, same habits, same language etc. God wants us to stand out, but in a way that draws attention to Him, not us! Daniel stood out, not because he tried to, but because he stuck to Heaven's values. He faced pressure to compromise like we all do. For him, it was pressure from the palace: to eat and drink certain stuff and then later, to worship a statue and crucially, to stop praying. To cut off his connection to his Power Source. The pressure was on to look and live like everyone else.

Where do you find yourself most under pressure to look like, sound like and live like everyone else? Is it in the way you speak? What you spend your money on? What you expect from the world? How you treat others? What you dream of? What you post online? Or even, how much time you give God? The key to Daniel's success is in the word 'resolved.' He'd made up his mind in advance, that God's word would shape his life. No matter what the pressure from the world. That decision caused him trouble here and there, but it didn't stop God increasing his influence and promoting him again. He wants to increase yours too. Don't give in to the pressure to blend in. Be brave, hold your nerve, pray hard and stick to His word. And you will stand out, for Heaven's sake.

PONDER
How do you blend in or stand out in your circles of influence? What is different about you?

PRAY
Ask the Father to show you where you'll need courage to stand out and live differently today. Ask the Holy Spirit to fill you with His strength to do that and to make any 'resolve' that you need to.

READ: Hebrews 10:24-25

You won't be able to live effectively as the woman of God you've been created to be on your own. You've been adopted into a family of fellow foreigners and you need them!

PUSH IN

From these two verses, note down what the Holy Spirit recommends for your health and your heart. Spend a few moments asking Him to show you if your life is in line with these verses. Then ask Him how He wants you to respond and what He wants you to do.

Talk to Him about what He says.

PUSH IN

Grab a pen and some paper, or use the space below.

– Create two columns: title one, 'culture of the world' and the other, 'culture of Heaven'. Identify a few attitudes or practices that are common in the lives of those around you, or that you see in the media / on social media, that contrast to what you know about the culture of Heaven. Write them in the first column. Then write the corresponding attitude or practice that Heaven would celebrate in the other column.

– Identify which attitudes or practices in the 'world' column you think influence the way you do things, or influence the attitudes you have.

– Ask Jesus to pinpoint one and to speak to you about it. Ask Him how you can live more in alignment with the corresponding attitude or practice of Heaven.

Use this prayer if it's helpful:

'Lord, where I look too much like the residents of this world, please forgive me. Help me to become more like You and to regain my 'different-ness'. I want to be effective in this world, not intimidated or compromised by it. Teach me how to live more fully with Heaven as my home. Thank you for Your patience with me. Please grow my faith and let me be a greater influence for Your kingdom. Amen.'

READ: Philippians 4:18-20
And my God will meet all your needs...

Have you noticed how some of the smallest things in life are the most precious? A special moment with one of your favourite people, a life-giving word at a desperate time, or even a sparkling diamond? Notice the small word 'all' in this promise. It's like a priceless jewel; little in size but great in value. It may only contain three letters, but it covers every need you'll ever have as long as you live on this earth. That's great news.

As a loving Father, God wants to provide for us, and His promise is that He will - for *every one* of our needs. He is more than able to. He 'owns the cattle on a thousand hills' (Ps 50:10). Imagine a landscape of 1,000 hills and then imagine every one of them covered in cows. That's a lot of milk and beef (my sons would be thrilled)! What do you think He's trying to tell us about His wealth and His ability to provide?

Whatever your needs friend, whether they're material or spiritual, they're covered by that little word 'all'. Notice, Paul doesn't spell out how the Father will provide for us. His provision comes in so many different shapes and sizes, and often in ways we're least expecting. But God says He will. Providing for you is an expression of His love for you.

The question is never will the Father provide, but do we trust Him to provide for us? When we do, we find strength and peace to face the day, knowing things don't depend on us. Spiritual orphans feel alone in the world, so believe they have to fight for or work for whatever they need. Daughters expect their Father will provide. Why wouldn't He if He loves His girls? God wants to increase that confidence in you. Don't you want more of it?

PONDER
Do you find it difficult to believe the Father will provide for 'all' of your needs? Can you identify which needs seem the most difficult to trust Him for?

PRAY
Ask the Holy Spirit to show you any lie you've believed about the Father's desire and ability to provide for you. Wait for a few moments. If He does, confess it. Declare this over yourself: 'I am confident that My God will meet all my needs.' Thank Him throughout today for this promise.

READ: Romans 8:31-32
**Since He did not spare even His own Son but gave Him up for us all,
won't He also give us everything else?**

My husband ran the London Marathon some time ago. 26 and a bit miles is a tough distance to cover. I went to support him, racing from one spot to another to cheer him on. I ended up exhausted just watching them all and I wasn't even competing! Respect to all you long-distance runners.

Running a few metres is a piece of cake if you can run a marathon. Paul draws a similar comparison with God. What was the toughest thing the Father could ever do? It was to give His own Son. To let His precious boy step forward and volunteer to be the human device in which He could destroy sin. What happened on the cross wasn't an outraged Father taking out His temper on His Son, just so He didn't have to take it out on anyone else. God isn't a Father with anger issues. The Bible tells us He's slow to anger (Ex 34:6). It was sin that needed destroying, not Jesus, so Jesus offered His body to be the place where it could happen. The devastating process cost Jesus, *and* it cost the Father. How do you think He must have felt watching His Son suffer so terribly and undeservedly?

The Father loved you enough to provide the way for you to experience His love and to become His daughter. Forever. As I write this, the race is on to produce an antidote, or vaccine, for Covid 19. Only then will we be safe from the virus. God produced the antidote for sin in what He did. It's what will protect us from the consequences of sin for eternity. The antidote is the blood of Jesus. Paul says, if He was going to hold anything back from us, wouldn't He have held back His Son? By contrast, our need for money, or guidance, or encouragement, or friendship, or a job, is a piece of cake. The Father is your provider. Trust Him. He didn't hold back Jesus, so He won't hold back anything else from you. The cross cries out that providing all you need is a no brainer every time.

PRAY
Imagine yourself at the foot of the cross. Spend a few moments thinking about what God the Father and Jesus the Son did for you in that place. Talk to them both. Let what's in your heart come out of your mouth. Thank the Father that the cross is a beautiful reminder that He will always provide for you because He gave Jesus for you.

READ: Matthew 6:5-11
...your Father knows exactly what you need even before you ask Him! (NLT)

God is your provider, but you need to ask. Have you noticed how small children don't have a problem asking for what they need, whatever it is? When I was little, I didn't sit down first and analyse how my parents would react to my requests. I didn't wonder what they'd think or how they'd fulfil them, I just asked and left the answering to them.

Some people say, 'What's the point in asking if God already knows?' Jesus says yep, He knows all about your needs and desires (how reassuring is that?) before you ask. But He spells it out: 'Go somewhere on your own and talk – not to some uncaring God, but to your loving Father. Ask Him and *be specific*.' Jesus' brother James said it a bit differently later on; 'You do not have because you do not ask' (Js 4:2). Sadly, I know too many people like the people James was talking to.

There's a connection, not between needing and receiving, but between asking and receiving. God wants you to ask Him for all (that little word again) you need, not just what you think is most essential or urgent. What do you need help with? Your sleep, your health, your kids, your temper, your money, your studies, your job, a relationship, an addiction? He's interested in everything, however unimportant we think it is. If we feel we don't deserve it, we've turned His provision into a reward. But it's never that. It's a gift. Since He's about relationship with us, we need to ask but there's no special way to do that. There's no prayer formula that will persuade Him to answer. Be yourself and speak from your heart. Remember, asking shows our dependence on His resources, not ours. It also demonstrates our confidence in His desire to provide for us. It's part of being like a child. Ask and keep on asking, friend. Like children do.

PONDER

How easy do you find it to ask the Father for what you need? Are there things you need or would like that you don't ask Him for? If so, why not?

PRAY

Talk to Him. Thank Him that He longs to provide for you and tell Him what you need today. Be specific. If there are things you haven't asked for before, for whatever reason, ask Him to forgive you for believing He wouldn't want to provide for you in those areas and ask away!

READ: Exodus 16:4-20
Now tell them, 'In the evening you will have meat to eat, and in the morning you will have all the bread you want.' (NLT)

I have a friend who was struggling financially. She had a job but not much money and hadn't had a holiday for years. She was getting to know God as her Father and one day, felt Him encourage her to trust Him with her money so He could provide for her. He encouraged her to give away a tenth of her salary and see what happened. She couldn't really afford to, but agreed to try it for three months. By the end of those three months, her overdraft had 'disappeared' and she'd been offered two holidays! She found her Father really does provide, and hasn't looked back.

As a loving God, He's not a slot machine, although He is generous. But He'll often invite us to take a risk to show we trust Him, *before* He provides. That risk sometimes involves doing something; my friend had to give away some money. Other times that risk involves not doing something. The Israelites were told not to gather more bread each day than they needed. That would show they trusted God to provide for them every day, not just once in a while. Some gathered more than they needed because they didn't trust Him. But it didn't go well for them.

The storehouses in Heaven are full of what we need for this life and so much more. But God releases much of that treasure *as* we trust Him. Asking is our first step. It shows we need Him. Often He asks us to take a next step too - a step in to a position of dependence or a step that feels risky; giving something away that you need, turning down a relationship because you trust Him for a better one or leaving a job before He's provided the next one. Friend, doing it your way might feel safer, but doing it His way positions you for His provision.

PONDER
Have you ever taken a step of faith before God provided what you'd been asking for? What happened? What stops you taking a 'next step into a position of dependence'?

PRAY
Ask God again for what you've identified. Thank Him that He loves to provide for you. Take a moment to ask Him if there's anything He wants you to do to show you trust Him as your Provider. Take note if something comes to mind and ask Him to help you do it.

READ: Luke 11:9-12
And so I tell you, keep on asking, and you will receive what you ask for. (NLT)

God wants to provide for you. Always. The cross settled that once and for all. A daughter who believes her Father's desire is to be the source of all she needs, will bring smaller and smaller more insignificant things to Him. That's because she knows no request is off limits or too small for a big God to care about. Is that you?

When my daughter was little, she was due to be a bridesmaid for a wedding that, for various reasons, didn't take place. She was so disappointed and of course, I couldn't fix it. I couldn't provide another opportunity, so I encouraged her to ask the Father who could. She did. Many, many times. Nine months and many prayers later, a young couple in our church (who didn't know about her disappointment) asked her to be their bridesmaid. That was such a great moment! It mattered to her, so it mattered to her Father in Heaven.

Let's just clear up some myths about asking God to provide for us. First, He's not a 'pie' God! He doesn't have limited resources so that when they're gone, they're gone, like the last piece of pie. We don't need to leave His resources to those in greater need. God has been providing for His children since time began and will continue to do so for ever from His unlimited resources. Second, His promise to provide doesn't depend on our performance but our position. We can't earn the favour of provision from Him, we can only ask as His daughter. His promises are for His children. And third, He doesn't compare needs. He's not moved to provide because your need is greater than someone else's, or less moved because it isn't. He's moved by faith. He's looking for those who will confidently bring their own needs (big and small) to Him, and the needs of others, because they know Him as their Provider.

PONDER
What would you love the Father to provide for you? Have you told Him? Have you fallen for any of the myths about asking Him to provide?

PRAY
Ask God to show you whose needs He wants you to bring before Him today. Pause while He shows you. Ask Him to provide for that person in every way they need. Be as specific as you can.

READ: John 2:1-11

PUSH IN

Take a few moments to think about this story. Imagine yourself sitting at the table where Jesus was. Imagine yourself watching this miracle unfold. Watch the servants go to the water jars and fill them with water. Notice the master taste what's in them and watch their response. Observe the reaction of the guests as they begin to discover what's happened.

– What's your reaction to this miracle of provision?

– Why do you think Mary had to ask Jesus when He could also see what was happening?

– Where was the confidence and where was the risk in this story?

– What does Jesus want to teach you from this event about His heart and His desire to provide for you and for others?

Note down whatever comes to mind. How does He want you to respond? Talk to Him about what comes up.

READ: Philippians 4:19
And my God will meet all your needs according to the riches of His glory in Christ Jesus.

PUSH IN

Plant this promise in your heart by committing it to memory. Declare it over yourself a few times (replacing 'your' with 'my'). Then cover it up and write it down on a piece of paper. You'll discover if it's in your heart that way!

Water it with thanks. Thank God this is His promise to you, for all of your life. Reflect on this week and how your life would look different if you were more confident He is *your* Provider. Talk to Him about it.

READ: Romans 1:7
To all who are in Rome, beloved of God, called to be saints... (NKJV)

Do you think of yourself as a saint or a sinner? If you associate the word 'saint' with someone outstanding like Mother Teresa who did totally inspiring things, then maybe, like me, you think, 'That word could never describe me.' But the Bible says you're a saint. Take a deep breath and believe it! It's part of your new identity as a daughter of the living God. The word 'sinner' describes an internal attitude, not outward actions. When the Bible uses the word 'sinner', it's describing people whose attitude is that they don't need a Saviour called Jesus. That's not you.

When you received His forgiveness, you received a new nature. You went from being spiritually dead to being alive, not from being bad to being good. Do you need to re-read that? Your old 'anti-God' nature was replaced with a new 'pro-God' one, with power to follow Him. It doesn't mean you won't sin again, it means you want to learn to live for Him. You know what it's like to experience mixed responses in your heart. Sometimes you give in to pleasing yourself rather than pleasing Him. But that doesn't mean you're a sinner. The conflict you experience within you is evidence your nature changed when the Holy Spirit came to live in you. He helps you follow Jesus and love Him. You. Are. A. Saint.

The enemy can't change the fact that your identity has changed, but he can try and hide it from you. Friend, it doesn't matter what you've done, you're a saint if you have a saviour. It may take years to unpack the implications of this, but that's not the point. Being a saint is not a measure of how spiritual you are, but a description of who you are. You sometimes mess up. But you're not what you do. Religion describes us in human terms (sinners) because we sometimes sin. Grace describes us in Heaven's terms. As saints. Don't let anyone, especially the enemy, ever tell you you're anything else.

PONDER
Do you think of yourself as a saint? If not, can you identify why not?

PRAY
Thank the Father for giving you a new nature and for making you a saint. Ask Him to help you believe it. It takes more faith to believe you're a saint than a sinner, and you walk by faith.

READ: Isaiah 61:10-11
For He has...draped me in a robe of righteousness. (NLT)

Not long ago, a young adult I know had to take an exam. She hadn't done any work during the year and didn't have any notes, so she borrowed some from a friend (isn't that a true friend?) who'd put in hours of hard work. She read through them a few times and came out of the exam with top marks, beating her friend. How unfair is that? She was successful, but only because of someone else's effort.

The cross was unfair. It was unfair for Jesus. He didn't deserve to die. He never put a foot wrong and trusted the Father completely. He didn't deserve to be crucified, He volunteered for our sake. Imagine His perfect life as a beautiful velvet cloak. Imagine ours as a dirty, ripped old cape. Imagine each of our ungodly attitudes or actions as a separate stain or tear on it. As Jesus was dying, God somehow transferred our selfishness and stubbornness, and all our flaws and failures, into His body. He dealt with them there, so He didn't have to deal with us. But He went further. In forgiving us, Jesus made sure we'd be blessed by God, as if we'd never done anything wrong. He swapped His lush cloak for our lousy cape. We get to wear His 'robe of righteousness'. That's grace. And grace is unfair.

Whenever we try and do life with God wearing our old cape, focusing on what we have or haven't done, we're expecting Him to respond to our own efforts. As the standard of Heaven is perfection, we won't have much luck with that! We can't be close to Him that way. But when we expect God to bless us because of Jesus' effort and what He's done, we wear His beautiful cloak and experience His presence powerfully. Saints wear royal cloaks. Sinners wear ragged capes. Which one are you wearing?

PAUSE
Imagine yourself at the foot of the cross with Jesus. Imagine Him taking off your cape of achievements, failures, sin, self-effort and all you try and do for Him. See Him put His cloak of righteousness on you.

PRAY
Thank Him that you can't earn anything from Him and that He has forgiven you. Declare: 'I am forgiven. I am a saint and I am clothed in a robe of righteousness.'

READ: Psalm 103:1-14
He doesn't treat us as our sins deserve... (MSG)

Big question: does our sin matter anymore? It's been punished at the cross, we've been washed clean, and God doesn't treat us as we deserve. We're free to come into His presence anytime, anywhere, as saints wearing royal cloaks that have nothing to do with our performance, only with His. So do our life choices matter? Is how we behave significant?

No. Access to God's presence and love has nothing to do with the way we live. Psalm 100 says we enter His gates with thanks and His courts with praise. Why? Because the way in is through what Jesus has done. Expressing our thanks and praise is the response that draws us near to Him. If you want to feel more connected to the Father, get thanking and praising Him for what He's done. He loves to hear from you about His beautiful Son. How we live and the choices we make make no difference to what He's done for us and how much He loves us. End of.

Yes! No one would expect to put milk in a car's fuel tank and for there to be no consequences – it wasn't designed for milk! Ignoring God's will for us has consequences; for us (because He doesn't protect us from them), for others, and for our connection with Him. Sin delays destiny and destroys intimacy. It's not possible to love the One who designed us without listening to Him or caring about what He cares about. If we ignore what He says, what does that say about how much we trust or respect Him? He won't make us pay, Jesus did that. And He'll never shame us. But He will change us as we walk with Him. If we haven't understood that, we haven't understood Him. If we ignore his voice and keep resisting the change He wants to bring, slowly our hearts go hard.

Life with God is not about behaviour, it's about relationship. But, if we've got a real, vibrant relationship with Him and we trust Him, the way we live will change because we will change.

PONDER
What would you say to someone who asked you if sin matters? Memorise the verse above, making it personal. Declare it out loud, a few times, and slowly.

PRAY
Thank Him He doesn't treat you as you deserve. Thank Him that He's merciful and kind to you.

READ: Hebrews 8:1-12
**They'll get to know Me by being kindly forgiven, with the slate of their
sins forever wiped clean.** (MSG)

The Father sees you with no sin. Do you need to read that again? To see yourself any differently is not humility, but a failure to trust what Jesus did on the cross. Saints aren't perfect people, they're forgiven people. If the Father sees us with no sin on our record (He's wiped our slate clean forever), what do we do when we mess up, disobey Him or let others down? What do we do when the Holy Spirit shines His loving light on something He wants to deal with in us?

My friend left a pot of chocolate icing out the other day. A few hours later, she discovered it empty, and confronted her four young children. All four denied knowing anything about it, although each one had chocolate icing smeared round their mouth! Crazy – except we can be like that with God. Our mistakes and our sin are not someone else's problem. Our choices are not caused by other people. And yet denial, blame-shifting or excuses are often routes we opt for over repentance. Just ask Eve!

Saints repent. Repenting doesn't mean we're not saints, it means we're not perfect! Beating ourselves up or self condemnation never helps. Neither does ignoring where we've gone wrong. But the Father's mercy always helps. And I need it so often. If there's a specific action or attitude we need to repent of, we must be quick to come to Him. Admit it, own it and hear Him tell you He's forgiven you. Receive His love and affection again. Don't promise Him you'll change, ask Him what He wants you to do next. At the core of who you are is a completely perfect Lord Jesus, not a dysfunctional person with a messy past or anything else. The more we believe this and at the same time, invite Him to work in us through repentance, the more of His life He can release in us.

PONDER
Do you believe your slate has been wiped clean? Ask the Holy Spirit if there is any action or attitude that you need to repent of so you can receive the Father's forgiveness and freedom. Do so now.

PRAY
Thank Jesus that He's wiped your slate clean. Thank Him that He has done for you what you could never do for yourself. Spend some time expressing your thanks and love to Him.

READ: Isaiah 54:14-17
You will silence every voice raised up to accuse you. (NLT)

Bad news: there will always be days when you're accused. You know what the pointing finger is like; pointing at your character, pointing out your faults, your weaknesses, your failings, your mistakes, your past and your imperfections. Sometimes you'll hear an actual human voice accusing you, but most of the time it'll be in your head. 'You're worthless, it's your fault, you don't pray enough, if you hadn't done ..., if only you were ...'

Good news: as a saint, you don't have to let these accusations haunt you and torment you. The Father has given you the authority to deal with them, and He expects you to use it.

STEP 1 – Remember it's *never* Jesus who's accusing you. He was accused Himself, even though He was perfect. He said, 'I will not accuse' (Jn 5:45). The accusations we hear against our heart don't come from God. He's waiting for us to grow strong in standing tall and silencing them.

STEP 2 – Remember the enemy is described as the accuser (Rev 12:10). He's the one undermining your confidence in who you are. Accusation is his language, and it never brings life or produces good fruit.

STEP 3 – Point your own finger – at Jesus. The Holy Spirit always points to Him so copy Him. Each time the accuser tells you, 'You're not good enough', point to Jesus and say, 'Jesus made me good enough'. When the accuser tells you, 'You don't deserve blessing', point to Jesus and say, 'I qualify for His blessings'. When the enemy says, 'You're useless', point to Jesus and say, 'He's chosen to use me'. You get the picture. The more confident you are in who He says you are, the easier this is.

You're a saint because of what Jesus has done for you. Believe it. As you point the finger at Him and at His obedience, and away from your shortcomings, you'll silence those voices and find yours.

PONDER
What happens to you when you feel accused? What do you do as a result? Declare over yourself 'I am a saint, I am loved and I will no longer listen to the voice of accusation.'

PRAY
Thank God He never accuses you. Ask Him to help you remember that, the next time you hear accusations. Decide to use the authority He's given you to silence every voice that accuses you.

READ: Micah 7:19
**Once again You will have compassion on us.
You will trample our sins under Your feet
and throw them into the depths of the ocean!** (NLT)

This is a prophetic declaration before Jesus came, about what God was going to do for His people through His Son's work on the cross.

PLAY the PART

Imagine yourself sitting in a small rowing boat out at sea. The sea is calm and the sun is shining.

– LOOK around you at the distant shoreline. Feel the heat on your skin. Hear the gentle lapping of the water against the side of the boat. Enjoy the moment. Watch as Jesus comes towards you. See the smile on His face as He gets closer and looks at you; watch as He climbs into the boat to join you.

– HEAR Him speak your name and tell you that your sins, everything you regret, everything you would change, everything you're ashamed of having done, and everything you're not even aware of, all of them are lying on the sea floor, way, way beneath you. They're out of reach and out of sight. Hear Him tell you He's thrown them into the depths of the ocean. Pause and let it sink in.

– ASK Him to show you if there is any sin you are still holding on to that you don't believe He's forgiven you for. Whatever He shows you, acknowledge it with Him, give it to Him, and watch what He does with it.

– LISTEN for anything else He wants to say to you.

Thank Him for what He's done for you and what He's shown you. Ask Him to increase your trust in His love and forgiveness. Commit to living in His forgiveness again. Begin to row back to shore and leave behind what's been thrown into the depths of the ocean.

RE-READ: Isaiah 54:17
You will silence every voice raised up to accuse you. (NLT)

It's important to know the difference between accusation and conviction. Accusation is the voice of the enemy telling you there's *something wrong with you* and *you* need dealing with. It results in condemnation. The enemy points at people, like you (Day 5). Remember, friend, *you* need to put him in his place and silence his voice. Jesus won't do it for you.

Conviction is the voice of the Holy Spirit telling you there's *something wrong with what you've done.* It's harmed you, your relationship with God, or someone else. And *it* needs dealing with. Conviction results in correction. The Holy Spirits points at a problem. When He does, we need to listen, remembering that *doing* something wrong doesn't mean there *is* something wrong with you. You're a saint; you are not what you do.

When we know we've gone wrong or the Holy Spirit is convicting us, we go quickly to the Father and ask for His forgiveness. He's already forgiven us, but we need to receive it to live in it. Otherwise our guilt or indifference will pull us away from Him. But let's not stop there. Let's remember to ask Him this: 'how do I live in Your power going forwards?'

PUSH IN
Jot down the main differences you need to remember between accusation and conviction and how the Holy Spirit wants you to respond to them both going forwards. Ask Him what else He wants you to remember from this week.

READ: Isaiah 51:9-13
I, yes I, am the One who comforts you. (TPT)

Is 'comfort' a word you link with God, or just one you associate with home, or chocolate, or sofa? The Father is always straight with us and nowhere in the Bible does He say life will be easy. Have you clocked that one? Jesus said we'll have trouble in this world because it's broken and messed up by sin. Heaven is where there'll be no more trouble, fear or pain. Jesus hasn't promised us a comfortable life, but He has promised to comfort us, always. He says He is our Comforter.

Our need for comfort isn't a weakness, it's part of being human. When we're in pain, or facing loss, or struggling, our need for comfort is meant to draw us to God, enabling Him to come close to us and be what we need. One definition of comfort is, 'easing or providing freedom from pain, distress and anxiety.' No matter how much faith we have, or how strong we feel, sometimes what we need is comfort. That's normal.

What do you do when you need comforting? When your heart is hurting or your soul is struggling? Most of us have our go-to comfort blankets that dull the pain or dial down the anxiety in the short term, making us feel better. Do you know what yours are? Maybe it's food, shopping, or someone you call. Perhaps it's exercise, social media or some other form of distraction or entertainment? Maybe it's something more dangerous. Friend, some of these are good things in themselves but not as a first resort. Our first step to knowing the Father as our Comforter is making Him our first resort when we need comfort. Make Him your go-to comfort blanket. Call out to Him. Don't fall for the lie that He expects you to have it all together. His arms are always wide open, ready to embrace you in your moment of need. When we don't go to Him first, we escape our pain or fear another way. And it always leaves us empty.

PONDER
How easily do you recognise or own your need for comfort? Can you identify your go-to comfort blankets?

PRAY
Ask God to forgive you for turning to false comforts before you turn to Him for comfort. Invite Him to come close and comfort you now if you need it. Pray for someone else who needs it too.

READ: 1 Kings 19:1-7
'I have had enough, Lord,' he said. 'Take my life...'

These are the words of a desperate man. This is the cry of someone in deep distress who needs comforting. Elijah's just had an epic showdown with the prophets of Baal, seeing God move in a mind-blowing way. Now he's on Jezebel's hit list and has an epic meltdown. He's had enough. He's exhausted and alone. This is not the best prayer anyone's ever prayed, but it's real and raw. Elijah knows God can handle his heart, and he knows God's strong arms are open wide to him, just as he is.

Elijah turned to God for comfort as his first resort. He prayed, asking Him for the comfort of an end to his life. That seemed like the best option to him in that moment. Not ideal, but his first move was still to pray. Look at the tender heart of the Father. He didn't say, 'Have more faith son', or 'Cheer up, it'll be OK in the morning when you've had some sleep.' He kindly and gently responded by providing what Elijah needed in that moment: food, drink and sleep. The Father is both caring and practical. Only later did He speak to Elijah, telling him what he needed to hear.

One of the enemy's biggest lies is that God is behind our hurt and pain. That He wants our hearts broken for some reason to prepare us for blessing. Let's wake up to that toxic lie which keeps us from the Father when we need Him most. Like Elijah, we have to feel and grieve our disappointments and losses or our hearts will harden, but God can't comfort us unless we go to Him with them. When we do, we discover His tender heart for us. He is big enough for you, friend. Let Him have access to your pain or fear, just as Elijah did. He may send His comfort through another person, through His word, through a sense of His nearness, or even through an angel as He did here. But the strength and relief you need are in God's arms alone. He gets your heartache and your humanity. Press in to Him, don't pull away.

PONDER
When were you last raw and real with God, asking Him to comfort you (excluding yesterday)?

PRAY
Imagine the Father's arms, flung wide to welcome you just as you are. Let Him embrace you. Spend a few moments in silence and enjoy His love.

READ: Psalm 119:49-56
Your promise revives me; it comforts me in all my troubles. (NLT)

God's heart is full of compassion for you. He's with you and working for good in all the things that are going on in your life, both good and bad. Nothing is beyond His reach. He is powerful, but has a soft heart for you. You may not have known comfort from your earthly father, but your Heavenly Father is different. He wants you to know Him as your Comforter so you don't shrink back from fear or pain, or bury it. He wants you confident enough to feel it and face it so He can grow you through it.

How do we experience Him as Comforter? First, we admit our need. That may be as simple as admitting to ourselves we're hurting or full of fear. Second, we admit to Him we want His comfort. Always be real about how you feel, friend. Remember, He can handle you. Elijah put his need into words by praying. We must do the same; God won't force His help on anyone. Third, we do what this psalmist did and let God comfort us with His word. His voice is like comfort food for our hearts.

As I've said, I've been through some dry times which I thought I'd never emerge from. I cried out to God for comfort, secretly hoping it would look like escape. I wanted Him to airlift me out! He didn't, but He did keep me going with His word. I'd open the book of Psalms, find one and keep reading through them until I found one where the words expressed my heart and described my experience. They're full of real, raw Elijah-type prayers of people in need of comfort. Not only did I find my voice in the words, I also found my Comforter's voice. He met me there repeatedly, and spoke to me with His promises. He comforted me in my trouble, just as the writer describes. Those promises were airlifted to my journal and fed my soul in the desert. God has no favourites. He was the psalm-writer's Comforter, He's my Comforter, and He's yours too.

PONDER

Can you remember a time when you found God's promises a source of comfort in your distress?

PRAY

Speak this verse out loud, back to God. Does it ring true for you? Does it stir up a longing within you? Let it to lead into an honest conversation with Him. Then ask the Holy Spirit to lead you to a verse for someone who needs comforting today. Message it to them.

READ: Deuteronomy 32:9-14
He was like an eagle...spreading its wings...teaching them to fly. (MSG)

God wants you to fly like an eagle. Eagles soar at great heights, flying higher and more effortlessly than other birds in the sky that flap hard to get to where they're going. Eagles let the air currents do the work for them. The Father intends for you to live in that same freedom, allowing the Holy Spirit to lift you above the challenges of life and lead you into the fullness of your purpose. But even eagles have to learn to fly.

God is described in this passage as being like an eagle, teaching His children to fly. An eagle gets its chicks flying by forcing them out of their comfort zone. She makes the cosy nest uncomfortable by stopping bringing them food there. The chicks realise that to eat, they've got to leave the safe place they're used to. So they start flapping their wings to learn to fly. At the outset, they begin to fall. The parent swoops down and flies underneath them, keeping the chicks from crashing.

God is the Comforter, but that doesn't mean He wants us comfortable. We only need a Comforter when we're uncomfortable. To grow into our potential, friend, we have to leave our comfort zones. He's called you to a purpose that lies beyond what you know and what you're capable of. Beyond your comfort zone is where it's at and where you learn to depend on the Holy Spirit more fully. Remaining in control of everything and playing it safe stunts your growth. Great lives don't emerge from great comfort. Some daughters are happier to take risks and embrace discomfort. Others need a gentle push. Jesus isn't afraid to give us one when He thinks we need it! But we'll be OK, because the Father is always waiting to catch us. Let's remember again, He's more concerned about our character than our comfort. So each time you're out of your comfort zone, learn to see it as a flying lesson.

PONDER
Is there a situation in your life at the moment where you feel out of control, or unsafe and insecure? Do you want to learn to fly?

PRAY
Ask the Holy Spirit to teach you to fly higher through this time. Thank Him He's the Comforter and won't let you crash. Ask Him to teach you to depend on Him more and give Him your fear.

READ: 2 Corinthians 1:3-5
He comforts us in all our troubles so that we can comfort others. (NLT)

Basic rule of life: you can't give away what you haven't got. As we experience the genuine comfort of God, He sets us up to pass it on. There are all kinds of people around us who are struggling and in pain because pain is part of life this side of Heaven. Not all the time, but much of the time, because we let pain into the world in Eden. God not only wants to comfort you, He's desperate to comfort others too. And His way of reaching out to others to comfort them is through His children, which means through you.

God has often comforted me in my most difficult moments through human skin. In response to my cries to Him, He's sent along people who have loved me, listened to me and chosen to hang out with me when I wasn't up for much else. People who would just love me in my mess. Explanations or direction rarely offer the same comfort in painful moments as the presence of another person. Someone who will hold back on questions and solutions and instead, just offer their attention. He's chosen you to be that someone for others.

He wants to comfort those around you when they've suffered loss, when they're struggling through trouble, when they're walking through difficulty and darkness, when they're facing ill-health and when they're anxious. There's no exception and no limit to His comfort. Most of the time, the greatest comfort you can offer to others is your presence. Being with them. You don't need to advise and you don't need answers, you just need to be available and give them your attention. If you try and put yourself in their shoes, it'll be even easier. The basic rule of life is that you can only give away what you've received. The Bible rule of life is that when you do, you receive back even more.

PONDER
Who is God wanting you to offer comfort to? How could you do that? Decide when you'll do it.

PRAY
Spend a bit of time praying for that person. Ask the Holy Spirit to open your eyes today to anyone else who may need God's comfort and remember to ask Him how you can bless them.

READ: Psalm 23: 4

Even though I walk through the darkest valley, I will fear no evil, for You are with me; Your rod and Your staff, they comfort me.

Valleys are part of life. The soil in them is very fertile and the Father does some of His best work in our valleys. Remember, they have a beginning and more importantly, they have an end.

When you're walking through a dark valley, as David says here, you need to keep walking. Don't set up camp there and don't assume it'll never end. Fear is part of the experience of a dark valley but David knows that the presence of the Comforter is the antidote.

PUSH IN

– If you're walking through a dark valley at the moment, read and re-read this verse a few times, out loud, and ask Jesus to reveal more of His presence to you. Ask Him to comfort you as He longs to, and ask Him to give you fresh strength today to keep going.

– Whether or not you're in your own personal valley, ask Him to bring to mind someone who is, and pray for them to know His deep comfort in their darkness. Ask Him to encourage them in a very specific way today, and ask Him if there's anything He wants you to do to be part of His comfort for them.

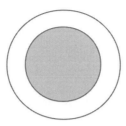

Imagine the shaded area represents your comfort zone. Your comfort zone is different to anyone else's. What you may be comfortable with, someone else will find uncomfortable and vice versa. So don't compare what you find uncomfortable with what others do! Your comfort zone reflects the areas of your life where you feel safe because things are predictable or under your control. You don't need to depend on the Comforter here because you're pretty comfortable. But that also means there's not a lot of room for Him to move in your life.

Sometimes life pushes us outside this zone through things beyond our control, like an illness, a pandemic, losing a job, a relationship crumbling, etc. At other times, we need to take an intentional step outside this zone to see God move and learn to depend on Him more. That might look like offering to pray with a colleague if you've never done that before. It might look like fasting from social media for a while to focus on your relationship with Jesus. It might mean making yourself vulnerable to someone when you're afraid of rejection. It might mean taking an opportunity fear or reason is urging you to refuse.

PUSH IN

Talk to Him. Ask Jesus if there's a step He's inviting you to take outside your comfort zone so that you can learn to depend on Him more fully. Spend a few moments waiting for His response. Ask Him to give you the courage you need and to reassure you that He'll catch you if you start to fall. Trust Him that He wants you to fly.

READ: John 4:21-24
...for they are the kind of worshippers the Father seeks.

What do you make of the word 'worship'? It's not an everyday word and yet worship is an everyday thing for you and me; we're wired to worship. God created us as worshippers, so everybody worships someone or something, even if they think they don't. Your heart is the truest and most precious part of you, and worship begins in your heart. God wired you to give your heart away, just as He gives His away. You can't help it.

The simplest definition of worship is admiration and adoration. When we admire and adore someone or something, our heart becomes attached to it. We admire and adore many things, but there will always be one that tops the list and gets us out of bed. Whatever it is, we guarantee it our time and energy. It's usually in our thoughts somewhere, whatever else is going on. Fame or success, our kids or career, possessions, pleasure or a partner, our image or a dream, all compete with Jesus for the top spot. A good question to check in with regularly is, who or what has your heart?

Jesus says something here that's easy to miss. He's not saying, 'The Father is looking for servants and evangelists'. He's not looking for preachers or missionaries, or leaders or entrepreneurs, or carers or campaigners. He's looking for worshippers. Does that surprise you? He doesn't need women who work for Him, He longs for daughters who love Him from the core of their being. Who make Him the centre of their admiration, adoration and affection. He's more interested in our mindset than our skill set and cares more about our connection with Him than our contribution for Him. He wants our whole heart because our heart is like a rudder. Whatever has our heart has our life. The Father loves you more than you know and He's the only One who won't break your heart and lead you astray. How much of it does He have?

PONDER
We can only give God our heart to the extent we haven't given it away to someone or something else. Who or what else is pulling at your heart today? Be brave and ask Him to show you.

PRAY
Talk to Jesus about what He's stirring in your heart today.

READ: Revelation 7:9-12
And they fell before the throne with their faces to the ground and worshipped God. (NLT)

We live down the road from a football stadium. When the local team scores, the crowd goes ballistic. I love hearing the roar of delight that suddenly fills the air. The admiration and adoration expressed in that moment is a reaction to what they've watched on the pitch. They can't contain their joy as they respond to their team and it's achievement. The greater their delight, the greater (and louder) their response.

Worship is your response to God; to what He's done for you, who He is and all He's promised you. The angels and the elders are on their faces in this passage, singing. They're expressing their reaction of awe and wonder to what they watched on the cross and in the tomb; to the eternal achievement of the Heavenly team. They're showing their delight and gratitude to the Father, His Son and the Holy Spirit in response to their deep love, supreme power, phenomenal mercy and endless kindness and commitment to each and every one of us. Wow.

Sometimes I struggle to worship, to get in touch with my affection and awe for Jesus, and express it from my heart. Just saying. It happens when I don't respond to what He's done for me and what He's promised, but do respond to something else. Often, it's my circumstances and how I feel about them. Other times, it's distractions. Worship music helps me in those times. It's a gift that has a power to stir up our affection for God, get us singing, and help us look back to the cross and the tomb. It helps get me in touch with what those moments in history mean for me, for those I love and for this world. Worship requires my heart, but it's a response, not a feeling. They're different. Sometimes the feelings aren't there. But I can *always* choose to worship.

PONDER
Picture yourself at the foot of the cross or looking into the tomb. What do you find yourself wanting to say? How do you feel?

PRAY
If you can, get on your knees and spend a few moments responding to Jesus from your heart. Why not put on a worship song and sing along?

READ: John 4:19-24

...He longs to have sincere worshippers who worship and adore Him in the realm of the Spirit and in truth. (TPT)

We discover the basis of our affection for Jesus when things go wrong in life. Are we still impressed with Him and what He's already done for us? Or are we only impressed with Him when life happens as we want? It's easy to worship Him when things are going well, less easy when they're not. When trouble comes, it can mute our expressions of admiration and adoration. And yet, the Father is looking for worshippers whose worship is rooted in spirit and in truth, not feelings or locations.

This Samaritan woman wanted to know about the 'right' way to worship God. Jesus told her that true worship isn't a religious ritual but an activity of the heart. It's not about what happens in a certain place, but about the place it happens from. Since worship is our response to the truth of who He is and what He's done, not to how we feel, He's looking for daughters who worship Him in every situation, even when it costs us. The Holy Spirit helps us worship Jesus, so He empowers us in every season, including the difficult ones. But first, we have to open our mouths.

The Father isn't after worshippers because He needs an ego trip to make Him feel bigger and better. He's not insecure like we can be. He's after connection with us. And since we're wired to worship, if we don't worship Him, our hearts go after something else. When we worship, we fix our eyes on Him. As we do, we open ourselves up to His presence and love, and we grow stronger. How we need that when life is hard. I've discovered the times I least feel like worshipping are often when I need to the most! How about you? How often do you tell Him how much He means to you? How often do you express your affection and admiration to Him? How often do you sing to Him? Worship and adore Him in spirit and in truth, in word and in song, in every situation and season. He is worth it.

PAUSE

Spend a few moments thinking about your relationship with Jesus. What proportion of your interaction with Him is you expressing your love and adoration to Him because He is worth it? Does that change with your circumstances? Ask Him to forgive you if it does. Identify if or how you'd like it to change. Ask Him to help you and tell Him why you love Him today.

READ: Mark 14:3-9
She has just done something wonderfully significant for Me. (MSG)

What does a God-worshipper look like? If you ask some people, they'll tell you a worshipper looks like someone with their hands raised in church, or someone on their knees by their bed praying. This may or may not be true. It depends what's happening in their heart. True worship isn't something that's done because of tradition, but begins in the core of our being. It's then shows as some outward expression of admiration and adoration. A worshipper can look like this woman with her alabaster jar.

The perfume she poured on His head that day was worth a year's salary. Where on earth did she get a fragrance like that? Even Harrods doesn't sell perfume that expensive! It must have smelled incredible. Wherever she got it, she chose to spend it on Jesus, all in one go. He'd changed her life and she was deeply thankful. She adored Him because of the way He'd loved her. Those watching called it a 'waste' since it could've been sold and the money used to help the poor. Others called it extravagant. An over-the-top demonstration of how much He meant to her. But it meant so much to Jesus He told the onlooking critics that her story would be told forever. That was the end of that conversation!

Friend, have you asked yourself lately how much you 'spend' on Jesus? Are you snatching moments with Him here and there that tick the relationship box or are you guilty of 'wasting' time on Him? Do you budget your energy and resources for Him, or could you 'waste' more of them on Him and His kingdom? Do you, like me, feel inspired by this woman's adoration and want to ask the Holy Spirit to increase yours? The opinion of the onlookers here sounded so reasonable, except that when you adore someone, you do unreasonable things. There is no right way to express your affection, it's deeply personal. But don't let others put you off by what they say or think, especially if they're not recommending extravagance!

PAUSE

Is your worship of Jesus ever 'wasteful' or 'extravagant'? How could you express your gratitude and love to Him today in an extravagant way?

READ: Philippians 4:4-9
Instead of worrying, pray. Let petitions and praises shape your worries into prayers, letting God know your concerns. (MSG)

Worry is optional, have you noticed that? It might not feel like that. When I'm in the midst of a worry fest, chewing over all the possible scenarios that I dread, it doesn't feel like an option I've chosen, it feels like worry has chosen me. But Jesus says, 'Don't worry.' (Matt 6:31) And if He says don't worry, it means I can choose not to worry. He never asks us to do what we can't do. The reason you have the option not to worry, friend, is because He's designed you as a worshipper, not a worrier.

When we worry, we're not living from our true identity as a daughter of God. We weren't created as worriers, so when we worry, it leaves us feeling anxious, stressed and troubled. We lose our peace, we lose sight of Jesus and we lose our joy. The Bible doesn't just give us good advice, it reminds us who we really are and how to live from that identity. Paul says here, *instead* of choosing worry, choose worship. Turn to Jesus and talk to Him. Tell Him about what's troubling you, be honest with Him, but praise Him at the same time. Praise Him as you pray. Express your adoration, your affection and your admiration to Him as you explain what's bothering you and what you need. And then crucially, in verse 7, you'll experience His peace. Yes please!

Option 1 is to pray and praise, option 2 is to panic. It's almost impossible to do both which is good news. Worshipping when we could opt for worry is choosing to live from our new identity not our old one. It's choosing to be more impressed with Him and what He wants to do, than with our problems. It's remembering we're His, instead of imagining we're on our own. Remember you're a worshipper not a worrier. Jesus doesn't want us worrying, He wants us worshipping. Friend, new habits are hard to create, but they're worth it. We can do it. Because He says so.

PRAY
Pick one thing that's worrying you at the moment. Tell God about it but as you do so, worship Him. Praise Him for who He is and how He cares for you and thank Him for what He's already done for you as you ask Him for His help. Each time you find yourself worrying about that thing today, be quick to turn it into a prayer, sprinkled with praise and gratitude.

RE-READ: Revelation 7:11-12
**All the angels were standing in a circle around the throne with the
elders and the four living creatures, and they all fell on their faces
before the throne and worshipped God, singing:
'Amen! Praise and glory, wisdom and thanksgiving, honour,
power, and might belong to our God forever and ever! Amen!'** (TPT)

The two main words for worship used in both the Old and New
Testaments contain the idea of some kind of physical expression. They
include bowing, kneeling, dancing, clapping, shouting, singing, standing
in awe and 'falling on their faces.' In themselves, these activities are not
worship. They need to be attached to an inward adoration and
admiration, however weak. But having an affection for the Father which
only involves our minds or hearts, and not our bodies, is equally empty.

PUSH IN

Spend some time worshipping Jesus today, using your body as well as your mind and heart. Be
bold and try something new or different!

RE-VISIT: Day 5
Instead of worrying, pray. Let petitions and praises shape your worries into prayers, letting God know your concerns. (MSG)

PUSH IN
− Commit this verse to memory in whichever version of the Bible you like most.

Grab a piece of paper or use the space below and write down the different things you're worried or anxious about. Be as specific as you can.

− Go through the list, one at a time, and tell Jesus why you're worried and what you want Him to do.

− Praise Him, as specifically as you can, for the different ways He's helped you in the past.

− Praise Him for any promises you can think of from the Bible that are relevant to the situations you've identified.

− Thank Him that He hears your prayers and that He's working for your good. Thank Him that all things are possible with Him, that He is for you, that He won't withhold any good thing from you and that He will give you everything you need.

READ: Genesis 18:1-14
Is anything too hard for God? (MSG)

God can do anything. Absolutely anything. Do you believe that? The Bible is full of stories of God demonstrating His wonder-working power in many different ways. From emptying Lazarus' tomb, to lighting Elijah's soaking wet bonfire, to walking on water. From making a way through the middle of a mini ocean to collapsing the vast walls of Jericho with a trumpet blast, to piercing the walls of a human heart. How did Saul the murderer become Paul the martyr?

The Father can do anything. And everything. Are you confident about that? Abraham's wife Sarah wasn't, and had trouble believing it. God said she'd have a baby. Nothing special about that if you're healthy and in your 20s or 30s. But Sarah was about 90. Imagine that! In her own words she was worn out and old (to put it politely). No wonder she laughed (as Abraham did a chapter earlier) when she heard what God was planning. In her mind, it was beyond the limits of both probability and possibility. God's reply was short: 'Sarah, when I'm involved, there are no limits.'

There are limits to everything. I have limits to what I can do, and so do you, friend. Part of accepting who we are is accepting our limitations (and those of others) and learning to live within them. But God isn't like us. There are no limits to what He can do. His power is so great, we can't get our heads round it. Nothing is too tricky for Him, not even destroying death. What's tricky for us is believing it. What's tricky is confidently rejecting the lies that, 'My situation is too hard for Him' or, 'God couldn't use me' or, 'Things won't ever be different'. If you're facing an impossible situation today, no matter how you feel about it, reconnect to this truth about the Father. He's all-powerful. His word to Sarah is His word to you.

PONDER

Hear the Father asking you the same question He asked Sarah (above). How does your heart reply? Does your faith in His power need a resurrection?

PRAY

Thank the Father in faith (even if it doesn't feel true) that He says nothing is too hard for Him. Confess the doubts you have and talk to Him about any 'impossibilities' you've given up on. Declare over each impossibility that, 'It's not too hard for God'.

READ: John 6:1-12
Where can we buy bread to feed all these people? (NLT)

The Father moves in power when we're weak, not strong. So the Holy Spirit tries to lead us into positions of God-reliance not self-reliance, have you noticed that? That's what's going on before this breathtaking miracle. God loves questions, and this question was for Philip, probably tongue in cheek. I imagine Jesus trying to hide His smile as He asked it. The text says, 'He already knew what He was going to do'. And that didn't involve a supermarket dash to find food for 5,000 families!

Why ask the question since this was a setup? Because Philip needed to hear himself process the situation. Jesus was teaching them to expect miracles, but Philip hadn't got it yet. His answer was telling. No expectation of Jesus. Philip was looking to himself and the others, and to their human ability (or lack of it) to fix the problem. 'We have no food and no money, so it can't be fixed.' The test (v6) was, did Philip have a kingdom mindset yet? Since God's kingdom is a kingdom of power, Jesus was hoping he might say, 'Lord, we can't fix it but you can. You can do anything'. But Philip still thought God expected them to do the fixing.

How big are your expectations of your all-powerful Father? The size of your prayers will tell you that. Do you limit Him because you think you're meant to be the fixer? Or because of your lack of faith? God said to Paul, 'My power works best in weakness' (2 Cor 12:9). What He's planned for your life is impossible in your strength. Your own limitations and those of your situation aren't meant to keep you down or keep you super busy, but keep you on your knees. They're a setup for Him. If we're making life happen in our own limited strength, we're actually limiting His. He wants His daughters to believe big and pray big, and bring a kingdom mindset to every situation. Don't look at what's possible or what's not, look at what He can do and what He has said. Then He'll do the impossible.

PONDER
Is there a situation you're feeling discouraged by at the moment, either in your life, someone else's life, or in your community or nation? What sized prayers are you praying?

PRAY
Ask God to show you what He'd like to do. Ask Him to move in power and do the impossible.

READ: Joshua 3:8-16
When you reach the banks of the Jordan River, take a few steps into the river and stop there. (NLT)

The world doesn't rate weakness, but it's a platform for God's power. Weakness doesn't move the Father, faith does, but when we partner with Him in our weakness, we make room for Him to move. Partnering with Him in weakness means He is Plan A, and if He doesn't show up and do what only He can do, there is no Plan B. Often, He asks us to make the first move. He invites us to show our weakness and make our faith in Him visible, before He shows His strength. And usually, that isn't comfortable.

Imagine how these priests felt. The land of their dreams, which God had promised them and all His people, was across the Jordan River. It wasn't far away, but the river was 60 metres wide in flood season and there was no way to cross it. God wanted to move in power and part it for them, but the priests had to move in to the river first. Imagine all the Israelites watching them. Imagine how clumsy they must have looked getting into the fast-flowing water with their long robes on. Imagine how foolish they would have looked if God hadn't then made His move.

To see God move in power, we need to be ready to make the first move. To take a step, expecting Him to take the second step, but without a backup plan if He doesn't. Like committing to a moving date from your home before you have a new one to go to. Like praying with a stranger for them to be healed. Like giving some money away even if you don't then have enough for all your needs. Like starting a new venture that you have no power to make succeed. Like speaking out and holding on to a promise of God when all looks hopeless. Like choosing to forgive when you don't have the strength to. If you're longing to see God move in power in your life, perhaps He's waiting for you to make your move.

PONDER
Can you think of a time when God moved in power after you'd had to make the first move? How did you feel as you made it? Is there a move God is currently asking you to make?

PRAY
Ask the Holy Spirit how you can partner with Him in weakness today. Talk to Him about your day.

READ: Matthew 26:47-56
Do you think I cannot call on My Father, and He will at once put at My disposal more than twelve legions of angels?

The Father doesn't always use His power how we think He should, but He is always good. The night before Jesus was killed, He was arrested in a dramatic way. As the guards arrived to take Him to His fate, a friend went for the counterattack and sliced off a soldier's ear. Gross! Jesus then says this: 'I could ask My all-powerful Father to send 72,000 angels (more than would fill a football stadium) to fight for Me. But I'm not going to.' 'Why on earth not?' the disciples would be forgiven for asking.

Question: was it more powerful to send 72,000 angels to protect the living Jesus, or to bring the body of the dead Jesus back to life inside a tomb? God can look powerless, even when He's working in power in your life. He didn't look powerful in Gethsemane, or as Jesus was dragged to the cross. But Jesus was relying on His power for each step towards His horrific death. The Father didn't look powerful as Jesus hung there, but the power of sin and the powers of darkness were being defeated in Jesus' body for all eternity. Only once the stone was rolled away was it obvious God had been moving in eternity-changing power, all the time.

Friend, the enemy whispers that the Father's not doing something powerful when He's not doing what we want or expect. The disciples' expectations of what God *should* have done blinded them to what He *was* doing. The way the Father works isn't always the way we would work. The way He thinks isn't always the way we think (although hopefully that's changing). Let's fight to hold on to our confidence today that He *is* working in power, where we are praying, and that one day we'll see what He was doing in our rear view mirror, just as the disciples did.

PONDER
Are you disappointed with something God isn't doing or hasn't done? How has it impacted your expectation of God?

PRAY
Be honest with God about it, He can take it. Ask Him to show you what to do to move forwards. Do whatever He tells you. Then ask Him to show you where He's working in power.

READ: 1 Corinthians 12:4-11, 14:1
Pursue love and desire spiritual gifts... (NKJV)

We belong to a kingdom of power. Jesus wants us to walk in the power of His kingdom so we can reveal Him and love others with His power, not our own. If He needed power to demonstrate the Father's love, then so do we. God is all-powerful but He's chosen to delegate His power to us for the benefit of those around us. Why else would Jesus require His followers to be clothed in His power (Lk 24:49)? He wants His power flowing through His people. Through you and me.

Paul says, 'The kingdom of God is not a matter of talk but of power' (1 Cor 4:20). Friend, words are not enough to enable us to encounter Jesus and His love and life. We need the Holy Spirit's power too. Paul compiles a list in this passage of spiritual gifts through which God's power and love flow. They're gifts from the Holy Spirit to us, for the benefit of others. Then, in case we're in any doubt, a chapter later he goes on to say, 'Oh, and make sure you desire these gifts.' God commands us to want them. He expects us to be convinced we need them so others can benefit from them. Only if we're convinced will we ask for these power-gifts.

God has demonstrated His love for me many times by moving in power in my life through other people using their spiritual gifts. Whether it's been healing, the phenomenal encouragement of prophecy, someone's gift of faith that released me from oppression, His word of wisdom in a situation that led to a breakthrough, or more, I'm so grateful for the way He's shown me the power of His love through others. He wants you to be that daughter, partnering with Him in greater ways, to see people saved, healed, set free, empowered, encouraged and equipped for kingdom life with Him. But for that to happen effectively, you need to be clothed in His power and walking in it.

PONDER
Review the list of spiritual gifts in 1 Corinthians 12. Do you have any personal experience of any of these gifts? Do you 'desire' any of them? If so, which ones?

PRAY
Ask Jesus any questions you have about walking in His power. Ask Him to come and clothe you in His power again and ask Him for the 'power-gift' you desire.

READ: Mark 5:21-24, 35-43

There is often a link between the power God can release and the faith we bring to the table. If there wasn't, there was no point in Jesus trying to teach Philip and the others the lesson He did at the picnic. He was continually trying to raise their expectations of what God could do. And it's why He continually tries to raise ours. It's also why the enemy tries so hard to do the opposite.

As Jesus came to the house to bring Jairus' little girl back to life, He made the crowd leave (v 40). He only took three disciples into the room with Him. Everyone else had to stay away. Resurrection power and reason don't work in the same room together. Reason is an enemy of faith. It's logical, it's compelling and it responds to and explains experience. But God is continually reminding me that reason suffocates my expectation of the impossible. Faith isn't reasonable. Jesus took an unusual step to protect His own expectation of a miracle in the midst of so much human response (v 38/v40). He longs for us to learn to do the same.

PUSH IN
Some things raise our expectations of God and what He will do, some things reduce our expectations. Identify what these factors are for you. Be specific. Looking at the two categories, decide what one thing you will do going forward to protect your confidence in His resurrection power, so you're better able to confront impossibilities like Jesus did.

READ: James 5:16(b)
The prayer of a righteous person is powerful and effective.

You're a royal daughter of the all-powerful One and you're a saint. That means your prayers are powerful and effective.

PUSH IN

– Commit this promise to memory and declare it over yourself.

– Ask God to highlight to you one or two situations He'd like you to pray for because your prayers are powerful. Take a few moments to ask Him to move powerfully in the scenarios He's shown you. Pray for His kingdom to come in them. Pray from your heart and with your imagination.

– Pray for anything or anyone else that's on your heart today.

READ: Luke 22:24-27
...the leader should be like a servant. (NLT)

How do you feel about the word servant? I'll be honest and say I'm not super keen! Take a room full of people and invite them to a leadership event and lots would be interested. Learning how to be a better servant would interest far less. Being served is one thing, but serving others? For some that conjures up images of doormats, being controlled or having to do things we don't want to. For others it's associated with feeling insignificant, inferior or taken for granted. But Jesus didn't give any of His children a new identity of leader, only of servant. Challenging!

Most of us want to be significant and recognised in some way. We want to live a life that counts, and the disciples were no different. Here, they're having a heated debate about which one of them would be the greatest. I'd love to have been a fly on the wall and heard what they thought would qualify them for the title. Maybe Peter thought being a supreme fisherman able to feed a community trumped collecting taxes. Perhaps Matthew felt making shed loads of money was more impressive. If they'd been having the discussion today, perhaps they'd be comparing personality types or the number of social media followers they had.

Jesus didn't squash their desire for greatness, and He doesn't squash yours. He put that longing into your DNA. He just challenges the route to getting there. Culture says we find greatness at the end of the road called status and success. Jesus says we find it at the end of the road called service. He should know. It may feel counterintuitive to put your energy into serving His purposes rather than yours, but the kingdom of God is upside down. The way down is actually the way up. The road down to serving is the one that leads up to significance. Let's make sure we take the right one.

PONDER

To what extent do you already see yourself as a servant? Of whom? And as a servant of *God*? How do you feel about this dimension of your new identity?

PRAY

Talk to Jesus about your desires and dreams to live a significant life and ask Him to grow a servant heart in you.

READ: Jude 1:1-2
Jude, a servant of Jesus Christ...

Jude may not be a well known dude, but he's great enough to have a letter published in the best-selling book in the world. Millions are still reading what he wrote 2,000 years after he wrote it. That is significance! Peter, Paul and James may be better known, but even Jude described himself as a servant of Jesus. He'd got the message that Jesus had called him to be a servant. But that led him towards greatness, not away from it.

The question is not, 'Are you a servant?' but, 'Whose servant are you?' We all serve an agenda, which is another way of saying we all have a master – something that motivates us and drives our decisions and destinies. Jesus talks about money being a common master, but there are others. If money's your master, then your financial agenda will drive your significant decisions. Career, influence, family, beauty, health, a dream, and your own needs or pleasure are other contenders for being the biggest motivating factor in your decision making. Jesus says we can't serve two masters. Only one can have our heart and hold the reins.

Jesus calls us to be His servant because He's the only master who cares about us selflessly enough to really look after us. We find our destiny in His agenda, and we walk in to it as *His* servant. Every other master will end up leaving us washed up on the shores of insignificance and emptiness. They'll block our route to greatness despite what they promise. Living as His servant isn't choosing to turn our back on money, or our career, or our own needs. It's choosing to love Him above all else, trust Him, and put His kingdom agenda first. Even when it clashes with ours. Do what He says, friend, and you'll find life.

PAUSE
Say the above phrase out loud a few times. Replace Jude's name with your own, try emphasising different words, and let the truth of this statement wash over your heart.

PRAY
Thank Jesus that you belong to Him and that He loves you. Ask Him, 'Lord, am I serving someone/something else? If so, what or who is it?' Pause for a few moments and notice what pops into your mind as you ask Him. Confess it and ask Him to help you serve Him first.

READ: Philippians 2:1-7
**And look out for one another's interests, not just for your own. The attitude
you should have is the one that Jesus Christ had.** (GNT)

A servant is identified by her heart rather than her actions. It's possible to perform an act of service and not be a servant. One time, I was clearing up a building on my own after a large gathering. Everyone had gone home, I had two small children with me and I'd volunteered to 'serve' the others; to do it myself and release them to leave. As I was in the kitchen, I was moaning in my spirit that it wasn't fair that it was taking so long and no one was there to appreciate my effort. The Holy Spirit interrupted my thinking and asked me who I was doing it for; me and the praise I would receive (or not), or Him? I learnt a bit more about myself that day!

A servant looks out for other people's needs or interests and then chooses to meet them. Paul says here that our attitude should be like that of Jesus. He was a great leader because He saw Himself as a servant. A servant asks herself the questions, 'What does the person (people) in front of me need? How can I help them?' Possibly Jesus' most controversial demonstration of this was when He washed His disciples' feet. What did they need as they sat down on the floor to supper? They needed clean feet! No one else was up for washing off the grime and the camel dung, so He did. It made them uncomfortable because they knew He was above such a thing. They thought they were too, so they didn't volunteer.

The people around you may not need camel dung wiping off their feet. But they might need a cup of coffee, or a listening ear, help with the kids or inviting round, some assistance moving house or some money, someone to speak up for them or someone to pray with them. Each time you choose to serve them for their benefit, you are serving Jesus. What a total privilege.

PONDER
Do you look for opportunities to serve or to be served? What do you consider to be beneath you?

PRAY
Tell Jesus you want to serve Him. Ask the Holy Spirit to point out an opportunity where you could be a servant to someone in your life today. Ask Him to show you what they need.

READ: Genesis 39:1-6

The Lord was with Joseph, so he succeeded in everything he did as he served in the home of his Egyptian master. (NLT)

Every now and again, someone will treat you like a servant. In your home or at work, at church or elsewhere, someone will ask you or expect you to do something you think is beneath you, or someone else should be doing. An easy way to tell if we have a servant heart is by how we react when we're treated like one. Is some stuff beneath us, or are we willing to do what's needed when it's needed? Even if crowds won't gather to thank us or our efforts aren't liked or retweeted on social media?

Joseph's life began with a dream – he saw his brothers bowing down to him. He enjoyed being served and honoured by others, so he told them. Problem: he didn't have a servant heart. He wasn't living from his true identity, so he wasn't ready for the great purposes God had for him. God used the cruel response of his brothers to grow Joseph into a true servant, preparing him for the greatness He'd chosen him for. The Father taught the son of a rich man who'd never served anyone, to be His servant. Through serving others. First, it was Potiphar. Then, it was prisoners. Finally, God promoted Joseph to a palace where Joseph could serve Him by serving an entire people.

What prepares us for the way up is how we respond on the way down. Leave the promoting to God and let Him use your current circumstances, your work environment, your home environment, your church and beyond, to grow a servant heart in you. Focus on what you can do for others rather than what they should/could do for you. Serve their dreams, not yours. The Lord will be with you as He was with Joseph, enlarging your heart and preparing you through the process. Your promotion will come when He knows you're ready.

PONDER
Can you identify any circumstances God has allowed in your life to grow a servant heart in you? How have you reacted to them?

PRAY
Thank God that He has a purpose and a destiny for you and that He's committed to preparing you for it. Ask Him to help you learn how to serve Him by serving others, so you're more prepared.

READ: Acts 2:14-18
'In the last days,' God says, 'I will pour out My Spirit upon all people.' (NLT)

There are times when the Holy Spirit will empower you to serve others in unusual ways. Four days before she died, my mother gave her heart to Jesus. For a few months, she'd been ill, and during that time, each time I saw her, I offered to pray with her. She was happy for me to do so. Amongst other things, I would ask the Father to help her know His presence and I would ask Jesus to give her His peace. She never said anything (except 'amen') until four days before she died. She described to me what she'd experienced each time I'd prayed. She had felt the reality of His presence and the power of His peace and because of that, she wanted to give Him her heart.

It was the Holy Spirit on me, touching her heart and life in those moments and revealing something of Jesus. Offering to pray with her was one of the ways I could serve her, knowing that experiencing His nearness was one of her greatest needs. I couldn't give her a touch from Heaven, but He could, as I prayed. The Father promised long ago that He would one day pour out His Spirit on all His servants. That includes you, friend. Why? Because we need Him and His power to serve the world as Jesus served it. Even Jesus couldn't fulfil His purposes on earth without the power of the Holy Spirit.

The Holy Spirit on you empowers you for service. The Holy Spirit in you shapes your heart into one of a servant. Jesus doesn't call us to live for Him and be a servant for Him just trying our best. He invites us to partner with Him so that His love and power can serve others through us. He is the One who increases our willingness to take the way down as we walk with Him. He is the One who highlights those He wants us to help. He is the One who whispers how we could serve them. And He is the One who gives us the power to connect them with Heaven. Live today conscious of His presence in you. Stay attentive and expect Him to work through you.

PRAY
Ask the Holy Spirit to fill you again, to empower you to be an effective servant. Ask Jesus if there is someone whose dreams He's wanting you to serve as a way of serving Him. Give Him a bit of time to respond. Notice any response in your heart to this, and talk to Him about it.

READ: John 13:1-17

PLAY the PART

Close your eyes and imagine yourself sitting amongst the disciples. Imagine Jesus getting to you and let Him wash your feet. Receive His love and feel His affection for you again.

– What does it feel like to have your Saviour wash your feet? Is it comfortable or uncomfortable? If it's uncomfortable, why is that?

– How do His actions speak of His love for you?

– What messy bits of your life and heart have you allowed Him to get involved in?

Spend some time thanking Him for the depth and breadth of His love for you and the way He longs to roll up His sleeves and head for the parts of your life you think are too messy for Him. Thank Him He doesn't leave you to wash your own feet. Tell Him about anything you'd like help with today.

READ: Joshua 24:14-16
But as for me and my household, we will serve the Lord.

Joshua confidently stood before the Israelites encouraging them to pick something or someone to serve; he knew they would serve someone or something anyway but he wanted them to be intentional about their decision. He then declared confidently that he'd made his decision (for himself and his family) about what the trajectory of their life would be; they would serve the Lord.

PUSH IN
– Can you say what Joshua said?

– If not, what would help you make your decision?

– Summarise what Jesus has been saying to you this week about being His servant.

Then turn your thoughts into prayer.

READ: Isaiah 6:1-5
Holy, holy, holy is the Lord-All-Powerful. His glory fills the whole earth. (NCV)

If we were chatting over a coffee and I said, 'I saw someone yesterday who was tall, tall, tall', you'd know immediately that the person I'd seen wasn't just your average version of tall. My repetition of the word 'tall' might make you think I'd never seen anyone taller! The only word used three times in a row about God is the word 'holy'. In both Isaiah and Revelation, the angels felt it wasn't enough just to say, 'God is holy'. They used the word on repeat to emphasise just how holy He is.

The word 'holy' has nothing to do with rules – it means 'separate.' It comes from an old word meaning to 'cut' or 'separate.' If you say someone's music is 'a cut above', you mean it's in a different league. When the angels cry, 'God is holy, holy, holy' they're saying, 'He's in a different league, He has no rival, no one even comes close'. Saying God is holy is saying He's nothing like us. He doesn't think like us, He doesn't react like us, He doesn't do things like us, He doesn't see things like we do. He is different. So different. He loves like no one we've ever known. The angels' repetition is meant to blow our minds with the idea that God is nothing like anyone or anything we've ever met. So much so that both Isaiah and the temple trembled!

We're not a good fit for God. But despite being in a league of His own, the Father loves us and has adopted us as daughters. Jesus paid the price for our un-holy-ness. The most powerful, pure, wise, patient, kind, gentle, generous, courageous, compassionate Being in the universe loves you. He longs to reveal more of His nature and His heart to you today. As He does, let that revelation stir up in you a fresh response of wonder and worship, and express it back to Him.

PONDER
What words do you associate with 'holy' when you think about God?

PRAY
You were not a good fit for God, but He loves you and chose you anyway. Re-read the verse above (out loud and slowly) a couple of times and invite Jesus to reveal more of Himself to you. Then express your heart back to Him.

READ: Luke 5:1-10

Master, leave. I'm a sinner and can't handle this holiness. Leave me to myself.

(MSG)

People say all kinds of strange things. My typing is so bad, my text messages often say weird and sometimes unrepeatable things! What Peter says to Jesus here is a different kind of strange. Jesus has just told him (Mr Career Fisherman) to go fishing again. Peter's been out all night with his crew, and they've caught zero fish. They're tired, discouraged, and probably annoyed. Jesus is a carpenter and doesn't know the water. But Peter obeys. Moments later the nets are virtually breaking with more fish (and therefore income) than they can handle, and the boats are beginning to sink. There are fish everywhere.

So what's with his reaction? *'Master leave. I'm a sinner.'* Did Jesus say something to Peter about his character, his past, his secret world? No! He just said, 'Have another go!' When we think about God being holy, it's easy to assume He wants to point out all our faults. Jesus doesn't do that. He just gives Peter a taste of His reckless generosity, His ridiculous kindness and His radical affection. It wrecks Peter, and suddenly, he feels unworthy. He knows he doesn't deserve loving like this. And He knows he doesn't love others like this either.

Do you ever feel unworthy of the reckless love of God? It's because you are. Friend, you can't earn Jesus' love and you never will, so quit trying. Unworthy is how Peter feels in this moment, aware of how holy (different) his friend Jesus really is. We can't reason why God loves us, we can only receive or reject His love. Trust what He's done and what He says, not how you feel or what you think. Trusting His love instead of trying to get our head round it is the only way into a deeper experience of it.

PAUSE

Do you struggle to accept God's love for you? Spend a few moments reflecting on this story, recognising Jesus loves you in the same way He loves Peter. Recklessly. Ridiculously. Radically. Acknowledge again that you're not worthy of such love, but He loves you anyway. Sit quietly and whisper a few times: 'Thank you Jesus that you love me like this.'

READ: Isaiah 55:8-9
My thoughts are not like your thoughts. Your ways are not like My ways. (NCV)

How do you handle the people in your life who are different to you? Your family members or your spouse, your friends or your boyfriend, your work colleagues or your neighbours? If social media is anything to go by, we're not always good at getting along with people who don't think like us or do things the way we would. God is holy. If He approved of cancel culture, He'd have no friends! But He's different to us. And He reminds us of that in these verses, just in case we're in any doubt.

The Father thinks differently to you; about you, about work, the future, your money, relationships, those around you, your problems, your challenges, your past, about the world and about how life works. He also does many things differently to the way we would. So that raises a question: our way or His way? One thing God doesn't do is negotiate, no matter how much we want Him to. Sometimes, when nothing is changing despite our best prayers or efforts, it's because He's waiting for us to whisper the words, 'OK Lord, let's do it Your way.'

Humility is a magnet for the grace and presence of our Father, who is not like us. If we want to be close to Him and see Him move, we need to be humble. He says as much in Isaiah 57:17. Humility looks like a number of things. It looks like being quick to learn, which involves admitting we don't have all the answers. Asking questions helps: 'Lord, how do I deal with this?' or, 'What would You do here?' or, 'Show me what You think about this?' or, 'Why am I not seeing this?' or, 'How do I love someone who is different to me?' Humility also looks like giving way when His way clashes with our way. That involves being ready to be corrected. There are our thoughts and there are His thoughts, our way and His way. His way is the high way but because He loves us, He won't force it on us.

PONDER
Can you identify something you think differently about now than you used to, because your thoughts are more like God's? How did that process happen?

PRAY
Moses asked God to teach him His ways and was known as God's friend. Ask God to teach you 'His way' in something you're currently wrestling with, so that you can know Him better.

READ: Ephesians 1:3-6

...He chose us before the world was made so that we would be His holy people... (NLT)

God is holy, and He chose us to be holy too, not so He'll like us better but because holy is how He designed us. He's more interested in our holiness than our happiness as happiness is connected to holiness. But how does holy happen? If you knew me as well as I know me, you'd think it was an impossible dream! Have you ever decided to be more patient? If you have, you'll know willpower doesn't work. It isn't enough to make us more like Him. Willpower alone won't make us more courageous, more loving, less insecure, more generous, more sensitive to His voice...

What Jesus has done is to give us a second chance to rely on Him, not a second chance to get our act together. Do you need to re-read that? He's already done the impossible and made us holy. That's the good news. We have His *Holy* Spirit living in us, so *He* makes us holy. That changed when our hearts changed. But learning to live holy is a process. The minute I said my vows on my wedding day, I became a wife. Sadly, I didn't then get a download and start living completely differently (poor husband!). I've had to learn how to be a wife and care about someone else's needs, not just mine. I've changed a lot, but I've got a way to go.

Few things are as crushing as trying hard to do your best to be like Jesus and succeeding for a while, just to fail again. Friend, remind yourself that learning to live holy is a day-at-a-time process. The Holy Spirit changes us gradually, which means we must be patient; with ourselves and with others. Let God heal your wounds, grow your strength and soften your heart. He does so as you make room for spiritual habits in your life. Give Him time in your diary, and He'll give you power in your life. Today is another day where He will work in you and with you, if you let Him.

PONDER

God chose you to be holy. Have you expected Jesus to leave you as you are? If not, have you expected to be able to change yourself, or do you expect the Holy Spirit to make you like Jesus?

PRAY

Pray, 'Holy Spirit, thank You that Your presence in me makes me holy. Thank you that You're making me holy. Soften my heart and help me to let You do what You want in me today.'

READ: 1 Peter 1:15-16
But just as He who called you is holy, so be holy in all you do.

Every day we get to choose who we live to please. You can choose to please yourself, please others or please the Father. Who are you hoping to please today? God has called you to be holy – to be like Him because that's how you were originally designed. Free from the need to please others, free from being controlled by your own needs and desires, and therefore free to love Him. Free to live the life He made you for.

How do we live holy? If holy means like God, not like the old me and not like the world, how do we do what Peter commands here? We work with the Holy Spirit. The Holy Spirit is in you and He wants to please the Father, so like a personal coach, He encourages you to make decisions that Jesus would make. When we become aware of a nudge to do something we wouldn't normally do, or a check in our spirits holding us back from doing or saying something that Jesus wouldn't, that's the Holy Spirit in us. He leads us. He whispers things like, 'Speak more kindly about others, I love them' or, 'Sexual immorality isn't for you – you're worth more than that' or, 'Don't worry about that, I've got it covered' or, 'Take the risk, I'm with you' or, 'Don't take that into your hands, leave it in Mine.'

Since the Spirit in us is holy, and He's like the Father who is holy, His promptings and nudges will often encourage us to do (or not do) things differently. Whether it's the way we use our bodies, our minds, our talents, our tongues or our time, the Holy Spirit will show us His way and empower us to obey. At times, He'll lead us to make different choices to those around us. But they always pave the way into the life and purpose we long for. Keep in step with Him and He'll guide your steps.

PONDER
When did you last feel a nudge or a prompt to do something different to what you were planning? What did it feel like? How did you respond to it?

PRAY
Invite the Holy Spirit to nudge and prompt you today to do things His way. Ask Him to help you to be more sensitive to Him.

READ: Revelation 4:1-11

PUSH IN

Read these verses and then re-read them, imagining yourself (like John who wrote this) in the scene. Picture the throne room as it's being described. Look around and listen for the sounds. Take note of your own reactions.

– What do you notice?

– What questions does it raise for you?

– What response does it stir in your heart?

Talk to Jesus about it. Spend some time worshipping Him with the angels.

READ: 2 Timothy 1:9
He has saved us and called us to a holy life.

Let's remember what holy means. Separate. A cut above. Different! God has called you to a life that's set apart and different. He's called you to a life of impact, purity, power, significance and love. To a life that leaves a legacy in eternity. The more He's able to work in you, the more He can work through you.

PUSH IN
Chat to Jesus about your dreams, your desires and anything else this verse makes you think about. Ask Him to show you something of what the 'holy life' He has called you to looks like. Note down anything you sense Him saying and talk to Him about it.

READ: Romans 5:6-11
But God demonstrates His own love for us in this: while we were still sinners, Christ died for us.

You are deeply loved. More than you'll ever know while you're on this earth. You're deeply loved by the Father, Jesus, and the Holy Spirit, and they want you to know more of their love. As it saturates your heart, they long for you to live 'much loved' rather than 'less loved.'

I love sitting on a beach watching the waves lap over the sand. The water rushes in and soaks it one minute, then withdraws until the next wave takes over. The enemy wants us to believe the Father's love is like that, ebbing and flowing, coming and going, depending on how well we're doing or what mood He's in. It doesn't help that often, the human love we've experienced has been like that. Conditional and inconsistent; more obvious one minute, less obvious the next. Greater when we've impressed, ticked the boxes and got the likes. It's easy to think God is like that and somehow we can make Him love us more or love us less.

Friend, settle it in your heart that you can't change the way God loves you. Sorry to break it to you, but you're not that powerful! He won't love you any more when you're perfect in Heaven than He does now. He doesn't love you less on your bad days than your good days. You have His heart, you're His beloved daughter. Paul says the proof is the cross. It's proof of His unchanging love. He didn't die for people who loved Him and impressed Him, but for people who'd turned their backs on Him. Your worst days were before you knew Him, but He loved you then as He loves you now. Enough to die for. His love for you doesn't ebb and flow, but your experience of it does. You've always been His beloved, and you always will be. He longs for you to trust Him and trust His love. Let it be what defines your day today.

PAUSE
This week, every time you find yourself struggling to believe that you're God's dearly loved daughter, make a choice to remember the cross and thank Him for it. It proves His love for you.

PRAY
Spend some time thanking God for showing His love for you on the cross. Ask Him to deepen your experience of His love and teach you to live 'much loved'.

READ: John 17:20-24
...the world will know...that You love them as much as You love Me. (NLT)

Whose approval are you after? Who do you try and impress? Many of us get stuck on a treadmill of some sort, trying to prove ourselves to others. Sometimes it's the approval of the significant people in our lives that drives us, other times it's approval on social media. Approval is like oxygen; we need it to survive as it validates us as human beings. Approval says, 'You're valuable, you've got something to offer, you matter.'

The danger of seeking approval from others, whoever they are, is that our sense of value gets tied to the way they react to us. 'If so-and-so is impressed by me, then I'm special and I matter'. 'If I don't get enough likes or affirmation, maybe I'm useless.' If what we do and the way we do it is done with other people's approval in mind, we've given them too much power over us. And Jesus doesn't want that.

The Father loves you as much as He loves Jesus. That's what Jesus says here. Pause a moment and re-read that. Remember that the Father declared His approval of Jesus at His baptism, *before* Jesus had done anything. Don't waste time trying to prove yourself to anyone, even the Father. He already approves of you; He died for you. He doesn't approve of every choice we make, but He adores His daughters.

Good news: you already have the Father's approval, and He's the One that really counts. Bad news: you won't always win the approval of others. So why not learn to live without it? Why care about the opinions of people who didn't die for you? Friend, let's live free from the need to prove ourselves and free to obey Jesus. To speak up for Him, to look different for Him and to step out for Him. We may not always feel the Father's approval, but we trust it when we live for His eyes only. Listen out for His approval today, not the disapproval of others.

PONDER
Whose approval do you long for? What do you do to try and win it?

PRAY
Ask God to show you one thing He wants you to stop doing, so you can live *from* His approval not *for* that person's. Ask Him to give you courage to take that step.

READ: Ephesians 3:14-21
Your roots will grow down into God's love and keep you strong. (NLT)

Imagine a tree on a stormy day. The wind is howling, and the battered tree is bending. The storm persists, and the tree resists. Finally, the storm ceases and the tree still stands. How come? Because of its roots. They've kept it anchored and alive. It's a picture of what Paul is praying in this famous prayer – that our roots dig down deep into the Father's love. A daughter who's rooted in His love is courageous, strong, and secure enough to live out the high kingdom purpose she's been called to.

But we all know it can be a challenge. Most days produce a battle of some sort to stay rooted in the Father's love rather than being uprooted from it. It's an inside battle, waged in our hearts which of course, affects the rest of our lives. On good days, when things go well and you get a promotion, or a new boyfriend, or an answer to prayer, it's easy to believe that Jesus really loves you. But when the test results are positive, when you watch someone suffer, when your prayer isn't answered, when the doors close around you or when you mess up, the enemy loves to whisper, 'If God really loved you, this wouldn't be happening.'

God never meant our circumstances to be a sign of how much He loves us. Many people carry scars and disappointments from life that convince them God doesn't truly care for them. But Jesus has His own scars to prove the opposite. The cross, not our circumstances, is where His love is most visible. Always. If you're convinced by His love poured out for you through His death, you'll be open to His love being poured in to you when the wind howls and your circumstances try and tell you otherwise. Turn up the volume on how loudly the cross is declaring the Father's love for you today and mute what anything else is trying to say.

PONDER
When do you find yourself questioning God's love the most? When are you most certain that He loves you?

PRAY
Invite Him to reveal more of the depths of His love for you and ask Him to help your roots go down deeper into His love. Let His love hold you and cover you now. Sit in silence for a bit.

READ: Ephesians 3:14-20
May you experience the love of Christ, though it is too great to understand fully.
(NLT)

Paul's prayer is too big not to revisit. He prays for our roots to go down deep into the Father's love because it's His love that keeps us anchored in the storms of life. We prosper when we're planted in the rich soil of His affection for us. But then he prays about a dual aspect to being rooted in God's love. He prays we'd understand it (as much as is possible in our small brains) and that we'd experience more of it.

If you want to discover more of the reality of God's love for you, no matter how you feel (about yourself or Him), you need to trust Him and who He is, even when you don't, if you know what I mean! Be quick to say to yourself, 'I don't like me, but God likes me.' 'I don't feel loveable but He loves me.' 'I am His and nothing can stop Him from loving me, not even my mistakes.' Instead of withdrawing from Him when you don't feel His love, be quick to draw near. We can't have deeper experiences of His love without holding on to what we know to be true about Him from His word. That's faith. And faith always positions us to receive more.

Although the Father wants us to trust He knows us and loves us because He says He does, He also wants us to experience His love. He wants us to feel it too. All kinds of things feed in to how we feel, like hormones and the day's events, so we can never rely on our feelings to tell us how God feels about us. But Paul prays here that we would experience His love. Friend, pray, like Paul, to feel more of it, as you trust what you already know to be true. Sometimes that sense of the Father's affection comes in a moment as we pray or listen to Him in His word. Other times, it comes as we open ourselves up to Him in worship, or to each other in vulnerability. Don't wait for it to happen. Pursue Him. And remember Paul's prayer. He's praying the Father's heart for you and for me.

PONDER
Can you identify anything that makes it difficult for you to believe that God loves you?

PRAY
Tell Him about it. Thank Him He's already forgiven you because He loves you. Ask Him to reassure you of His love today. Pray Paul's prayer for yourself now, and anyone else on your heart.

READ: Genesis 32:22-32
Just as it is written: 'Jacob I loved...' (Rom 9:13)

My friend has an unusual hip condition, but it wasn't caused by a tussle with God. Most people's hip problems aren't. Jacob was different. 'Jacob' means deceiver, and he certainly lived up to his name since all his life, he tricked others and lied to them to get out of tricky situations.

One night, he wrestled with a man who was actually God. Jacob longed for more of God's blessing on his life, so he didn't let go until God blessed him. But mid-tussle the man asked Jacob, 'What's your name?' Why did God ask what He already knew? Because He wanted to give Jacob a chance. To be honest about himself. To own his weakness, his flaws and his brokenness with his Father. 'I'm Jacob, I'm deceptive, I manipulate people and I cheat them.' Fortunately, Jacob went for it.

God doesn't want us to pretend with Him. He didn't gasp in surprise and back off in shock and disapproval. He knew exactly what Jacob was like. But He couldn't fully bless him and make Jacob into the patriarch He'd planned until Jacob was real and honest with Him about who he was. Jacob could only know God's love and blessing when he absolutely knew it had nothing to do with him. What was with the hip? It represented a man's strength. In dislocating it, God was letting Jacob know, 'I don't need your strength.' He pours His blessing into brokenness.

The Father loves you. As with Jacob, He knows all about your weaknesses, your flaws, your failures and your stubbornness; they don't disqualify you from what He's got for you. And as with Jacob, He's after a relationship with the true you. He wants to bless the real you. But we have to be honest with Him about our weaknesses and our flaws. No blaming others for them, no excusing them, and no hiding them.

PONDER
Are there any parts of you that you think God couldn't love? How easy do you find it to admit your flaws and failures to yourself and to Him? What do you think He wants you to admit today?

PRAY
Be honest with Him about an area of weakness; own it without excusing it. Thank Him that He loves you despite it, ask Him to bless you anyway. Invite Him to transform that part of you.

READ: 1 John 4:7-10, Isaiah 49:16

See, I have written your name on the palms of My hands. (TPT)

PUSH IN

Ask God to give you a fresh revelation today of His love for you as He demonstrated it on the cross.

– Close your eyes and picture yourself at the foot of the cross. What comes to mind when you think about the death of Jesus for you?

– What does it mean to you that Jesus has signed your name onto Himself, in the palms of His hands?

– Ask Him to speak to you through His hands; how do they speak of His love for you?

Spend a bit of time letting His love wash over you. Let His love flood the dry places in your heart. Respond by thanking the Father and Jesus for the extreme lengths they went to, not only to demonstrate their love for you, but to enable you to know that love and live in it. Let your delight in their love be stirred up again today.

– Ask Him to help you love others today in the way that He has loved you.

PUSH IN

Grab a bit of paper or use the space below..

– Ask the Holy Spirit to show you (and then write down) what you're trying to do in your relationship with the Father to get Him to love you more, or what you feel you need to do to make Him love you more. Be honest with yourself.

Look at what you've written. Talk to Jesus about anything that's on there and acknowledge that none of these things makes any difference to how much He loves you.

Ask Him what He wants you to do instead of what's on your list. Write down what He says.

– Is there anything you would do if you were more convinced God loved you completely?

Make a note of it!

READ: Psalm 103:1-5
He forgives your sins – every one. He heals your diseases – every one. (MSG)

God is a healer. His word says He's the One who heals and here, that He heals every one of our diseases. In Exodus 15:26 (MSG) He says, 'I am God *your* Healer.' Sometimes He heals sovereignly and supernaturally. Other times He uses the gifts and skills He's given others, but His desire is for us to be well. Mentally, spiritually, emotionally and physically.

Think for a moment how He's designed our bodies. A mind-blowing masterpiece of art and science which has an immune system (which comprises cells, proteins, tissues and organs) built into its software. Why? To protect and defend us against the tiniest organisms, germs, and toxins that would make us sick. Its repair mechanism also knows how to kill diseased cells, slow ageing, fix broken bones and keep us healthy. Wow! Sometimes, these in-built, self-repair systems don't work properly. We live in a broken world and our bodies get broken too. But our design reveals the heart of our Designer. The Father wants us well. Which is why one day, we'll get a new and perfect body that will last us forever.

Why does this matter? Because if we think God wants us sick or broken, we'll misunderstand Him. We'll miss His heart for us and for others. Sickness is part of this world, but God didn't create it and doesn't wish it on us. I've spoken to many who believe the lie that the Father doesn't want to heal them, or others. And yet they go to the doctor because they believe the doctor does, or would give it their best shot. Why would we think doctors want more for us than our loving Father? We don't see the fullness of healing until Heaven, but that doesn't change the fact that God cares about our bodies, our minds and our hearts. Whoever He uses and however He does it, the Father heals because He wants us well. Let the truth of this beautiful psalm bring hope to your heart today.

PONDER
How do you respond to the statement 'God wants us well'?

PRAY
Ask God to heal you wherever you need healing (body, mind or soul), or if someone else you know needs healing, ask Him to heal them.

READ: Matthew 4:23-25
And He healed every kind of disease and illness. (NLT)

Picture those people you know well. You wouldn't have been able to truly get to know them without hanging out with them, would you? No amount of social media contact, texting, or hearsay helps us discover who they really are. It's spending time with them, watching them navigate different circumstances and react under different pressures that gives us a picture of what they're really like.

Jesus came to show us what the Father is like. God came in a human body so we could see Him, touch Him, listen to Him, hang out with Him, and watch Him in different scenarios to get to know Him. There's no record in the gospels of Jesus refusing to heal anyone. Or of Jesus being unable to. Except where there was no faith (Mk 6:4-6). And I imagine that was because no one really asked for healing. Faith feeds our requests. Jesus healed everyone who was brought to Him, never telling anyone the Father wanted them sick. He showed the crowds that God took no pleasure in people being ill. He wanted them well, so He healed them. And if that wasn't enough evidence of His heart for them, He told His followers to carry on doing what He'd done. That mandate hasn't changed because He hasn't changed.

The enemy wants us to draw conclusions about Jesus' heart for us by looking at our circumstances. 'His will' must be for me to be sick because I am. God wants us to draw conclusions about His heart for us by looking at Jesus and looking into His word. The enemy's way is easy; it requires no faith. God's way is harder. It takes faith and pushes us to seek His will worked out on earth, just as it is in Heaven (Matt 6:10). How do you draw your conclusions, friend? The pain, the disappointment and the hardship when healing doesn't happen in this life is difficult and real. It can raise all kinds of questions, and we don't get all the answers. But don't fall for the lie that God doesn't want you well.

PONDER
Do you tend to draw your conclusions about Jesus from your circumstances or His word?

PRAY
Ask the Holy Spirit to show you what lie you've believed about His desires for you. Ask Him to forgive you. Ask Him to help you discover more of His heart (through His word) and agree with it.

READ: James 5:13-18
Confess your sins to each other and pray for each other so that you may be healed. (NLT)

I have a friend who Jesus healed supernaturally. Her husband had abandoned her and her three children years earlier. Then, to make it worse, her husband's family had been extremely cruel to her. She ended up very bitter towards them. One day, my friend got ill, and over time, the sickness got worse. Eventually, she ended up in a coma in hospital. Jesus sovereignly spoke to her in the coma and told her He wanted to heal her. But before He could move in her body, she had to let go of her bitterness. She had to forgive her husband and his family for how they'd wounded and rejected her. She was desperate to get well, so she did. The next day, to everyone's surprise, she was ready to leave hospital.

Her story illustrates what James is saying here. Sometimes, there is something we need to confess (own) or let go of before we can receive the blessing of physical or emotional or spiritual healing God has for us. My friend's heart-wound had become infected with unforgiveness and resentment, and it was affecting her receiving her physical healing. Before Jesus could heal her, she had to let go of some stuff; the Holy Spirit showed her what that was. The temptation for us can be to take a passage or a story and turn it into a formula. Let's not do that! The Father doesn't do relationship by formula. But remember, these verses make it clear that sin can block what He wants to do for us.

Since God is a loving Father who speaks, let's not make assumptions about our circumstances (or those of others for that matter). Instead, let's ask the Holy Spirit, 'Is there anything blocking the blessing You have for me?' If we're serious about our questions, He'll be serious about answering them. We don't need to dig, only to wait for His response. If you're open to whatever He might say, He'll make sure you hear. He wants to bless you and He will.

PRAY

Ask the Holy Spirit, 'Am I holding resentment in my heart towards anyone?' If someone pops into your mind as you pray, ask the Holy Spirit to help you let go of that resentment. You might like to picture yourself at the cross, leaving it there. Ask Jesus to bless anyone connected with it today.

READ: Psalm 147:1-6

He heals the heartbroken and bandages their wounds. (MSG)

My heart has been broken in ways I didn't know were possible. It has felt like it was shattered into lots of little pieces and sometimes the pain was so acute, I felt it physically. I couldn't imagine recovering. I've heard others say, 'If I started crying I would never stop.' That speaks volumes. When our hearts are broken and our souls are wounded, it feels like the bleeding will never end and the pain will never go. Some say time heals. I'm not convinced. The Bible says God heals. The Father is not only close to us when we're hurting, but He heals our broken hearts.

What is your heartache today? Can you feel the tenderness of God's heart for you in these words? He feels our pain and knows what it's like to be heartbroken. He has been too. When Eve ate the apple, when Cain killed his brother, when His people turned their backs on Him, when His Son hung on a cross. God can heal our hearts, but He needs access to them to do so. Which means, friend, if He's going to deal with our pain, we have to be willing to feel our pain. Instead of denying it, or burying it, or medicating it, or blaming others for it (even Him), we need to feel it and be real about it – with ourselves and with Jesus. If we're afraid of expressing our emotion and refuse to engage with our pain, we'll end up stuck, right where we got hurt. We have to uncover our wounds for the Father to heal them.

There is no hurt we can experience that Jesus doesn't understand and the Father can't heal. More than that, He uses our healing to bring healing to others. He intends for our wounds to become scars and for our scars to tell stories; of His grace and power, just as Jesus' scars do. Don't fear your pain, give up in it, or lash out in it. It's not too big for Him even when it feels too big for you. And don't let your pain come between you and your Healer.

PONDER
Have you ever seen God heal a broken heart? Is there a wound in your heart that you need to invite Him to heal today?

PRAY
Pray for your own heart and for someone you know who's hurting. Ask the Father to comfort them too, and to fully heal their broken heart.

READ: 2 Kings 5:1, 9-15
So...Naaman dipped himself seven times...and he was healed. (NLT)

I have lots of questions about lots of things. I also have questions about this story. Why seven times? Why not ten or three or one? Surely one would have been simpler? Why the Jordan River? I agree with Naaman's analysis. Why couldn't it be another river? And I sympathise with his assumption that the 'man of God' Elisha could have just come out of his house, prayed a prayer, and that would have been that. Why the drama? Why the weirdness? Why the delay on a hot summer's day?

Naaman wanted the quick fix, instant healing. He believed that if there was a God, newness and wholeness could happen instantaneously. Good belief! And yet, because of that belief, he nearly missed it. If he hadn't been persuaded by his officers, his impatience would've got the better of him. God longs to heal our wounds, our relationships, and even our land, but He rarely does it overnight. Healing takes time and is a process. And it often takes work. We probably won't have to get in a river, but we will need to forgive those who've hurt us. We will need to let go of our ideas about how God will heal us. We will need to trust His strength not ours, and we will certainly need to be listening to what He's saying.

What if Naaman had given up after six times? What if his doubt or impatience had got the better of him? Fortunately, it didn't. He persevered and discovered a God who was real, who loved him and who wanted him free and whole. Part of trusting the Healer means trusting His timing and trusting His process. That means keeping on keeping on, resisting the whisper of the enemy that it won't happen. And it means believing you'll end up stronger and with a story; of His faithfulness to you and His love for you.

PONDER
Do you have a question about the way Naaman's healing happened? Is doubt getting the better of you over some scenario, and assaulting your ability to persevere in trusting God?

PRAY
Talk to God about what He's saying to you through this story and how it affects your own journey with Him. Ask Him to give you strength today to persevere, if that's what you need.

READ: Luke 5:18-25

Think about how this man got to Jesus to be healed by Him – he was dependent on friends who had faith that Jesus could help. They played an important part for him. What these friends did in the visible, we do in the invisible when we pray for each other.

PUSH IN

- Who are the friends that you show your wounds to?

- Are they people who pray with you and with faith, 'bring you to Jesus'?

- Do you need to share your pain with them?

- Are you this kind of friend to others?

- How could you grow these kind of friendships in your life?

Talk to Jesus about this today.

PRAY:

- A prayer for any friend of yours who is sick:

Precious Father,

It doesn't seem fair that _____ is needing to cope with so much pain and I find it really hard to see her suffering in the way that she is. Please heal her. I believe You're powerful and that You can break into this situation and change it. I'm trusting Your promises in Your word about healing and restoration and I'm also trusting that You hear my prayers. I bring my friend before You and ask You to make her well. Thank You that You promise complete healing in eternity but I ask that You'd intervene this side of Heaven and bring healing to her body / mind / spirit. Reach out and touch her powerfully, give her strength and peace and may she know Your presence with her. Amen.

- A prayer for your own heart:

Loving Father,

Thank You for Your patience with me and that You love me in my brokenness; thank You that You gently love me to wholeness. Thank You that You love me when I'm immature and thank You that You love me as I grow. Thank You that my weaknesses and limitations don't take You by surprise, but You meet me in them when I acknowledge them, and You're the One who makes me strong. Thank You that You want to bind up my wounds and heal my heart. Please heal the wounds in my heart that aren't yet healed. Please give me courage to let You do so, even if it's not comfortable. Please move in my heart so it can grow stronger; please do a miracle in me and make me whole.
I want to live a life that is bigger than I could live without You. Make me more like You. Thank You that I can trust You with my heart because You love me. Amen.

READ: Genesis 1:26-28
God spoke: 'Let Us make human beings in Our image, make them reflecting Our nature.' (MSG)

You were created to bear the image of God. His image lies at the heart of who you are. To let our identity be defined by how we look, what our body can / can't do, our sexuality, our political preferences, our ethnicity, our relationship status, what we do, how many followers we have, or anything else, is to live with a lesser identity created by culture (Gal 3:28). God designed us to reflect His image to the world, not be defined by it.

I have a mirror in my bedroom. When my husband stands in front of it, I can still see his reflection in it, even if I'm outside the room and can't see him. You and I are like that mirror. We're designed to reflect the heart of our invisible God to those around us. He wanted to be seen on earth, so He chose to reveal His power and beauty through you and me. God made us like Him; as thinking, feeling, moral, relational beings. So others could catch sight of Him. Catch your breath – it's a total privilege.

As a daughter, you reflect the image of your Father. Don't evaluate your identity by looking in the mirror, remember you are like that mirror. Friend, let this truth sink in a little deeper today. Don't listen to the enemy telling you you're worthless. Don't listen to the lies that you have no value or you're less important. Don't get upset by what others say about you or to you. You carry His image and the blood of Jesus is your price tag. Be confident in who God says you are. However others have treated you, and whatever the world tells you, you're precious and needed. Because you reveal the likeness of the Father. The value of a mirror is in its potential to let other things be seen. That's you, beautiful image-bearer! Believe it, whether or not others believe it about you.

PAUSE
Let the Father remind you again now that He made you to bear His image to the world. Confess any lie you've believed that you have to strive to be significant or valuable. Every time you pass or see a mirror today, let it remind you that you're God's mirror to the world.

PRAY
Ask the Father to help those around you see Him when they see you today. Ask Him to help you be that mirror and reflect His heart. Thank Him for the honour of being His image-bearer.

READ: Colossians 3:5-14

...put on the new self, which is being renewed in knowledge in the image of its Creator.

Something I love to do is update old bits of furniture. I have two beautiful mirrors in my home that had frames that needed painting. Being me, I did the job a bit messily and got paint on the edge of the mirror. If you've ever used oil based paint, you'll know it's difficult to get off. Imagine if I'd painted most of the surface of the mirror with it!

We're designed to reflect the image of Jesus to the world, but we don't reveal Him like we were made to. The clear glass God originally put within us to reflect Him changed as Adam and Eve chose disobedience. Sin didn't destroy His image in us, but it distorted it. It was as if the glass got covered in oil-based paint. Instead of reflecting His face, we wanted to take His place. So His reflection became hard to see. Suddenly things like pride, fear, shame, guilt and insecurity blurred His image in us.

The Holy Spirit patiently removes bits of that paint so His reflection becomes increasingly visible again. We need to be patient with this process too. It's like making good coffee – it takes time. I used to get so frustrated by the gap between the kind of friend I want to be and the witness I want to be, and the kind I currently am. Between the way I want to love others and the way I want to love Jesus, and the way I actually do. I'm learning to let my longing remind me that deep in my soul, He made me to reflect His image in all its fullness. I'm just not there yet.

The process is a partnership as this passage reminds us. It's not all His work, and it's not all ours. A 'taking off' of things such as a need for approval, is like the paint being scraped off. A 'putting on' of things like love, is like the glass being polished. The more we surrender to the Holy Spirit's process, the clearer His reflection becomes. He's renewing His image in you today whether He's scraping or polishing. Welcome Him.

PONDER

How has the Holy Spirit already enabled more of His image to be seen in you since you met Him?

PRAY

Spend some time thanking Him for what He's done in your heart and what He's doing now.

READ: Genesis 1:27
In the image of God He created them; male and female He created them. (NLT)

God has planted an expression of Himself in you. You carry something of His uniqueness, strength and creativity. He has set something of His courage, compassion, and purity into you. Each one of us is made in the image of the wisest, kindest, most genuine Being that ever lived. But we each reflect different facets of His image like different sides of a diamond.

Here, the Father says the first difference in us is being male and female. Men and women reflect different elements of His nature. We weren't created the same so we don't reflect Him in the same way. To say that is not sexist but biblical! Women have the ability to nurture new life. The nurturing side of God's nature is more visible in women. He meant it that way. But neither men nor women are more significant than the other. How could we be? How could one part of God's image be more important than another? He didn't create us the same, but He created us with equal value. And for the world to see the fullness of His image, it needs to see men and women partnering together. Celebrating one another, and lifting each other up, not putting each other down.

Our differences continue. Our nationalities are different, as are our skin colours, our backgrounds and our skill sets. Our ages and our strengths are also different. So are our natures, our dreams and our desires, because we each reflect different facets of the Father's magnificence. If we see each other as image-bearers, there is no room for any kind of prejudice in our heart towards those that are different to us. Let's celebrate our differences and look for the reflection of Jesus in the person in front of us, whoever they are. Let's treat each other as image-bearers. And let's honour and value one another and our differences, the same way the Father does.

PONDER
Do you look at everyone around you, whether you know them or get on with them, as image-bearers? How would it change the way you treated them if you did?

PRAY
Ask the Father to reveal something of Himself to you today through everyone you meet. Pray for Him to help you celebrate the differences you find in others today.

READ: Genesis 1:28
**Then God blessed them and said, 'Be fruitful and multiply. Fill the earth
and govern it.'** (NLT)

Wherever we go, we're assigned to release the life of the kingdom
because we carry the image of the King. God made us in His image and
then gave us authority to rule on His behalf. Not over each other, but
over the earth. The Father always brings order and life. Wherever His
kingdom comes, people prosper. As His image-bearers, God made us to
bring order and life to our environments, so everything and everyone can
prosper as He intends. The mandate has never changed. Jesus gave us
back the authority God meant us to have, which we gave away in Eden.

The Father has appointed us to rule over environments, atmospheres,
problems and impossibilities. He's designed us to rule so He can release
life. To be effective, we need to remember who we are and the spiritual
authority He's given us.

I have a friend who's a primary school teacher. She's had some tough
classes in her time, but she knows she's more than a teacher. She's an
image-bearer called to rule. One thing she does each morning is to pray
over each chair in her classroom. She invites the presence of God to fill
the room and declares His peace over the lives of the children. Her
experience of her classes is different to that of others. The kids behave
better and get an upgrade in their learning experience. Why? Because
she exercises her spiritual authority to rule over her environment.

Friend, whether it's in your home, or your workplace, God has appointed
you to work with Him to bring transformation and life in a variety of ways.
You have the authority to bring benefit and blessing to others and to
contribute to an environment where others thrive. Just as the original
image-bearers were created to shape things with God, so are you. He's
inviting you again today to take your place alongside Him.

PAUSE

Ask the Father to show you in which 'environment, atmosphere, problem or impossibility' He
wants you to exercise the authority He's given you. Ask Him how to do that. What is He wanting
you to pray in that place or over that circumstance? What scripture or truth is He wanting you to
speak out in faith until you see His kingdom break in? Go for it, confidently.

READ: Genesis 3:1-9
So they sewed fig leaves together to cover themselves.

'Image is everything'. So said the Wimbledon champion Andre Agassi in an advert he did. Do you believe it? It's caught on and it's now a philosophy that permeates much of current culture. Companies and individuals invest much time and money into perfecting the image that will sell their brand to the world. The brand image is intended to create and communicate value. And we all know a successful image sells.

How do you measure your value? Do you measure your value by the success you have or the impact you make? By the followers you collect or the bank balance you accumulate? By the way others treat you or who you know? Or by what others say about you? Friend, the enemy tries to lure us into these traps because when we forget our true value, we project an image to the world. To sell ourselves. To prove our worth. To produce the feedback we're longing for. To reassure us that yes, we matter, and yes, we're valuable. But the images we project, by definition, hide our true selves. And they hide the image of God in us.

The enemy successfully persuaded Eve to build a new image as part of the tragedy in the Garden. Her fig leaf might have been her idea of an image to make her look good to the world (Adam) and to God, but it covered the image she was created to bear. When Jesus died for you, He proved once and for all how valuable you are. Our worth is measured by what someone will pay for us when we offer nothing in return. He's proved yours, so you don't need to. Remember again today, Jesus wants you free from the need to prove your worth. So you can reflect His image, not project yours. So you can live in response to Him, instead of in response to your need for validation. Does He need to release you further from the pressure to prove who you are?

PAUSE
In which of the ways above are you tempted to measure your value? How do you want to be seen by others? What difference would it make to you to let go of that 'image'? Ask Jesus to lead you into a new freedom by trusting more fully your true value. As His image-bearer. Hear Him tell you again today that He paid the highest price for you, gladly. You were worth it. Literally.

READ: Isaiah 40:18
To whom can you compare God? What image can you find to resemble Him?

God made us in His image. It's one of the reasons the world can see Him in us. The process of revealing His image in us more clearly can be a painful one at times. When it is, He often deals with some of the false images and ideas we have about Him – about how He works and what He's like. Sometimes, when He's *not doing* something we expected or moving how we'd hoped, or when He *does* let something happen that we'd hoped He'd protect us from, He is dismantling the false images we have of Him.

Unknowingly we can 'make Him' in our image. We can imagine He thinks like us, feels like us or acts like us, or like other people we know. Because we're on a journey of knowing Him better, He makes us let go of those wrong images and ideas we have. He replaces them with the truth about what He's really like. And as He does, His image in us becomes clearer.

PUSH IN
– Ask the Holy Spirit to show you a picture that you hold in your mind of God which is actually a false image of Him. (e.g. a bully, a taskmaster, unsympathetic, a 'yes man', a frail grandpa, etc). Trust what pops into your mind.

– Ask Him to show you what effect that wrong image of Him has had on your relationship with Him.

– Ask Him to show you what effect it's had on the way you live.

– Ask the Holy Spirit to show you the true picture of what the Father is like. Ask Him to show you a scripture that confirms what He's shown you.

– Let go of the false image and ask Him to forgive you for believing He was like that; trust what He's shown you and ask Him to help you know Him better as He truly is.

PONDER

Write down in three sentences what the Holy Spirit has been saying to you this week about being an image-bearer. Write down a declaration to speak out over yourself today, affirming this dimension of your identity.

READ: Psalm 54
But God is my helper. The Lord keeps me alive! (NLT)

Where do you need help? Needing help in different sizes is a regular feature of life. Help with the washing up speeds up the job; help moving a wardrobe you couldn't shift on your own finishes the job. Help getting out of debt is life-changing; help getting out of a car on fire is life-saving. Needing help is part of being human. How easy do you find it to admit you need help? If that's a toughie for you, then maybe you live under a pressure to be self-sufficient that God wants to lift off you this week.

The Father says He's the Helper. Pause and let this amazing truth wow you again for a moment. The Architect of the universe, the One who's existed since time began, has promised to be your helper. Why would He promise that? Because first, He didn't design you to be able to do life on your own without needing help. Second, He hasn't called you to a life so ordinary that you don't need His help.

David was struggling. Life was tricky. As he wrote this psalm, he declared, 'God is my helper.' He intentionally reminded himself he was not alone and help was at hand. To David, God wasn't just the helper, or a helper, but *his* helper. The Father wants you saying the same. He wants you confident that He is *your* helper and He wants your prayer life to reflect it. What kind of help does God provide? Whatever help you need. Do you have trouble with your temper? He'll help you. Do you need wisdom? He'll guide you. Do you need to make friends? He'll assist you. Do you have a financial need? He'll provide for you. Do you need help with your prayer life? He'll encourage you. Whatever you're struggling with, whatever's stretching you, God is *your* helper, however big or small your need. All you need to do is ask.

PONDER
How confidently can you say 'God is my helper?' Have you believed there is something God wouldn't help you with? Why? What do you most need help with at the moment?

PRAY
Thank God that He's your helper and you're never on your own. Identify a time that He's helped you in the past and thank Him for what He did for you. Ask Him for the help you need right now and ask Him to grow your confidence that He will always help you.

READ: Mark 4:35-41
Teacher, don't You care that we're going to drown? (NLT)

Let's translate what the disciples are saying (or shouting) here, just in case we're unclear. '*Heelllpppp!*' How do *you* ask for help? There are different ways of asking; the simplest is to say, 'Please help'. Less healthy is trying to put pressure on someone to help by making them feel bad: 'If you loved me you wouldn't leave me to clear up on my own!' The disciples go for this option (been there, done that!). Perhaps they felt ashamed to be so scared and needing help. Maybe they saw it as weakness or failure.

The cry of 'help' is one of the most prayed prayers in the world, even by unbelievers. Sadly, it's often prayed as a last resort when other options have failed, rather than as a first resort. Jesus wants you to pray it more; to develop a 'help' habit. Learn to turn aside and ask for His assistance throughout the day, whatever you're facing, whether it's planning your day, a simple problem, deep pain, a perplexing situation, a difficult conversation, a momentous moment or a powerful storm. He normally waits to be invited to help His daughters, even though He's eager to step in and help with anything and everything.

He was as gracious with the disciples as He is with us. He responded to the cry of their hearts rather than the cry on their lips. I might have got offended at the accusation, 'Don't you care?' Jesus got into action. They'd disturbed Him because they needed Him and that's the bit that counts. The Father knows what help we need but we need to ask. Asking for help is admitting our dependence and owning our limitations. There's no shame in asking, only humility. God draws near to the humble, not because He loves them more but because they make more room for Him. Friend, He won't force His help on you if you want to go it alone! Whether you're feeling overwhelmed, overjoyed or somewhere in between, how can you live more dependently on the Helper today?

PAUSE
How easy do you find it asking for help? What could it look like if Jesus helped you with everything you need to do and be today? How might things look and feel different? Ask Him to help you with each thing facing you today, even if that thing feels insignificant. Continue to whisper those precious words, 'Please help me', at various points during your day.

READ: John 14:15-27
This Helper is the Holy Spirit whom the Father will send in My name... (NCV)

Self-help books are all the rage. It's a huge and growing industry, but God didn't design us for a self-help, self-dependent, or self-sufficient life, no matter how much the culture raves about it. He made us to live a Spirit-helped, Spirit-dependent, Spirit-sufficient life. The Helper will take us places self-help material or a self-dependent approach never can. Because only He knows the way. In the Garden, the enemy persuaded Eve to help herself; to the apple and to the life she wanted. In helping herself, she cut herself off from her Helper, and His ability to lead her into that life. Tragically, she couldn't find it on her own. We've all followed suit. But Jesus came to give us a second chance.

God has called you to live a big life. But He hasn't created you to live it on your own or work it out by yourself. You can't. Think for a moment of some of the stretching things God has called you to do. Pray for the sick, love the people you most dislike, forgive those who've wounded you and believe for the impossible. Disciple nations, walk on water and trust Him in the storms. Persevere when you want to give up, stop worrying and obey when you feel like doing the opposite. I could go on. As a friend used to say, 'Good luck with that!'

Luckily, Jesus doesn't wish us good luck! He promised to send the Helper to live in us, to help us live the big, bold life He made us for. Friend, if you've fallen for the enemy's lie that you can help yourself to this life, recognise it today and let go of it. Self-dependence is the opposite of Spirit-dependence. It's one of the enemy's ways of tricking you into living a life with little or no eternal legacy. If you don't need His help on a daily basis, perhaps it's time to review what kind of life you're living, or what kind of life you're after.

PONDER
Would you say you live more self-dependent or more Spirit-dependent? What are the reasons for your answer? What does it mean for you that you're made to need the Helper?

PRAY
Thank the Father for sending the Helper to you and talk to Him about what's on your heart today.

READ: Matthew 14:22-33

Jumping out of the boat, Peter walked on the water to Jesus. (MSG)

The chocolates in my tin at home are wrapped in lots of different wrappers. God's help comes wrapped in different ways. Sometimes it's wrapped in the form of another person; other times it comes wrapped in a miracle. Sometimes it's in the form of His power at work in us; other times it's hidden in a whisper from Scripture.

We don't get to decide how Heaven's help comes, but we do have to ask for it and expect it to arrive. More often than not, it comes *as* we step forward in that expectation. When I ask God to help me hear His voice, He does so *as* I open my Bible. Peter wanted to walk on water. Asking Jesus to call him out of the boat was like saying, 'Jesus, I want to do that, will you help me?' When do you think the water went solid so Peter could walk on it? I reckon it was each time he took a step, *as* he put his foot down! Peter had to move, and *as* he did, the Helper moved too.

I have a friend who was suddenly abandoned by her husband and left with two small kids. She sat on the end of her bed, totally broken, not knowing how to get through it. She called out to her Father and said, 'You know what to do so please help me get through this. Show me what to do.' She prayed that prayer every day for 18 months, inviting God to help her with each decision and situation she faced. At the end of that time, she looked back and was astounded at how He'd helped her *as* she did each day. In both supernatural and straightforward ways, in big things and small, He'd put her life back together in an amazing and unpredictable way. She had walked on water.

Doing impossible things in impossible ways, is part of our calling as daughters. But often, it's *as* (not before) we take a difficult step forward, asking and then expecting Him to help, that He does what He's promised.

PAUSE

Is there a step you need to take, asking Jesus to help you, that will enable you to do something that seems impossible right now? Ask the Holy Spirit to show you what that step is. Spend a few moments waiting for Him to speak. Then talk to Jesus about anything He's brought to mind and thank Him that He invites you to walk on water.

READ: Psalm 146
Don't put your confidence in powerful people; there is no help for you there.
(NLT)

Who are the powerful people in your life? They may be people you know personally, like a family member or a friend. They may be people you've empowered by giving them a voice in your life, like those on social media you listen to. Or they may be people who have power in your life because of a relationship you have with them whether you've chosen it or not. Like a political leader, a doctor, or a boss. God warns us, 'Don't put your confidence in those powerful people, whoever they are.'

Why not? Because no matter how much we like them or rate them, no matter how many resources they have, the Father says they can't really help us. They can't deliver what we really need. He may choose to use them as we ask Him for help, but He says, 'Put your confidence in Me, because in the end, they'll let you down and disappoint you'. Politicians are limited. Scientists only know so much and doctors can only go so far (as a pandemic reminds us). The members of our family, our boss, our church leader or the celebrities we follow are all human beings who make mistakes. They are limited in what they can do, however great they are.

Verse 5 says, 'Joyful are those who have the God of Israel as their helper, whose hope is in the Lord their God.' The Father is the One who has what you need, who will fulfil His purposes for you and who will take care of you. He is the One who'll work things out for you. Believing this and trusting Him releases joy. Depending on others to make life work for you doesn't. Friend, if you're hoping that someone else will provide for you, heal you, open a door for you, make a dream come true for you, or make you happy, you need to shift your confidence again today. Joy is waiting for you as you trust the Father as your helper.

PONDER
Who are the 'powerful people' in your life and to what extent have you put your confidence in them rather than God?

PRAY
Ask Him to forgive you for putting your confidence in anyone other than Him. Thank Him that He is your helper. Ask Him to release a new joy in you as you trust Him to look after you.

READ: Hebrews 13:5-6
So we can say with confidence 'The Lord is my helper, so I will have no fear.'
(NLT)

PUSH IN

– Make a list of the three things you are most afraid of.

– Ask the Holy Spirit to show what lie you believe about the Father's ability to help you or His willingness to help you for each one.

– Re-read Hebrews 13:5-6 and then write down alongside each fear, what the Father is saying to you through these verses.

Memorise the verse above and ask God to grow your confidence in each of the areas you've identified. Play your part in standing on the truth He's shown you.

READ: Romans 12:13
When God's people are in need, be ready to help them. Always be eager to practise hospitality. (NLT)

God is the Helper but He often sends His help in human skin. You are that human skin for others.

PAUSE

Spend a few moments asking the Holy Spirit who He wants to help in your life, through you. Note down any people that come to mind. Ask Him how He wants to help them and what He's asking you to do for them. Offer yourself to Him as His hands and feet and decide when you will do what He's asked you to. Pray for that person / those people.

READ: Romans 8:31-37
No, in all these things we have complete victory through Him who loved us!
(GNT)

If you want to live out the purposes God has for you, you will have to overcome some things in your life and gain victory. Good job He's set you up as an overcomer. It's not an optional extra like a side order of chips – it's part of who you are as His daughter. You're no longer a victim but a victor because the powerful One lives in you.

To live as an overcomer, you have to think like one. That doesn't make you one; you're an overcomer because of what God has done in you. But to experience victory in your life, you must refuse to agree with the enemy, or others, or your circumstances, or your feelings about who you are. Agree with God. He says you're actually *more* than an overcomer!

If 'overcomer' (or more) is who you are, then 'victim' is who you are not! You are not powerless. Painful experiences have taught us we can't control much of what happens to us. Many of us have been on the receiving end of things like injustice or illness and felt utterly powerless. But being powerless in one situation doesn't make us powerless in every situation, unless we fall for that lie. While we can't always control what happens to us (cue a pandemic), we can always control our response; the choices *we* make and the actions *we* take. When we blame what we do or say on our circumstances (or on others), we're thinking like victims. It gets us nowhere. When we take responsibility for the way we act and react, we're thinking like victors. Our lives are shaped by our choices more than they are shaped by our circumstances.

No one can stop God fulfilling His plan and purpose for you (Job 42:2). But you must live as an overcomer to walk into it. That means taking a rain check on your mindset.

PONDER
Do you live as an overcomer or as someone who's more easily overcome? What current situation in your life requires you to be an overcomer? Are you thinking like a victim or a victor?

PRAY
Thank God He empowers you to be an overcomer no matter what the situation. Talk to Him about your specific scenario and ask Him to show you how to live as the overcomer you are.

READ: Romans 8:31-37
...we are more than conquerors through Him who loved us.

Let's face it, overcomers have things to overcome. Paul lists hard times, trouble, hatred, hunger, extreme poverty and danger to name a few! What would you add to that list from your life? Paul wasn't battling to overcome the hatred that he faced and get everyone to like him. He was battling to overcome the fear, self pity, resentment, discouragement, and doubt that threatened to overcome him from facing such hatred.

What do you have to overcome? Like Paul, it's not primarily our actual circumstances, but the giants that go with them. Fear, discouragement, temptation, shame, doubt, bitterness... They rise up from our circumstances to assault our hearts and attack our confidence; in our identity, the Father's goodness and His calling on our lives. Be encouraged, friend. You're not alone. These giants assault all God's people. And we all have the potential to be overcome by them. Peter says (1 Pet 5:8), 'Your enemy is...looking for someone to wipe out. Resist him.' The difference between those who are overcome and those who aren't is not a personality type. It's resistance. 'Resist him.' Overcomers get resisting. They refuse to give in and lie down. They rise up and fight back. They fight the giant, whatever it is.

Remember this: whenever you engage in a fightback, you're never fighting for victory. Jesus defeated what's threatening to overcome you and nailed it to the cross. You're fighting to enforce His victory in your heart and life by believing Him. Whatever you're facing that's threatening to overwhelm your confidence in the Father's great love for you – hear Him tell you again today, 'You *are* an overcomer.' You need to put up a fight, choose hope and remember who you are. He is in you, so you will overcome because He has overcome.

PONDER
Ask the Holy Spirit to show you what giant is assaulting your confidence in God's love or calling at the moment? Look at the list above. Is it fear? Is it shame? Is it unbelief? Remember, you're not powerless – what one thing can you do today to resist and fight back?

PRAY
Think of someone else you know who's currently engaged in a fightback. Ask God to bless, strengthen and encourage both you and them today. How could you encourage them too?

READ: Revelation 12:10-11
And they overcame him by the blood of the Lamb, and by the word of their testimony... (NKJV)

'You've got nothing to offer.' 'It's all your fault.' 'You're not good enough.' 'If only you were...' 'You did such-and-such so you don't deserve...' When you hear those accusations, in your head, remember the Bible says the enemy is the 'accuser' (v10). He loves to accuse us of all kinds of things to keep us stuck or make us shrink back, *especially* when we've chosen to fight back.

It's not a voice to be ignored but to be overcome if we're going to move forwards. We cannot conquer what we do not confront, and accusation is no different. Friend, fight back and silence that voice. This verse says they (God's sons and daughters) overcame him (the accuser) with two things: the blood of Jesus and their testimony. How do you silence that voice with the blood of Jesus? What does that mean? It means reminding yourself those accusations may or may not be true, but it doesn't matter. Jesus' blood paid for all your mistakes and failures, past, present and future. He's forgiven you for the lot. The Father's desire to bless you no longer depends on your performance but on Jesus' performance on the cross. That's the good news of the kingdom.

But you also need to pick up the weapon of your testimony. In fact, you need to speak it out as it's the word of your testimony, not the fact that you have one, that empowers you to overcome. What has Jesus done for you? Where have you seen Him work in your life? What do you believe about Him? What do you know about Him? That's your story, not someone else's. As you speak it out and turn it into a prayer of praise, the truth on your lips will defeat the accusation in your ears.

PONDER

Can you identify the accusations that you 'hear' more frequently? How do they make you feel?

PRAY

Thank Jesus for the power of His blood and that you have a testimony. Declare His truth about your identity, speak out what you've seen Him do in your life and what you know about Him. Be specific! Do the same again if you face any accusation today.

READ: 2 Corinthians 12:9-10
My strength comes into its own in your weakness. (MSG)

Whatever you're needing to overcome, whether it's an assault on your heart or a habit you want to break, you won't do it on your own, and you won't do it in your own strength. I find this promise so comforting, like a hot chocolate on a cold day! Yes, we must fight back, but victory doesn't depend on our strength, it depends on His. You are an overcomer, not because you're strong but because He is. He who is in you is greater than he who is in the world (1 Jn 4:4), or anything else for that matter!

How does His strength 'come into its own in our weakness'? It comes when we bring our weakness to Him like we might bring an empty cup back for a refill. His strength and His power work in us and through us only when we say to Him, 'Help me Lord. I need you, I can't do this on my own.' That's how His power is released into our lives. In a world that celebrates strength and success, it's not always an easy thing to do. And when we're weak, the enemy tries to convince us we're failing. But in the kingdom, recognising weakness comes before receiving strength. And recognising weakness means asking for help, sometimes from others too.

Where are you feeling weak today? You may feel that overcoming is about as likely as finding a tasty, calorie-free chocolate. The opposite is true. You're perfectly positioned to overcome. Be honest with yourself, tell God and open up to others. Admit your vulnerability and your need of help. That's often the hardest part. Paul says he didn't just own up about his weaknesses, he bragged about them. In a culture that brags about achievements, that is radical. But he'd discovered this secret to God's strength and was excited by it. So let's not despise our weaknesses, friend. Why not get real about what you can't make happen, and get ready for an upgrade of His strength in your life.

PONDER
Identify something you need help with, where you're weak. How easy do you find it to talk to others about your weaknesses? Who could you tell, that could pray for you or with you?

PRAY
Acknowledge your weakness with God and ask Him to help. Ask Him to give you the courage to be open with others about your weaknesses and ask Him for an opportunity to do that today.

READ: Romans 12:17-21
Do not be overcome by evil, but overcome evil with good...

The Father has set you up to be an overcomer at all times. Both when you face tricky circumstances that threaten your joy, your hope, your peace and your connection with Jesus, *and* when you face tricky people! Let's be honest – we all have those people in our lives who, at best, rub us up the wrong way, or who at worst, have actively and sometimes deliberately, bruised us, betrayed us, burnt us or broken us.

God is clear about how overcomers respond to such people – they fight back with good. Love is God's weapon of choice. In the Bible, the word 'evil' means anything that isn't in God's heart – stuff that He wouldn't think or do or say. You'll often be on the receiving end of stuff that God wouldn't think about you, do to you, or say to you. How are you meant to fight back in those moments and respond to those people? He says, 'Don't try and get your own back or get even. Instead, fight back with kindness and do something different – do something good.'

As an overcomer, you need to be savvy. In this case, being savvy means realising you won't always find a huge amount of support for such a countercultural response. It's easier to retaliate or do nothing. A counterstrike of kindness to those who've been unkind to you is counter-intuitive. And it's costly! But Jesus is a radical. He's kind to us when we don't deserve it and expects us to follow His example. Remember, He said to love those who make life difficult and pray for those who hurt us (Matt 5:44).

Jesus always lays out a path to victory for us, but along the way we'll be irritated, offended and wounded by others. Staying on His path requires us to respond to them with radical grace to make sure we overcome.

PONDER
Is there anyone who has irritated, offended or wounded you lately? What kind thing could you do for them? Decide when you will do it!

PRAY
Ask the Holy Spirit to strengthen you to live as the overcomer you are and ask Him to bless the person that has come to mind.

READ: James 1:2-8, 12
Anyone who meets a testing challenge head-on and manages to stick it out is mighty fortunate. (MSG)

Overcoming rarely happens overnight. James says those who 'stick it out are fortunate.' That doesn't mean they end up lucky! It means they end up blessed. God promises that when we stick things out, when we keep on keeping on, we get favour – life and more life.

Overcomers are gritters not quitters. Sometimes, all we need to do to overcome is stick it out by taking another step in the same direction; of forgiveness, of praying the same prayer, of choosing to trust, of declaring out loud the promise we're believing for, of putting ourself out there again, of choosing to bless someone else, whatever the step is.

Picture a beautiful pearl. They may be valuable, but they're formed from a piece of grit getting stuck in the oyster's shell. The grit acts like an irritant that the oyster can't get rid of. The oyster fights back by coating it with a fluid and it keeps going; it keeps producing layer upon layer of the stuff until eventually, the oyster overcomes and a lustrous pearl is formed.

PUSH IN
– Ask God what pearl He is growing in your life right now through what you have identified this week you as needing to overcome.

– Do you need to adjust your expectations about how quickly overcoming happens?

– Let Him remind you that overcoming is the result of sticking it out; of keeping on taking another step and another step and another step.....

– Re-read the verse above a few times, slowly, out loud over yourself. Which word(s) stands out to you and why?

Talk to Him.

READ: 1 Samuel 17:32-50

So David triumphed over the Philistine with only a sling and a stone... (NLT)

Let this phenomenal story encourage you today. David had a giant to overcome, and despite his size disadvantage, David believed he was an overcomer. The rest of the Israelites were guilty of victim thinking; they let their circumstances determine their response (doing nothing) and blamed Goliath's size for their fear. The Israelites shrank back. David fought back.

Like a true overcomer, he had to silence the voice of the accuser whispering in his ear. And he had to make room for God's power to work. So he fought Goliath in weakness, not strength; he refused Saul's armour and spear for stones and a sling. His confidence in God enabled him to step forward to fight, and then to victory. David's God is your God and He is for you as He was for David.

PUSH IN

– Take a moment to think about what defeating your giant would mean for you. What would it feel like for it not to be there? What new freedom would it bring for you? What would it enable you to do?

– Read the verse above replacing David's name with your name and 'the Philistine' with the name of your giant.

– Spend some time thanking God in faith for the victory He's going to give you. Ask Him what fighting it in weakness means for you. What is He asking you to do?

READ: Genesis 3:1-7
Then God blessed them... (NLT)

Have you ever been misunderstood? Do you know what it's like to say something and have it taken out of context or misquoted so you look like someone you're not? Do you know what it's like to do something to bless someone, only for your motives to be questioned and for everything to go pear-shaped? If so, the Father identifies with you. And you'll know it's particularly painful when it's people you love who misinterpret you.

The Father's heart has always been to bless. The very first thing God did after He created Adam and Eve was to bless them. We too were created to receive His blessing, which is why we long to know the affirmation and favour of God on our lives. God loves to bless us. He's always looking for ways to do good to us and to direct His power towards us. He treasures us as a good Father would. And yet here in the Garden, the enemy called His heart into question; and he hasn't stopped.

God said to Adam and Eve, 'Avoid the fruit on that one tree because it'll harm you and your relationship with Me.' That command was a blessing to protect them, but the enemy wanted to wreck things (like usual) between them and God. So he made Eve unsure about God's motive for saying it. 'How sure are you that He loves to bless you and that this is for your good? Maybe He's not on your side? Maybe He's keeping good stuff back from you?' She wasn't sure, so she took a bite. Fatal.

The fiercest battle is waged over this simple question: 'Can I be sure God will bless me today, tomorrow and every other day of my life?' The Father longs for you to be sure. The enemy doesn't, because how you live your life hinges on your answer. So let's wrestle with it this week.

PONDER
On a scale of 1-10, what is your level of confidence that God wants to bless you today, tomorrow and beyond?

PRAY
Ask God to forgive you where you've doubted His desire to bless you. Invite Him to grow a deeper conviction in you that this is His heart for you. Ask Him to open your eyes to His blessings today.

READ: Psalm 23:1-6
Surely Your goodness and love will follow me all the days of my life.

One day when I was young, I went to a local park with a friend. As I said goodbye and began the six minute walk home, I noticed a man following me. I sped up and took a slightly unusual route out of the park. When I looked over my shoulder, he was still behind me. At that point, as the adrenalin kicked in, I legged it home and didn't look back until I was inside! I have no idea if he was actually following me, but I wasn't hanging around to find out.

David says in this famous psalm that God's goodness and love will follow us all the days of our lives. He was convinced of it. Think about that for a moment. Picture two angels called Goodness and Love following you around every day. Where did you go yesterday? What did you do? Imagine them on your tail, trying to catch up with you, trying to get your attention, trying to get you to stop. Imagine if it was for one reason only – to put a blessing into your hands.

God is a good Father who loves to bless His children, and He convinced David of it, as his words make clear. If you look over your shoulder at any given moment, you'll find blessings behind you ready to be poured into your life. They come in all kinds of shapes and sizes; one of David's blessings was a feast in the presence of his enemies (v5). Personally, I'd prefer the blessing of no enemies at all, but God doesn't prescribe what His goodness and love will look like. When has He promised to bless you? Each day of your life. I was filled with fear as I thought I was being followed that day. God wants us filled with confidence because of what's following us. That confidence grows the more we lean into this promise of blessing.

PONDER
What difference would it make if you believed God's goodness and love were following you every day? How would you act differently? Would you feel different? Try memorising this verse.

PRAY
Thank God for the truth of this promise. Do so throughout the day and as you do, declare it over yourself. Consider encouraging someone else by messaging it to them too.

READ: John 11:1-44
Yet when He heard that Lazarus was sick, He stayed where He was two more days.

What defines what you believe about God and what you believe about yourself? Is it His word or what you're going through? It's a simple choice, but the difference between them makes all the difference. When you're wading through treacle, how sure are you that God is blessing you even if it doesn't look like it from what's happening in your life?

This verse is troubling. Jesus didn't rush to rescue Lazarus. He took His time to get to Mary and Martha's after getting their message (aka prayer) about their brother's illness. Tragedy: Lazarus died. How do you think the sisters felt when He didn't come immediately? Although they didn't know it, Jesus had already responded to their cry and declared Lazarus would be OK (v4). That blessing was dispatched immediately. But there was a delay in its delivery. A delay between the declaration of Heaven that Lazarus would be healed, and the demonstration of it on earth.

We've seen that God's heart is to bless us every day and His desire doesn't change. But sometimes He keeps us waiting for things we've been crying out for. He's not like Amazon! It's not because He doesn't care or isn't in control, or because He's changed His mind. It's because He's at work in another way to bring glory to His name. Often the blessing is for many others as well. He's working to bless us, but frequently, a process precedes it.

When God makes us wait, He's at work. He hasn't logged off, or deleted our requests. The waiting is for our good, but it doesn't feel like it at the time. Are you waiting for Him at the moment? Are you wondering if He's logged off? Believe me, friend, He hasn't. His delivery is on its way and it will glorify Him and bless both you and others. Let Him grow your patience and confidence while you wait.

PONDER
What blessing(s) are you asking God for that you're having to wait for?

PRAY
Thank God in faith that He's working while you're waiting. Thank Him that He's blessing you through it too. Ask Him if there is anything He wants you to do while you wait, apart from pray.

READ: Psalm 84:8-12
O Lord Almighty, blessed is the one who trusts in You.

You cannot earn God's favour or His blessings. They're not a reward for good behaviour like the stars you get on a chart when you're a little girl. The Father smiles on you because you're His. He wants to bless your heart, your mind, your work, your relationships, your home life, your finances, your future, and your relationship with Him. He wants to bless you and others through you because you were born to carry His blessing.

Trusting His heart for you and His word to you opens the door to more of His blessings. When I look at me, I recognise I don't deserve His radical kindness and generosity. That can push me to try and earn His blessings by filling a loyalty card with good choices! But friend, it doesn't work like that. When we doubt God's desire to bless us, with our faults and flaws, the place to look is not in at me, but up at the cross where Jesus showed us how He felt about us. He got what we deserved, so we could get what He'd earned. His blessings for our curses. Let the cross remind you again today that as His precious daughter, that's the truth over your life.

Some people focus on the blessings of God and go after only them. They care more about the gifts than the Giver. The Bible says nothing to those who want the former without the latter. There's something wrong when that happens, like it did in the prodigal son's case. His blessings became empty and unfulfilling and eventually dried up. But desiring God's gifts is normal. This verse (12) reminds us that blessing is linked to trusting, and trust is a relationship issue. So let the expectation of His blessing in your life increase, but let your desire for Him grow even greater. The biggest blessing of all is knowing Jesus Himself and His love for you.

PONDER
How did the Father bless you yesterday? Ask Him to show you.

PRAY
Let those blessings, which were an expression of His love for you, lead you into His presence now. Thank Him for them and express your love to Him today, however you feel led.

READ: Genesis 39:1-6

The Lord was with Joseph, so he succeeded in everything he did as he served in the home of his Egyptian master. (NLT)

Joseph didn't get off to a good start. He was his dad's favourite kid, which made his brothers super jealous. They hatched a plot to get rid of him and dumped him in a pit. Next, he was sold on as a slave. How did the son of a very rich man end up as the personal property of Potiphar? Where was God and where was His blessing in all that went on?

The text says God continued to *bless* Joseph. We can easily get stuck on what the Father's blessings look like if we're not careful. Some are convinced they only look like health, wealth and happiness. Life is more complicated than that, and God has bigger plans for us than that. But those plans *do* involve blessing. Joseph didn't want to be there; things hadn't turned out how he expected. But despite his circumstances, God kept blessing him, making him successful in everything he did. He made sure he was promoted and given more and more responsibility. God didn't change Joseph's circumstances for a while, but continued to show him great favour. So much so that everyone around him noticed.

The verse above highlights a kingdom principle: God's blessing flows most freely into our lives when it flows on out, to others. From the day Joseph was put in charge, God blessed Potiphar's household – for Joseph's sake. He loves to bless others through us too. Joseph was the pipeline through which God sent the oil of His favour into Potiphar's household. We are pipelines too. Joseph blessed the household by offering his best despite his circumstances. Will we do that too? If you want more of God's blessing flowing into your life, step out, offer your best and bless those around you. You're blessed to be a blessing, and He is with you as He was with Joseph.

PONDER
Who are you going to come into contact with today? What could you do to bless those people so God can bless their lives through you?

PRAY
Ask God to bless others through you today. Offer yourself to Him for that purpose. Ask Him to make you sensitive to His promptings and ask Him to bless you as you bless them.

READ: Numbers 6:22-27

PUSH IN

Listen to the heartbeat of the Father as you read these verses. This is a prayer He wants prayed over your life and the lives of others. Hear His intention for you in these words.

– Read these verses aloud a few times and slowly; as you do so, ask the Holy Spirit to write the truth of His desire to bless you on the walls of your heart.

– Pray this prayer over your own life and over the lives of those you know who need God's touch.

– Think about writing it out and sticking it somewhere where you see it to remind you of the Father's heart for you.

Consider messaging this blessing to someone you love today.

READ: James 1:17
Every desirable and beneficial gift comes out of Heaven. The gifts are rivers of light cascading down from the Father of Light. (MSG)

Are you a complainer or a counter? Those who expect the goodness of God to follow them around, and who trust His heart to bless them, have learnt to count their blessings. It lets us see how He's blessed us already.

PUSH IN
Grab some paper and a pen (or a note app on your phone) and a stopwatch. For five minutes, write down as many blessings as you can that God has poured into your life. Ask the Holy Spirit to help you identify them and especially to see those that you have taken for granted. Include answers to prayer as well as the many things He's given you that you didn't even ask for.

Look at your sheet of paper. Turn it to prayer and thank Him individually for each blessing you've identified.

Then thank Him for the many more that are coming your way that you don't yet know about.

READ: Isaiah 61:1-3
They will be called oaks of righteousness...

When did you last see an oak tree? They're beautiful big trees that stand out and stand tall, and they're a picture of how God sees you and what He's doing with your life. Oaks are known for their strength and resilience. If you own any oak furniture, you'll know that oak is heavy, super strong wood. The Father wants you strong. His desire is always to strengthen you not squash you, whatever you're facing right now.

What does 'strong' look like? It doesn't look like being controlling or domineering, independent or intimidating. It doesn't look like power dressing and a loud voice. It doesn't look like super woman, spinning 60 plates, not showing emotion or not feeling weak. And it doesn't look like only eating one piece of chocolate when you could have five! Biblical strength isn't intellectual or physical or emotional strength. It's having a strong spirit. A strong confidence in God's love and power in every situation. A strong spirit dives deep into His Spirit for help and courage, to stand strong and step forward no matter what's going on around you or inside you!

'Strong' looks like being determined to: trust despite your doubt, take risks despite your fear, love despite your pain, resist temptation despite your desire, stay the course when you feel like quitting, get up when you've fallen down, admit your weakness, lift others up, own your mistakes, confront difficulty and darkness, and surrender again and again to God. Why does God want us strong? For what's ahead today and tomorrow. To experience the fullness of what He's promised us and live out our calling, in our relationships, our workplaces, our streets, our ministry, our communities and beyond, we need strength, friend. To stand firm, stay steady and step up.

PONDER
In the same way you could do various physical exercises to strengthen your core, think of one spiritual exercise you could do more of to increase your core spiritual strength.

PRAY
Put your hand on your heart and ask God to grow a stronger spirit within you. Ask Him to help you do that spiritual exercise, so He can do what He needs to do in you to strengthen you.

READ: Jeremiah 17:7-8

They are like trees planted along a riverbank, with roots that reach deep into the water. (NLT)

I was out for a walk the other day. As I walked past a young tree that was planted a few years ago, I noticed all its leaves were dry and crispy. Sadly, the recent hot weather and lack of rain had clearly taken its toll and proved too much for it. Its roots just hadn't been able to find water.

You may have visible roots, depending on your hair colour, but you also have invisible roots. God uses this picture of a tree to help us grasp how life works. Our roots represent our hidden relationship with Jesus that no one else sees, on social media or anywhere else. We tend to focus on fruit, He focuses on our roots. If they're good, fruit will grow. This particular tree prospers in all circumstances because it's roots go deep enough to always find water. Friend, roots are the key to our life and health. The deeper they go, the bigger and more fruitful our life will be. Jeremiah describes a life that's producing kingdom fruit, even in tough times. Our roots need to be strong and deep like this tree's.

Let's be honest, without regular time with Jesus, we dry up. And when the pressure's on, we struggle; to live from His love, to remain confident of His goodness, to be sure of His word over us and to stay in the centre of His will for us. We can't change the weather conditions but we can choose what kind of relationship with God we have. We make time to surf the net, do we make time to read the Bible? We always have time to scroll and swipe, do we have time to pray? When we dry up spiritually, we end up drying up emotionally and mentally. And that's never the Father's purpose for us. Our private life with Jesus fuels our public life. Make your relationship with Him your priority. It's costly to make time for Him in the private place, but it'll be a *lot* more costly if you don't.

PONDER
Find a flower or a weed(!) today and pull it up. Put it somewhere you can see it and watch what happens as it no longer has access to water. Note how long it takes. Let God speak through it.

PRAY
Ask the Holy Spirit to show you an X-ray of your root system. Wait for Him to show you. How deep do the roots go? Talk to God about how He wants to grow them.

READ: Isaiah 61:1-3
...they will be known as Mighty Oaks of righteousness... (TPT)

The Father loves growing things, just look at nature. Your long-term 'outside' influence for Him grows as your 'inside' life with Him grows. It can't help it. But the opportunities He uses as growing seasons aren't the ones we'd choose. At least, they're not what I'd choose!

A few years ago some research was done on oak trees. Several small trees were put in a greenhouse and divided into three groups. Some were tied to a stake, others were left unsupported. The trees in the third group were left unsupported but waved to and fro every day, simulating windy conditions. After a few months, the trees measured for the strongest trunks were those in the last group. Conclusion: oak trees get stronger when they're exposed to storms. And so do we, when we stay connected to the Father.

Instead of the storms in your life blowing you over, Jesus wants to use them to build you up. We can either get upset that the Father would let us go through storms, or we can be grateful for what He can grow in us through those storms. Storms are part of life. Mighty oaks don't just survive them, they grow stronger through them by sticking close to Jesus in them. Fewer storms might be nice, but greater resilience is necessary for you, friend, to handle influence, authority, difficulty, opposition and peer pressure without them shaping you. Jesus wants you to bring His life to that stuff, not get blown over by the freak winds of life.

Perhaps you're going through some kind of storm right now. Maybe you're wondering if it will destroy you. Remember again today that your Father is stronger than the storm and He's in you and for you. His heart is to grow you through it and His promise is to bring you through it. So let the storm make you stronger not stroppier! Listen for His voice, trust His plan for you and surrender again today to His purposes for you.

PONDER
What is Jesus saying to you today?

PRAY
Ask the Holy Spirit to help you trust the Father to grow you through the storms, both big and small, when they come. Then, write out a prayer of surrender to God on your phone or on paper.

READ: John 15:1-4

He cares for the branches connected to Me by...pruning every fruitful branch to yield a greater harvest. (TPT)

Yes, I know, Jesus is talking about a vine here, not an oak! But God is the Gardener, and He likes to prune the plants in His garden. And, believe it or not, oak trees also need pruning. Dead and diseased branches have to be removed, and both the weak branches and some fruitful ones also need cutting back. This is to make sure enough sunlight and airflow get to the tree, stimulating it to grow stronger and produce more fruit. So when the time is right, God gets out His secateurs. Ouch!

Pruning is painful and can feel like punishment. But notice God doesn't just prune dead branches, but ones that are already fruitful. When the Father prunes us, it's not a punishment, but the product of bearing fruit. For a season, He cuts back or removes our capacity for what may seem like some good stuff. He might ask us to give up something that's fruitful. Our opportunities may dry up or doors may close on us. But it's to grow more fruit in our life. Some people think painful pruning isn't from the Father because they don't believe a loving God would do that to them. So they resist it. Others get discouraged and think, 'Well if that's how God's going to treat me, I may as well give up.' But when He does it, it's because it's what's best for us. He's on our side.

There are different seasons in life but don't let your season shape your response to the Father. Whether or not you're being pruned, draw near to Him with a heart full of praise today. He knows you. He knows your needs. He knows exactly how to take care of you. And He knows when to prune you and how. When He does, He's ensuring greater beauty, greater growth and greater fruit will emerge from your life than ever before.

PONDER
Do you trust that God knows what He's doing with you? If you don't but you did, what difference would it make to you?

PRAY
Spend some time praising God. Praise Him He's the Gardener, that He cares for you and that He knows exactly how to bring an increase of fruitfulness in your life.

READ: Isaiah 61:1-4

They will be...a planting of the Lord for the display of His splendour.

'Have you had any work done?' That seems to be a question asked increasingly of celebrities in particular, whose looks don't seem to match their age. But it's the kind of question to which mighty oaks should always be able to answer 'yes.' Strange, I know, but let me explain.

Your life is designed to be a shop window for the world to see the splendour of God. You're a planting of the Lord so He can display His goodness through your life. Other people see His nature as He works in you. Therefore, the more 'work' He's done in you, the more His nature is visible to others. When He set my friend free from an addiction, I saw His power. When He comforted another friend through great loss, I saw His compassion. When He turned a friend's despair into praise, I saw His goodness. I could go on. Look back at some of the things He promises to do for you in these verses. They include turning the ashes of your life into beauty, replacing your tears with joy and leading you into true freedom.

Have you had any work done? What would you point to? Have you looked back and thought about it? If you have, but you're not sure what you'd point to, do you need to ask yourself if you're trying to do all the work? Are you sure that Jesus can bring radical change to your life? The greater the work He does in you, the greater the work He does through you. His work through you includes restoring, rebuilding and renewing devastated places and people (v4) which is a high calling. But He needs to do the work in you first. As a mighty oak, you're called to mighty work, but only because of the Mighty One doing His mighty work in you.

PONDER

What 'work' have you had done in your heart and life? Do you see what He does *in* you, or what He does *through* you, as being more important?

PRAY

Invite Him to display His splendour more fully in your life. Tell Him your desires to be more involved in restoring, rebuilding and renewing devastated places and people. Surrender again to His work in you that is connected to His calling on your life.

READ: Psalm 1
They are like trees planted along the riverbank, bearing fruit each season. (NLT)

The contrast in this psalm is between those who delight in God and His ways, and those who don't.

PUSH IN

– What enables this tree to prosper and bear fruit in each season?

– How, and how often, do you think about and chew over what you've read in God's word?

– What things could you do differently, or what changes could you make in your schedule that would help you to do that more?

Fun fact: The Hebrew word translated as 'meditate' is the word 'hagah'. It's an onomatopoeic word and is the same word used to describe the growling, or the pleasurable murmuring of a lioness as she eats her prey. Therefore, when the psalmist says those who meditate on the word of God are like prosperous trees, he's assuming that we'll regularly speak out the word we're meditating on, rather than just thinking about it.

– To what extent do you do this?

– Speak this verse out over yourself a couple of times, replacing the first three words with 'I am like a...'

Talk to God about what's on your heart today.

READ: Isaiah 61:3
You will be called an oak of righteousness.

PUSH IN

Be still for a few moments and hear the Father speaking this word over you. Thank Him that this is who you are and declare it out loud with confidence: 'I am an oak of righteousness.'

Get outside today and find an oak tree. If you can't find one, find another big tree. Stand in front of it, spend some time looking at it and ask God to speak to you through it, bearing in mind some of the things He's been showing you this week.

READ: Psalm 103:19-22
God has set His throne in Heaven; He rules over us all. He's the King! (MSG)

Life is not about you, and it's not about me. Anyone who tells you it is, is living in cloud cuckoo land! Life doesn't revolve around human beings (no matter how loud we shout or how much influence we have), any more than the universe revolves around the earth. Life is about God, His kingdom and His purposes. There is one throne, high above every other power, and Jesus is sitting on it. He was sat there long before we were born, and will be long after we've gone. The story of life is about Him and His story. To follow Jesus is not to follow good advice; it's to follow the King of kings and to join His kingdom.

The psalmist often addresses Him as 'my God *and* my King'. He has made God His Lord. Have you? To follow Jesus is to appoint Him as ruler over us. It means releasing the reins of life to Him and letting Him be the CEO. It means obeying His orders and submitting to His authority. We don't tend to like orders or authority, so let's be real about what this means. Having a new king also means being part of a new kingdom. That means signing up to a new culture; a new way of thinking and doing things. The King's way. And of course, it means a new, royal identity.

God is our Father but He's also the King of the cosmos. How do we relate to Him as both? How do we relate to God with the familiarity and closeness of a good father, and yet with the respect and honour required of a powerful king? It happens as we recognise He is both, and register which one we lean towards more heavily. Then, we need to make sure we have times when we consciously lean in to the other. This week is a chance for that. Both realities are essential for a healthy relationship with God. He is your Father, He is the King of all, and He is your King!

PAUSE
Get on your knees if you can. As you kneel before Him, declare this personalised verse to God three times: 'You have set Your throne in Heaven; You rule over us all. You are the King.'

PRAY
Spend some time praising Him. Thank Him that He's established His throne in Heaven, that He rules over us all and no one can challenge Him. Summit to Him as your King. Tell Him what that means to you. Pray the Lord's prayer, slowly. You can find it in Matthew 6:9-13.

READ: 2 Kings 6:8-17

...he looked and saw all the hills full of horses and chariots of fire all around Elisha.

Wouldn't you love to see what Elisha's servant saw? Imagine one minute all you can see is a massive army that's come to attack you and you're terrified. Then, after a quick prayer, you open your eyes and see hillsides covered with horses and chariots that belong to the King of Heaven. And they're there for your moment of need. What a roller coaster of emotion! There's nothing like a change of perspective to release confidence.

There's no room for a victim mindset in the kingdom of God. That mindset is rooted in a lie of powerlessness, and an assumption that our future is in the hands of circumstances or people beyond our control. Elisha's servant expected defeat. Luckily, he was with a prophet who knew the Father as the powerful King. So Elisha asked his King to let his servant see the true reality of their circumstances. What a contrast! God was in control after all. Friend, whatever challenges you face today, God rules over them. He's more powerful than your biggest problem and He's prepared for it. God never thinks, 'Oh, I hadn't seen that coming - what do we do now?' He's got your challenges covered.

God says nothing and no one (not even the enemy) can stop Him fulfilling His plans and purposes for us (Job 42:2 MSG) if we trust Him. That remains true no matter what authority or power other people have over us. It doesn't change however challenging our circumstances, however big the opposition we face or however out of control we feel. We have a lot going for us today. Heaven's forces are on our side. They're working for us *if* we're living for the King. We may not see the armies like the servant did, but Elisha was confident they were there *without* seeing them. And that's the kind of confidence the Father's looking for in us. It grows each time we submit to Him as our King.

PONDER

Is there a situation in your life that you feel overwhelmed or defeated by at the moment?

PRAY

Ask God to show you how He sees it and pause. Then, hear Him tell you, 'I've got it covered.' Leave it with Him, thank Him for His power at work for you, and ask Him for what you need today.

READ: Psalm 47
God reigns above the nations, sitting on His holy throne. (NLT)

Take a deep breath. Don't worry today. If Jesus is your King, then today and what it brings are in His hands. If you're trusting *Him* to reign over your life, *you* don't have to. Put your confidence in Him. We humans love to be in control, have you noticed that? Worry or anxiety only come out to play when we're facing situations and outcomes we can't control.

Don't let your trust in God's sovereignty over your life be shaken because He doesn't do things the way you expect. He's not a dictator, forcing His ways on us. And He's not like Alexa or Siri, there to carry out our wishes. We're here to carry out His. But this psalm reminds us He does have full authority. He is working His purposes out, for our good and His glory. Somehow, He's always in control, even when it looks as if He's not. Think of the cross. The priests persuaded the crowd to cry, 'Crucify Jesus.' They thought they had the power. Pilate believed he did, as he sentenced Jesus to death. The enemy thought he was in control as Jesus was finally nailed to the cross. Jesus' friends and family thought everything had spiralled *out* of control, leaving them scared, scarred and scattered.

Who was right? None of them. Jesus and the Father were in control the whole time. A true king never let's go of his power. Jesus said, 'I lay down My life, only to take it up again' (Jn 10:17). He put His life into God's hands. The Father was still ruling. He never dropped the ball. He brought His dead Son back to life, completing His master plan to defeat death.

Whatever you're anxious about that's beyond your reach today, remember it's not beyond His. Don't focus on what it looks like, or what you can't do or can't change. Fix your eyes on the King who can do all things. Put it into His hands. Trust Him that He's working His purposes out for your good and His glory, and breathe in His peace.

PRAY
Ask the Holy Spirit for a fresh revelation of the sovereignty of God today. Where do you need to trust He is in control, so you can let go of anxiety? Over your family? Your future? Your finances? Your relationships? Your work(place)? Your health? Praise Him, in faith, for what He's doing and say, 'Thank You Jesus that you reign over my _____ . I trust You with it/them.'

READ: Matthew 6:25-34

Seek first His kingdom and His righteousness and all these things will be given to you as well.

To experience the fullness of life in the kingdom, we must be willing to let go of our agendas and our timetables. If we want Jesus' power and sovereignty to show up in our lives, we have to do things His way. Jesus talks about putting first things first. He says, 'If you put going after My ways at the top of your list, then all the other things you need in life will come to you as well. Put Me first, follow Me and let Me be in charge.'

I've learnt that since Jesus is great enough to be King, He has good reasons for doing things I don't understand. That includes letting me experience things (and timings) I don't understand. Peter tried to stop Jesus going to the cross (Matt 16:21-23). He expected Jesus to rule like a human king, and defeat evil and injustice the human way. Human kings don't give up their lives! But Jesus had the sternest words for Peter. If Peter was going to follow Him as King, he had to let go of his agenda and get used to Jesus doing things differently.

Friend, His kingdom doesn't give a green light to our way of life. It slowly affects everything in our life, like a fragrance spreading through a room. Where the King rules, change comes. He changes how we approach problems and how we bring change. How we treat others and how we speak about them. What we post and what we watch. What we do with our bodies, our wallets and our diaries. Who we listen to and who we learn from. What we pray and what we proclaim. And how we see God's timing. Are we switching agendas? His for ours? He asks us to do things we don't understand, and He works in ways we don't get. Peter had to work through what he found difficult because he loved Jesus as his King more than he loved his own agenda. Will the same be said for us?

PONDER
Why is switching to God's agenda a challenge? Can you identify a time when you surrendered something specific and did things His way, when you wanted to do it your way? What happened? Is pursuing His agenda your priority?

PRAY
Ask Jesus to grow your love for Him as a good King who has your best interests at heart.

READ: John 18:36-37
My kingdom is not of this world...My kingdom is from another place. (NLT)

Do you ever look at your world, or out at the big wide world, and wonder whether God really is sovereign? If He is the powerful King the Bible says He is, do you wonder why life can be such a struggle? Why innocent people suffer? Jesus came saying His kingdom had come and described it as being from 'another place'. In other words, His kingdom isn't like human realms of power where leaders impose their will. It's a spiritual kingdom which invades hearts and lives where it's invited. It *is* visible, but for now, only to those who have eyes to see it. One day it will be obvious to everyone, everywhere. That's the day when Jesus will come back.

When He returns, Jesus says the entire world will see Him as the cosmic King He is (Matt 25:30). His arrival will fill the skies. Imagine that! But it will also be a day of great grief for everyone who rejected Him as King. Until then, there's an ongoing struggle between the kingdom of this world and His kingdom. Between what we can see, and what we can't. Don't be thrown by it, but recognise it. We're caught up in this struggle around us, and we experience it within us. Victory was secured at the cross, but its reality is still being rolled out. His kingdom is *still* advancing.

Jesus calls us and empowers us to continue this work of rolling out His kingdom. Of bringing Heaven to earth, throughout the earth. That's our mandate as kingdom women. Like rays of sunlight breaking through the clouds, His kingdom life breaks in and becomes visible where we serve others in love and where we confront what others struggle with. That looks like meeting practical needs, such as feeding the hungry, caring for the orphan and providing shelter for the homeless. Doing what Jesus did. And it looks like disease being healed, oppression being lifted, bondage being broken and captives being freed. Jesus has given us authority and power to show the world its loving King. Let's make sure we use them.

PONDER
How have you seen His kingdom breaking in to the lives of others as you have served them in love?

PRAY
Think about the different situations you'll be in today. Pray for His kingdom to come in each one.

READ: Matthew 21:1-11, Revelation 19:11-16

PUSH IN

Ask the Holy Spirit to reveal something new to you about your King today as you read these two short passages. Each one describes the same King. The first is from Jesus' first time on earth. The second is when He'll come again.

– What differences between the two scenes strike you most?

– What word(s) would you associate with each scene?

– What does it mean for you and your life that Jesus is King in both these different ways?

Write down whatever you sense the Holy Spirit saying to you today.

PUSH IN

Grab a bit of paper or use the space below. Do you remember pie charts from your school days? Draw a big circle and divide it up into different segments reflecting the different areas of your life. You might want to think about family, friendships, career, studies, free time, money, sex life, online life, church commitment, health, etc.

When you've done that, ask God to show you which ones you've not submitted to Him and are still trying to rule. There can only be one ruler! Ask Him to highlight one that He wants you to surrender today. Ask Him to show you how, and what He wants you to do. He'll show you what you're afraid of and the Holy Spirit will help you hand it over to Him. Take note of what He says to you. He may well ask you to do something differently going forward.

You might find this a helpful prayer to pray:

'Lord Jesus, thank You that You're a good King and that You know best. Please forgive me for trying to manage this area of my life independently from You. I want You to be king over my _____. I surrender it to You now and ask You to rule over it as my Lord. Please govern my life with Your power and Your love. I love You and I thank You. Amen.'

READ: 2 Corinthians 5:18-21
So we are Christ's ambassadors; God is making His appeal through us. (NLT)

As a daughter of the King, you have a never-ending supply of love, grace and mercy available on tap 24/7 because you belong to Him. He's also called us to make this love, grace and mercy known and accessible to others. You're His daughter and you're called to live on assignment for your Father. And He has appointed you to be His ambassador.

Paul reminds the Corinthian followers of an important part of their identity. No matter what their everyday roles, they are ambassadors for Jesus; as parents, teachers, scientists, artists, medical professionals, carers, or personal trainers (not sure if they had them way back!). So are you. Whatever you do, you're His personal ambassador. You work for Him. The role of an ambassador is to accurately represent someone or something that's not physically present. A brand ambassador represents a product. A national ambassador represents a government or leader.

Since we're instructed to represent Jesus, our assignment is to re-present Him and His government wherever we are. We're His ambassador to our generation and our peers. In the classroom, in our home, in our office, in the supermarket, in the gym, at the school gate, at the dentist, in the boardroom, and online. He's appointed you and anointed you to re-present Him so that when others look at you, they see what Jesus is like. They can't see Him or His kingdom, they can only see Him through His people. And they can only hear about Him from His ambassadors. Since being one is part of our new identity, we re-present Him everywhere. Whether or not we're aware of it, and whether or not we're doing a good job of it! Remember, everything we say and do has a bigger impact than we intend because we represent the King and His kingdom.

PONDER
Spend a moment letting this truth about this dimension of your identity sink in. Declare this verse over yourself. What does it mean for you to be His ambassador? Where will you be re-presenting Jesus today?

PRAY
Thank Jesus for the privilege of re-presenting Him wherever you go. Ask Him to help you do it well today.

READ: Proverbs 3:3-4

Never let loyalty and kindness leave you...then you will find favour with both God and people... (NLT)

Ambassadors from foreign nations need permission from their host country to work and have influence there. For an ambassador to get that permission, they need to convince the foreign power that something of value that will benefit them is on offer. As Jesus' ambassadors, we can learn a lot from this principle. The more those around us, especially those who don't know Jesus, believe that we value them, the more they'll be open to the kingdom we represent.

Solomon was one of the wisest kings ever, and he knew about influence. He wrote this: 'Love and loyalty pave the way for favour with God and with people.' In other words, if we're loyal to others, if we're kind, paying attention to what they need and doing good to them, they'll allow us more access to their life. They're more likely to listen to what we have to say. As His ambassador, He wants you using your influence for Him. He wants to tell others He loves them and is offering them eternal life. Through you.

Loyalty is expressed in actions. Are you someone who is dependable in good times and in bad? What would your friends and colleagues say? Can you be relied on to follow through on what you've said? Or is your support conditional? Loyalty is also expressed in words. Do you speak well of others behind their backs even if you disagree with them? Yesterday, a friend told me that she's tried to be kind and loyal to a housemate who was initially hostile to her because of her faith. Recently he's been honest about some personal struggles. He's now opened up to her influence because she's been loyal to him. We're to be kind and loyal to everyone, not just those we think deserve it. We're to be loyal because we're God's ambassadors. The Bible says, 'Don't let loyalty and kindness ever leave you; write them on your heart.' Why not make that a goal.

PAUSE

Try committing the verse above to memory. Call it back to mind during the day.

PRAY

Ask the Father to highlight someone to you today with whom He wants to increase your influence. Pray for them. Ask Him to show you how you can express His kindness to them.

READObject: Colossians 3:13-17
And whatever you do or say, do it as a representative of the Lord Jesus... (NLT)

Jesus knows you completely and trusts you to represent Him. But as ambassadors, we have to be careful how we act and speak. So He gives us guidance on how to do it well. This brief passage identifies several characteristics our King asks us to display for Him. They include forgiveness, love, peace and thankfulness. The phrase above sums up His mandate: *whatever* we do or say, we're to do it as His representative.

That means, are we doing it as if He was doing it? When we post on line, it's as if He was posting. When we're with our friends, we're His presence amongst them. When we show up at work, we're showing up for Jesus. When our colleagues see us, God hopes they'll see how Jesus would do our job. We're really on Heaven's payroll, just deployed in the world. Friend, let's turn away from blaming and shaming one another and overlook what offends us. Let's not focus on how we've been mistreated, but focus on how we treat others. Let's not talk about what we haven't got, but speak out our thanks for what we have. Let's stop rehearsing our rights and remember our needs are met from Heaven, not earth. Let's go the extra mile, demonstrating we're here on assignment from another kingdom instead of living as if we're not. Let's look more like Him, because others are looking at us.

Jesus has a purpose for us wherever we are. Many people spend their lives being their own boss, following their own path and prioritising their own passions. But when we embrace our identity as ambassadors, we embrace Him as boss. Our true boss. It's liberating and life-changing. Whoever we live with and wherever we work, we are on the King's business (Col 3:23). Are we giving Him our best?

PAUSE

If those around you were interviewed, and asked what you represented, what might they say? What might you be doing or saying that's making it hard for others to see Jesus in you? How would it change things if you believed Jesus was your boss, and you were doing and saying things for Him? Ask Jesus to help you live out this verse and spend some time talking to Him about it.

READ: Acts 9:1-7

He fell to the ground and heard a voice saying to him, 'Saul! Saul! Why are you persecuting Me?' (NLT)

Once upon a time, the Paul (formerly known as Saul) who wrote 'We are ambassadors', was not an ambassador. Others were, but Saul was out to get them. He believed they were deceived and dangerous. He made life super tough for them and even watched some of them die. But when Jesus showed up in his life and confronted him, Jesus didn't say, 'Why are you persecuting *them*?' but, 'Why are you persecuting *Me*?' Jesus treats what's done to you as being done to Him. Because you're His ambassador. Because you represent Him to this world. That's big.

In His timing, Jesus intervened and defended His first ambassadors. He confronted Saul. In His timing, He will intervene and defend and protect you. God sees any assault against us as an assault against Heaven. Ambassadors of this world are given government protection, and Jesus commands His angelic hosts to protect His ambassadors in the same way (Ps 91:11). If we're about the Father's business, no one can take us out until our time is up. The enemy wants to trip us up with anxiety and bury us under burdens. He wants to distract us from representing Jesus by keeping us looking after ourselves. Knowing you're an ambassador on Heaven's business is believing Heaven has promised to take care of you while you're on assignment. The more we confident we are of this, the more we know His peace.

Jesus will look after us. He'll take care of our needs and answer our call if we're seeking to represent Him. Take a deep breath and let that truth sink in again today. Check in with Him often, send every concern His way. Then let His concerns be your concerns. Ask Him to show you what's on His heart and He'll look after what's on yours. It may feel counterintuitive, but that's the way of the kingdom.

PRAY

Imagine yourself at the foot of the cross with Jesus. Spend a few moments handing Him the things that are worrying you at the moment. Then invite Him to hand you what He wants you to hold today. Does He have a specific request of you?

READ: Matthew 28:16-20
All the authority of the universe has been given to Me. Now go in My authority... (TPT)

If you ever found yourself in the French ambassador's presence, you would be in the presence of the government of France. In the same way, anyone who finds themselves in your presence is actually in the presence of Jesus and His kingdom. When people meet you, God intends them to meet the One in you. If you're letting the Holy Spirit lead you, they get the chance to hear Him speak and see Him act through you.

Jesus has been misrepresented in this world by the enemy and his strategies, and He's chosen us as His counterattack. To set the record straight! And He has given us power and authority to do so. An ambassador has authority to act on behalf of his government and when he makes a decision, his government backs him up by doing what he's said. The same applies to us. The Holy Spirit is in us as the presence of Heaven, and when we act on His behalf, His power will back us up. It's His power, but it's under our control; like the power supplied by the national grid which we control as we turn on the kettle.

As this verse says, He's given you authority to heal and authority to declare blessing over those around you. Authority to overcome the power of the enemy and authority to teach, comfort and encourage others. Authority to tell others about Him, authority to release hope, authority to do what Jesus did and make disciples. You have more influence and authority to reveal His kingdom and His nature than you know or are using. The question is not, 'How much authority do we have?', but, 'How much do we believe we have authority?' It flows through faith. It's not a reward but a gift to His ambassadors so they can do their job. That's you, friend! Be confident and use it.

PONDER
Re-read the verse above and hear Jesus speaking these words to you. How do you use the authority He has given you? Do you expect His power to back you up?

PRAY
Talk to Him about whatever is on your heart today.

RE-READ: 2 Corinthians 5:16-21

We are ambassadors of the Anointed One who carry the message of Christ to the world, as though God were tenderly pleading with them directly through our lips. (TPT)

PUSH IN

Read the passage slowly and ask the Holy Spirit to come and speak to you today, as His ambassador.

– Which part of it stands out to you?

– How would you put it into your own words if you were trying to explain it to someone else?

– For it to become more of a reality for you, what do you need to do?
- Do you need to let go of a lie?
- Do you need to start doing something?
- Do you need to stop doing something?
- Do you need to confess something?
- Do you need to make a declaration over yourself?

Write down what you sense the Holy Spirit showing you.

PONDER

If you had to describe in three sentences what Jesus has been saying to you this week, what would you say? Write it down and then identify one thing you can do to represent Him better. How will you begin to do that?

READ: Daniel 6:25-27
His rule continues eternally. He is a saviour and rescuer. (MSG)

God has always been a rescuer. He has continually rescued His people from what the world has hurled at them and the traps they've fallen into. Whether it was rescuing the Israelites from the Egyptians, Rahab from Jericho, Daniel from the lions, or Lazarus from death, there are times when only a rescue will do. He's able to do whatever it takes to rescue you from sin and pain, oppression and addiction, affliction, lies and torment, sickness and hopelessness, mistakes and more.

Most times, a rescue follows a cry for help. When the gearbox on my car went on the motorway, I ended up stranded on the hard shoulder in freezing conditions. I had to call the breakdown people to come and rescue me and I could have hugged them when they arrived (even though they took a while)! In all the scenarios above, someone called out to God for rescue (except Lazarus, but his sisters did!). Psalm 34 says, 'The Lord hears His people when they call to Him for help. He rescues them from all their troubles.' What a promise.

We end up in deep waters for all kinds of reasons. Or is it only me? Whether it happens from choices we've made or not, sometimes we end up out of our depth. How do we get our feet back on solid ground? There are three keys to being rescued: *admitting* our need of rescue to ourselves and to God; *asking* for rescue, and then *accepting* His help when it comes. We may need patience for His rescue, as I did on that motorway. But God's timing is both perfect and a mystery. Whatever you need rescuing from, don't give in to the lies that you must grin and bear it, or that you should fix it on your own. However impossible a situation may seem to you, call out and keep calling out to your Rescuer. Believe He wants to rescue you, and that He's more than able to.

PONDER
Everyone needs rescuing from time to time. Some just find it easier to admit than others. How easy do you find it? Are you quick to ask Jesus to rescue you? How easily do you accept help?

PRAY
Thank Jesus He's your personal Rescuer. Ask Him to forgive you if you haven't believed He would come through for you when you've needed it or if you've believed you don't need a rescuer.

READ: Psalm 18:6,16-19
He rescued me because He delights in me.

David knew the Rescuer. He knew where to turn and he knew how to turn (v6). He knew God wouldn't rescue him against his will, but would when he called. But the Holy Spirit had also given him a revelation of the Father's love. This revelation fuelled David's confidence. He connects his rescue to the way God felt about him. David wrote, 'God rescued me because He treasures me. I'm precious to Him and I delight Him. So He came through for me.'

Friend, if you think your circumstances or even your life might be beyond rescue or beyond help, think again. If you're facing a test, a temptation or a trial that's too big for you, look to your Rescuer. He delights in you. That's why you can be confident He'll step in. You are precious to Him. He doesn't promise to prevent those trials from coming, but He promises to walk through them with you. And He promises to prevent them from taking you out. The enemy wants us to believe we wouldn't experience such things if God really delighted in us. The Father wants us to trust He'll bring us through them because He does.

David knew the delight of his Father. It was what kept him confident that God would rise up and rescue him, however long he had to wait for that rescue. That time of waiting for God to move is a fertile place for the Holy Spirit to give us fresh insight into God's pleasure in us. Ask Him to give you a deeper revelation of His delight in you today. Trust His love for you. Remember, you're His treasured daughter. He will sustain you, He will deliver you and He will bring you through. Because He delights in you.

PONDER
God's rescue comes to us in all kinds of different ways. What has He rescued you from in the past and how did He do that? Have you associated that rescue with His delight in you? Read the verse above out loud.

PRAY
Spend some time praying about whatever or whoever is on your heart today.

READ: Galatians 1:1-5
Jesus gave His life for our sins, just as God our Father planned, in order to rescue us from this evil world in which we live.

Why not let the greatest rescue fill your heart with joy again today? Jesus has come for you and rescued you out of this world, into His kingdom. As He made His way onto earth that first Christmas, under the cover of night and hidden in human skin, the execution of His plan to rescue us had begun. His long journey from Heaven to earth ended as He invaded our sin-wrecked world to rescue us. There was no hope for us otherwise.

Many people think entry to Heaven depends on being a good person and living a good life. As this verse reminds us, it doesn't. It depends on faith in a rescue. A child of God is someone who's been rescued, not someone who's been good. Jesus died to save our lives. Literally. To rescue us from an eternal future without Him; from the sentence of the sin-disease we were born with. To rescue us from the power of that sin. To rescue us from ourself and our ego. To rescue us from the enemy and his schemes and all that assaults our heart and identity. To rescue us into His arms, into His kingdom and into life with Him. The reason behind His rescue? Love. The Father rescued you because He loves you. Because you matter. Because you're deeply precious to Him. And the lengths He went to spell out just how much.

The Father is a rescuer. Our relationship with Him is based on trusting His rescue. When we drift into religious effort or a response of 'You owe me' to Jesus, we've moved away from a rescue-based relationship. He's done something for us we could never do for ourselves. He's rescued us from separation to intimacy, guilt to forgiveness, bondage to freedom, despair to hope, and pain to restoration. What a stunning rescue, what a stunning rescuer. Let His rescue shape your day today.

PONDER
Re-read the verse above, aloud and slowly, two or three times. Replace 'our' with 'my', and 'us' with 'me'.

PRAY
Spend some time thanking Jesus for His rescue of you. If you've taken it for granted, confess that and let it remind you afresh how much you matter to Him. Put your adoration into words.

READ: 2 Timothy 4:14-18
The Lord will rescue me from every evil attack and will bring me safely to His heavenly kingdom.

There are certain types of people that are very difficult to rescue. When a person is drowning and someone tries to rescue them, the rescue becomes much harder if that person keeps struggling to save themselves. What they think will help them harms them and makes things worse. Rescue is only possible once they're willing to surrender and let the rescuer take over.

Paul had been opposed, and in his words, harmed by a chap called Alexander (v14/15). No one had come to his defence, no one had stepped up to support him. No one had fought for Paul and rescued him from the unjust situation he found himself in. Was he being criticised, insulted or slandered? Was his reputation at stake? Was his future under threat? We aren't told. But we know that instead of fighting back and fighting his own corner, he let Jesus fight for him. He didn't let anger or bitterness or self pity get the upper hand. You can hear his previous experience of the Father rescuing him in his confident declaration.

What do you do when you're feeling threatened or under attack? Or when you feel you're on your own and no one's looking out for you? Do you fight back to rescue your reputation or your image when they're questioned or undermined by others? When we do, we're not trusting God to do His job, we're trying to do it for Him. Fighting back, blaming others or defending ourselves makes it harder for Jesus to rescue us Himself. Which He will, in His time, if our purpose is good and our heart is right. But we cannot stay on the kingdom offensive if we're busy being defensive. Friend, evil attacks *will* come, as they did for Paul. They're designed by the enemy to discourage and defeat us. I've had plenty of practice at this in recent years. But hard as it is to do, surrendering to Jesus is always better. If we're on His side, He is on ours.

PAUSE
How confidently can you make this declaration that Paul makes? Imagine yourself in a situation where you want to fight back and defend your reputation or integrity. What practical step could you take so next time, Jesus has a chance to rescue you rather than you trying yourself? If you need help with a suggestion, ask the Holy Spirit to give you one.

READ: Mark 14:22-33
...he was terrified and began to sink. 'Save me, Lord!' he shouted. (NLT)

My first white water rafting trip was a disaster or a success depending on how you look at it. As we bounced over the rapids in Malaysia, I fell overboard into the water! I was only under the swirling water for a few seconds before a hand grabbed the top of my life jacket and pulled me back into the raft. Before I'd had time to work out what was happening to me, I was out of the water and back with the others. Jeremy, the professional raftsman, had skilfully rescued me with spectacular speed.

The reason I got into the boat in the first place was Jeremy. All my 'what ifs' were silenced by his presence. His being in charge gave me enough confidence that everything would be ok – so I had a go. Peter got out of his boat because of Jesus. He knew he was trying something risky. But his 'what ifs' were nothing compared to his confidence that Jesus would rescue him if he got into trouble. So he had a go.

All kinds of miracles and breakthroughs in our lives are the other side of us 'having a go'. Fear of rejection, of failure, of pain, or of a disaster of some sort, will hold us back. Faith in our Rescuer pulls us forwards into our assignments. Jesus doesn't guarantee we won't begin to sink, but He does promise rescue. He's willing us on just as He did Peter. Friend. the supernatural life He made us for is outside the boat. Trying to eliminate risk and stay in control guarantees us nothing except a life that doesn't satisfy. No one walks on water without taking a risk. The presence of our Rescuer and the promise of rescue frees us to take those risks and get out of the boat. Do you trust He'll rescue you? If you do, that confidence in Him will take you places that fear will always keep you from.

PONDER
If you were 100% confident that Jesus would rescue you if you needed it, what would you do? What would getting out of your boat involve?

PRAY
Thank Jesus that He's set you free to take risks and step out by promising to rescue you. Ask Him to help you get out of your boat, trusting that He'll be there to rescue you when you need it.

READ: Psalm 31:1-5

David had a great call on his life but was very familiar with struggle. Despite the fact he'd been chosen and anointed by God, he was chased and regularly threatened by king Saul who was so jealous of him, he wanted to kill him. On one occasion, David had the chance to defend himself and get rid of Saul (you can read it in 1 Samuel 24:1-10). David refused to disobey God by taking Saul out, and trusted that God would rescue him properly, in His way and in His time. David had to wait for his rescue which did come, but in the meantime, wrote lots of prayers and songs pouring his heart out to God. His amazing psalms encourage us and help us to pray, but we wouldn't have them if he'd organised his own rescue and refused to wait for God.

PUSH IN

Reflect on your own life. Where could you do you with a rescue today? Also ask the Father to show you what *He* wants to rescue you from. Spend a few moments waiting for Him to speak. Use the words of Psalm 31 and pray them as your prayer to Him.

Pray boldly and from your heart, as David did.

READ: Esther 4:12-17

God invites His daughters to join Him in His rescuing activity of others. Usually, His rescue is clothed in human skin, and sometimes that skin is yours and mine.

Esther's uncle Mordecai discovered a plot to kill the Jews and he told her about it. He then encouraged her to play her part (v14) in rescuing them by using her influence with her husband, the king. It was costly for her, as approaching the king without being invited to could be punished by death. But her response is a powerful one (v16). She was willing to get involved in the rescue of others, despite the risk to herself.

PUSH IN

You may not be called by God to rescue a nation, but reflect with God on what sort of rescue activity He's called you to join Him in, or given you a heart for. It could be helping Him rescue someone or some people from suffering, unbelief, loneliness, poverty, oppression, spiritual captivity, hopelessness ... (you get the idea)!

Jot down anything He shows you today, note what He's prompting you to do and talk to Him about those He has put on your heart.

READ: Galatians 4:1-7
And since you are His child, God has made you His heir. (NLT)

OK – so technically you're an heiress, but let's stick with Bible language. Pause and think about what you've inherited from your biological parents. We all inherit plenty from them. Whether it's your mum's eye colour or her skin type, your dad's curly hair or his hay fever, you've inherited stuff from them which you got no say in. Maybe you like the deal you got, maybe you don't! Perhaps you'll inherit more from family down the line, whether that's a financial sum or a family heirloom. That's because, more often than not, inheriting is connected to family ties.

This stunning verse says we're heirs of the King of the universe because we're daughters. No one ever earns an inheritance, they just receive it. The moment you turned your life over to God, He made you His heir. In Bible times there was only one heir: the oldest son. No matter how many other children there were, *all* the family wealth went to the oldest. But the Father always does things differently. We're told we're co-heirs with Jesus. We get everything Jesus gets and have access to all He has access to (Lk 15:31). Wow!

Do we live like heirs of a rich King, or as orphans? The Father wants us confident of our inheritance. Spiritual orphans beg and plead with God. They worry about how their next need will be met, unsure whether He'll come through for them. Spiritual orphans try and manage on their own, fearing there won't be enough. They fight for themselves and struggle to be generous because resources feel scarce. Heirs with an inheritance pray and trust a Father who is wealthy beyond belief and good to all who rely on Him. Heirs always expect to have what they need and more, so they're free to be concerned about the needs of others. How we pray and how we live shows us how confident we are in our identity as His heirs.

PONDER
Reread the above verse a few times. What does it mean for you to be an heir of God?

PRAY
Thank Him that you belong to Him, that He's a good Father and that He's made you His heir alongside Jesus. Thank Him for providing for every need of yours. Ask Him to teach you how to live in the knowledge and reality of the rich inheritance you have as His heir.

READ: Romans 4:13-16

For if keeping the law earns the inheritance, then faith is robbed of its power and the promise becomes useless. (TPT)

When you go to work, you get paid a wage. If you worked for a month and then your employer decided not to pay you, you'd be troubled at best, livid at worst! And rightly so. You deserved that money. A bargain was struck: you put in the hours, so you'd get paid for those hours. If your employer did pay you but tried to claim the money was a gift, you'd be having none of that either! Payment was part of the contract.

The Father doesn't do contracts. He's given each of His children an inheritance; all the promises in the Bible. Jesus died to make sure every one could be owned by us and fulfilled by Him (2 Cor 1:20). Each promise is like a voucher from the Argos catalogue that we've been freely given. We have thousands of them, paid for with His blood. They're not just nice words on paper, they're doorways into experiences. But we have to lift them off the pages of the Bible, and start praying and believing them, to receive what's in the promise. We have to slap 'mine' on it and take it to the Father to cash it in. God has filled our pockets full of promises and He's waiting for us to do something with them.

Friend, Paul reminds the Romans that we can be tricked into believing that the way we perform for God will affect how He performs for us, as if there's a contract going on. The enemy whispers we deserve something because we've been good. Or we don't because we haven't. But this mindset makes faith powerless and pointless. Learn to reject those lies as soon as you hear them. Jesus did all the performing necessary for us. *His* work earned *our* inheritance. We need to put our effort into believing His promises to see God move, not bargaining with Him by how we behave.

PONDER

How easily do you get tricked into thinking you can perform for God to persuade Him to perform for you? How would your relationship with Him change if you never fell for it?

PRAY

Ask the Father to help you trust His radical grace more radically. Ask Him to show you what is available to you, and what you think you 'don't deserve' so don't ask for. Dare to ask Him now.

READ: Romans 8:12-17
Now if we are children, then we are heirs – heirs of God and co-heirs with Christ...

Do you know that feeling of envy? That desire for what someone else is enjoying (that you want(ed)) tinged with a green sense of resentment that they have it and you don't? Maybe you've heard the question that goes alongside that feeling. 'Why them, and not me?' God makes it clear that envy never leads us anywhere good – in fact the opposite is true. It paves the way for trouble in our heart and life.

As a co-heir with Jesus, we have access to the same privileges and blessings as Jesus and every other child of His. But when we envy others, we forget this. Envy tells us our inheritance has been given away to another at our expense. Friend, the Father doesn't give away what He's promised us. We don't have to work for it, we have to wait for it with faith. And we have to pray. When Jesus was in the wilderness, the enemy offered Him the kingdoms of the world. Jesus knew they were His inheritance, God had promised them to Him. But He had to wait and trust He'd receive them in God's timing. There is so much God has promised us that we have to wait *and* trust for too. Knowing you're an heir releases you from striving for what He's promised to release to you. And it will release you from envying others when their timing or blessing is different from yours.

The way to defeat envy is not only to admit it to yourself and to the Father, but to remember you're His heir. He has no favourites. Choose to celebrate with others over their blessings and benefits, especially when they are blessings and benefits you'd love too. And celebrate your own inheritance, in faith, before you see what you're believing for in your own circumstances.

PONDER
Are you envious of anyone at the moment? Ask Him to show you if you're not sure.

PRAY
Thank God that you have access to all the resources and blessings of Heaven because they're part of your inheritance. Confess any envy He shows you and ask Him to bless that person with more. Thank Him for what He's lined up for you as His heir. Declare this verse over yourself, confidently.

READ: Romans 8:17

In fact, together with Christ we are heirs of God's glory. But if we are to share His glory, we must also share His suffering. (NLT)

I can't say I wake up in the morning (or the middle of the night for that matter) in a tough season and think, 'I'm really struggling, I don't know if I can face today – but luckily that reminds me I'm an heir of the King of kings.' You won't be surprised to know I never think that! In fact I'm often tempted to think the opposite.

Look at this verse again. Children and heirs of God share everything that is His, including suffering. Being an heir is not an exit pass from suffering. It's a guarantee of it. Yes, we have an incredible kingdom inheritance, which we will receive in greater measure when we die. Yes, we are invited into a kingdom adventure with Him while we're on this earth. But that also includes going through hard times with Him, not just good ones. If He wasn't exempt from pain and difficulty here, then neither are we. He experienced it all. Betrayal. Abandonment. Injustice. Loss. Loneliness. False accusation. Humiliation. Rejection. And excruciating physical pain. He doesn't promise us a pain free life just because we're His. If you've fallen for that lie, dear friend, it's time to let it go.

If you're going through a tough time right now or next time you do, remember Jesus has walked where you're walking. Remember that as a co-heir, you have access to the same love, the same comfort, the same hope, the same strength and the same power of the Holy Spirit as Jesus did. Draw close to Him to keep going and keep believing. Ask for what you need. Don't give in to despair or discouragement. And don't give in to doubt. Don't listen to what they tell you. The same joy lies ahead of you. You're an heir of the kingdom and your resolve to keep walking with Him proves it.

PONDER
How does it make you feel to know that Jesus has already walked through what you're walking through? What questions do you have about this?

PRAY
Talk to the Father about whatever is on your heart today. Be honest and don't hold back. Then, spend a couple of minutes in silence, just enjoying His presence.

READ: Luke 19:12-27
...and to those who use well what they are given, even more will be given. (NLT)

Much of our inheritance as heirs of the kingdom is available to us now. But the Bible also talks about an inheritance waiting for us in Heaven. It's not often talked about, but part of what we stand to inherit will only be put into our hands in the next world. And how we live this side of the grave affects what we'll be entrusted with on the other side.

One of my kids started off handling money pretty badly! Most of it went into their stomach (not literally!) or got lost. Nobody in their right mind would have given that child a large sum to look after until they'd learnt to manage it better. And they did. But they practised with small amounts first. The story that Jesus told illustrates this principle. The extent of the inheritance He'll trust us with in Heaven (when the Master returns) depends on what we've done with what we've already inherited from Him in this life. Our time, our resources, our gifts, our experiences and our opportunities are all part of what He's freely given us now. We haven't all been given the same amount, but He won't reward how much we've had. He'll reward what we've done with what we've had.

What are you doing with the relationships He's given you? What are you doing with the wealth He's trusted you with? How are you using your gifts and your time? Are you using them and investing them for His purposes or just your own? Are you seeking to honour Him with what's in your hand since it's come from Him? When we do well with what we've already got, He entrusts us with more. That's His heart for us. He's a God of increase. But as a kind and loving Father, He makes sure we can handle what we've got in our hands before He let's us handle more.

PONDER
What's in your hand? How are you investing what He's already given you for His kingdom?

PRAY
Talk to Jesus about what this story brings up. Ask Him if there are ways you could invest more wisely and ask for whatever help you need.

READ: Ephesians 1:3

All praise to God, the Father of our Lord Jesus Christ, who has blessed us with every spiritual blessing in the heavenly realms because we are united with Christ. (NLT)

Imagine the cross of Jesus as a place of exchange. Imagine it covered in vouchers with your name on. On every voucher there is written a different blessing. Provision. Forgiveness. Peace. Acceptance. Mercy. Freedom. Courage. Joy. Hope. Favour. Compassion. Power. Healing. Life. Purity. Fullness. Abundance. Comfort. Wholeness. Presence. Guidance. Wisdom. Friendship...

Our inheritance was released at the cross but it's possible to live without transferring it in to the current account of our experience with God. Jesus invites us to bring our lack, our burden or our need to Him and exchange it for the inheritance He's given us. But it needs taking hold of through faith. That means believing it's ours because of His grace, and receiving it with gratitude and expectation before we experience it.

PUSH IN
– What do you need to exchange today?
Do you need to swap your shame for His acceptance? Do you need to swap your anxiety for His peace? Do you need to swap your financial lack for His provision? Do you need to swap your bondage for His freedom?

Spend some time in His presence, imagine yourself at the cross and go for it.

READ: Matthew 6:25-34
...do not worry...

PUSH IN

Read this passage, remembering you're an heir of God.

– Ask the Holy Spirit to speak to you as you read it. Note down any thoughts you have, or anything you sense Him saying to you.

– What is He wanting you to do in response to what He's drawn your attention to?

Ask Him to help you live out of the fullness of the inheritance He won for you at the cross. Thank Him there's no way you could ever repay Him for what He's done for you. Ask Him to help you honour Him by living as someone who has great expectations of Him because of what He's promised you. Ask Him to make you someone who talks more about what He's promised you than about your problems.

READ: John 14:1-6
Jesus told him, 'I am the Way, the Truth, and the Life.' (NLT)

Truth is essential for life. If we want to know how to protect our skin, we need the truth about the sun's rays. If we want the doctor to sort us out, they need the truth about our condition. If we want healthy relationships, they need to be built on truth. A lot is said about healthy eating for healthy living, but what about healthy thinking? We may be what we eat, but we are even more what we think. Healthy thinking needs truth. It leads to healthy living, so question: what do you feed you mind on?

Our world is full of ideas, opinions, theories and points of view and we spend a lot of time consuming them. And while many of these perspectives claim to be truth, let's be clear, many are not. Jesus declares, 'I am the Truth'. This is hugely significant. Truth *isn't* primarily an idea, an opinion or a point of view. It's a person. Jesus. Notice He sandwiches this dimension of His identity between 'Way' and 'Life'. The way to life is *through* truth. He is the Truth. He alone decides what's true. He decides what's right and wrong. We can't believe what we like and do what we like and call it truth. Even if it works for us. He is the Truth: about how relationships work, how life works, who we are, what matters in life, what's in and what's out, and what happens after this life.

Friend, we must treasure the truth if we love Jesus. Even when it's uncomfortable. Even when it clashes with what other voices around us are saying, whoever they are. Sometimes His truth is comforting, sometimes it's confronting. Do you need to re-read that? He lost His life for speaking the truth. Truth has never been popular. But Jesus loves us too much to trick us. He tells us what we need to hear, not what we want to. Because truth frees us (Jn 8:32). It strengthens us, releases us, heals us and empowers us. His role is to be the Truth. To speak it and lead us into it. Ours is to let it shape the way we think and the way we live.

PONDER
Re-read the verse above a few times and let Jesus speak to you through it. He is the Truth. Do you accept and trust what He says, or does it depend? If so, on what?

PRAY
Thank Jesus that He'll always be straight with you. Tell Him what that means to you. If you need to, lay down your desire to decide what's true and what isn't, and submit to Him today.

READ: Matthew 7:24-27

Rain poured down, the river flooded, a tornado hit – but nothing moved that house. (MSG)

There are lots of voices in our world. There are outside voices that tell us what skin care to use. How we should parent. How to have better relationships. What makes us significant. What we can say and what we can't. How to save the planet. How to reduce stress or increase influence. What cause we should fight for. What matters and what doesn't. What's right and what's wrong. And then there are inside voices that tell us things like, 'Do this because it feels right.' Or, 'You feel useless because you are useless.' Or, 'Praying doesn't make any difference.'

Friend, remember that life is shaped by the voices we listen to. Because those voices shape the way we think. How do we you know which ones to listen to? Jesus tells us this parable to make the point that our lives will only work if His voice is the loudest in our life. He says life storms will come like weather storms come. Difficulty, disappointment, injustice, offence, loss or confusion will assault our hearts like hurricanes assault a house. If we've built our lives on His word, these things won't flatten us when they hit. We'll be able to recognise what's truly going on around us, and how to walk forward into life.

Are you building your life on His word? Does His word shape your decisions, inform your choices and filter the other voices in your life? It has the ability to direct you, protect you and transform your life. It *is* truth, and every time you engage with it and obey it, you pick up your spade and dig a deeper foundation to your life. Treasure it. Treat it with respect. And trust it. Thankfully, every day doesn't bring a storm. But it does bring an opportunity. To build. Each day offers us a chance to dig in to His word and do what He says. Whatever any other voices are saying. And what we do today prepares us for the storms of tomorrow.

PONDER

Are you building your life on God's word? How do you do that? Which voices compete with it?

PRAY

Declare this verse over yourself a couple of times, emphasising the word 'nothing.' Ask Jesus to show you what you can do today to build your life on His truth, not anyone else's.

READ: Genesis 3:1-7
The serpent told the woman, 'You won't die.' (MSG)

I've recently found some vinyl records that belonged to my father. As he stuck them on his gramophone years ago, I'm sure he didn't expect he'd one day be listening to digital music on a different phone. Some things in life change rapidly. Some things never change. The enemy has been lying to God's daughters since way back. He knows the connection between truth and life. If he got Eve to question the truth, she'd then be open to believing his lies. And once she fell for the lies, the life God had for her would be over. The rest, as they say, is history.

The enemy hasn't changed. He used the same tactics in the wilderness on Jesus, and uses the same tactics on you and me. Jesus calls him the father of lies (Jn 8:44). He lies to you about who you are. About what the Father's like. About what God has and hasn't said. About what's right and wrong. About what makes life work. About the way to happiness. He even lies about himself. He knows the havoc he can cause if we believe his lies. They're like a virus on a laptop. But he also knows the havoc we can cause him when we reject his lies and walk in God's truth. So let's make every effort to do that, using the protection Jesus has given us.

In Ephesians 6:17 God says His word is a 'sword'. John 17:17 says His word is 'truth'. Jesus wielded this sword, reminding the enemy of what God had said. Eve didn't bother. Let's not do the same. If we're not confident in God's word, it will show up when ignoring it looks more convenient, like it did for Eve. Have you decided you will live under its authority? Or do you decide which bits you like and which you don't? And therefore which bits must be 'true'? Jesus has put a weapon in our hand because we live in a world full of lies. It's not our opinion, or someone else's version or interpretation of truth that will keep us safe. Only *His* truth will protect us. Friend, the power is always in what *He* says.

PAUSE
Ask the Holy Spirit to show you if there's a lie you believe about the Father, or something He's said, that He wants to free you from today. Spend a moment waiting for Him to speak.

PRAY
Acknowledge any lie He has shown you. Ask Him to reveal the truth to you from His word and declare it over yourself today. Ask the Holy Spirit to increase your love for God's word.

READ: John 16:7-15

But when He, the Spirit of truth, comes, He will guide you into all the truth. (NLT)

How do you know what Jesus is saying to you? How do you know what's true in your situation? How do you know you're on His path? We can't live the life God has made us for without His word, the Bible. He's made that clear. But we can't live the life God's made us for with only the Bible. Of course His word is true since He is the Truth. But Jesus says something surprising here to His friends. He says it's not the Bible that will lead us to the truth, but the Holy Spirit.

Remember the wilderness? The enemy lies, but he also misapplies. He quoted scripture at Jesus, wrongly applying Psalm 91 to His situation. He said, 'Go on, jump. The angels will look after you.' If Jesus had thought to Himself, 'Well it's in the Bible so it's what I should do now', He'd have disobeyed the Father and destroyed His destiny. He didn't. He relied on the Holy Spirit to lead Him to the truth for that moment. 'Don't put God to the test' was the scripture He was led to. We need both scripture *and* the Spirit to hear God. To get free and stay free.

You have the Holy Spirit living within you, friend. But to hear Him, you must lend Him your ear. If you want to know God's way for you and will for you in any situation, you have to ask the Spirit of truth to speak to you. He won't control you and He won't compete with other voices. My experience is that when I ask Him, He'll show me (most often from His word) what I should do. Either He'll bring a verse to mind, or one will stand out to me as I read my Bible. It may not happen immediately depending on the situation. Sometimes He waits to see if I'll wait for Him to speak (I'm quite impatient!) before I act. Only the Holy Spirit can lead us into truth. No matter how much we know or understand, we can't find it on our own.

PONDER
What is your relationship with the Holy Spirit like? How often do you ask Him to lead you to what's true, or to show you what to think or do in any given situation?

PRAY
Thank the Holy Spirit that He's able to lead you into the truth. Reaffirm your trust in Him to do so. Ask Him to show you the truth about a particular situation in your life at the moment.

READ: John 8:31-42
You will know the truth, and the truth will set you free. (CEV)

Jesus wants us free. Free to live in His love and free to love. Free to be all we were designed to be. Freedom is fantastic but it comes at a cost. Jesus paid the highest price at Calvary. But there's a price for us too: to face certain truths about ourselves and about His kingdom. Sometimes that truth is troubling. A few years ago, doctors diagnosed a malignant lump in my left breast. It wasn't what I wanted to hear. But if they'd kept it quiet to keep me happy, who knows where I might be now.

Not everyone wants to face the truth. It can be painful, although not as painful as the consequences of ignoring it! The people listening to Jesus didn't value truth. Their own needs and desires controlled them, so they were on their way to an eternity without Him. Jesus told them, 'You want to get rid of Me because I'm telling you the truth' (v40). They were offended, even though He wanted to help them. Did I get offended at my doctors because they told me something I didn't want to hear? Duh!

Do you want to see a breakthrough in an area of your life? Maybe Jesus needs to tell you the truth; that there's bitterness in your heart, that self pity is suffocating you, that disobedience is disempowering you, or that unbelief is holding you back. He will confront our unbelief, our disobedience or our fear, as well as confirm our identity as His treasured daughters. If we want freeing by the Truth, we have to face the truth. And sometimes that crashes into our pride. I'm personally so glad He's willing to be honest with me; through His word and through others. But I have to make sure offence doesn't block my ears. If it does, I stay in my trap. Minimising what He confronts me with, excusing it or blaming others stop the truth from helping me. Friend, remember Jesus is like a good doctor. What He tells us is *always* for our good, however painful it may be.

PONDER
Reality check: on a scale of 1-10, how easily offended are you? Do you actively invite Jesus to speak truth to you? Even if He uses others as His mouthpiece? If not, do you know why not?

PRAY
Ask the Holy Spirit to show you if there's something true He's spoken to you that you're not paying attention to. Talk to Him about anything He brings to mind.

READ: John 18:33-40, 3 John 1:1-4

Jesus' friend John wrote both of these passages. Knowing Jesus as the Truth was obviously very important to him. In the second passage, he refers to believers 'walking in the truth' twice and connects it to the health of their souls (v2).

PUSH IN

Pilate says to Jesus in John 18:38, 'What is truth?' John's encouragement raises the question, 'How do we walk in truth?'
How would you answer if one of your family members, friends or colleagues asked you either of these questions? What would you say, looking back on this week?

READ: Colossians 2:1-8

In these verses, Paul mentions his concern that the believers he's writing to in Colossae could end up being deceived. Twice. The same was true of John yesterday. Perhaps there's a theme here...

PUSH IN

– If truth is the antidote to deception, and these believers knew the Truth, why do you think it was possible that they could be deceived?

– Do you take it seriously that the enemy wants to deceive you too? Why do you think that is?

– If you had to identify 'fine-sounding arguments' and 'hollow and deceptive philosophies' that might deceive believers today, what would they be?

– How would you know if you were deceived?

– Does anything else in these verses catch your attention?

– Note down anything you want to remember.

Pray about anything this passage raises for you. Thank Jesus that He is the Truth and ask the Spirit of Truth to lead you into all truth today.

READ: 1 Corinthians 6:18-20
Don't you realise that your body is the temple of the Holy Spirit who lives in you and was given to you by God? (NLT)

Pause a moment and look at your hands. Look at your feet. How are they looking today? Take a look at your legs, your arms, and look down at your chest. Look at any other part of your body that you can see right now. You're looking at God's temple, isn't that extraordinary? You're looking at where the King of Heaven has made His home. In you. Because of Jesus' work on the cross. Let that blow your mind a bit!

Paul was against any kind of mistreatment of the body and was strong in his advice to us as followers of Jesus to treat our bodies as the residence of the Holy Spirit. To avoid things like sexual immorality, overeating, drinking too much and more. As he says in this passage, 'You do not belong to yourself.' In other words, my body now belongs to Jesus and because He lives in me, I am His. I am now His home. I am now a temple. So are you. When the Holy Spirit came to live in you, you didn't become a better version of you, you became a new you. He moved in, and His presence in you changes everything.

If your body is His home, how are you taking care of it? Do you take His instruction to honour it, seriously? Do you love and care for it, controlling it and using it in the way He desires? He wants the best for you and has plans and purposes for you. Being a temple of His, carrying His presence has all kinds of incredible implications, but they're connected to the way you treat your body. Instead of telling the Corinthian believers this, Paul asks them a rhetorical question: 'Do you realise your bodies are now temples?' They clearly didn't. So they were experiencing confusion and defeat in their lives. They weren't living out of their true identity. Friend, you host the Holy Spirit. You are a temple. Do you realise it?

PONDER
Take a deep breath, be still for a moment and 'realise' again that *you* are a temple of the Holy Spirit. Let that truth about who you are sink in again today.

PRAY
Put your hand on your heart and thank the Holy Spirit that He lives in you. Ask Him to show you if there is anything He wants you to do differently, to take better care of His temple.

READ: John 14:15-21
**...you know Him already because He has been staying with you,
and will even be *in* you!** (MSG)

When did you last give someone your address? It's something I seem to have to recite or fill out regularly. The Holy Spirit gives your heart as His address. On the day of Pentecost, God fulfilled His plan to make sure He could live in each of His children. The Holy Spirit came down to earth as a person to fill each heart where the door was opened and He was welcomed in. He's done so ever since and is still doing so today.

When visitors come to my home, I tend to clear up. I put things away, vacuum the carpets, put better food in the fridge and shove the stuff I haven't got time to sort somewhere hidden! It's generally a bit of a rush. We can think we need to do the same for God. Clean ourselves up and sort ourselves out so we can meet with Him and pursue relationship with Him. But it doesn't work like that. The Holy Spirit isn't a visitor, so He doesn't need us to clean up for Him. He's a resident. He hasn't come to visit, He's come to stay. When we opened our heart to Him, He moved in regardless of the state of the home we were offering Him. He's good with mess; remember He was born in a stable? Nothing puts Him off.

Once He's moved in, He gets to work. He brings order and beauty to the house of our heart, clearing and cleaning up, getting rid of rubbish and renovating, rebuilding and redecorating where it's needed. He's a high calibre interior designer, and it's His home after all! Sometimes that work is exciting, sometimes it's excruciating and sometimes it's somewhere in between. But when He's at work, it's always for our benefit. Which part of the house of your heart is He working in right now? What would you like Him to do? Like any craftsman, the more permission He has, the more He can accomplish. Why not surrender to Him again today?

PAUSE

Think back to when you first opened the door to Jesus and invited Him in. Thank Him that He doesn't leave you to do the 'housework' on your own, but that He takes the lead. Is anywhere out of bounds for Him? Ask His forgiveness if you've lived as if 'clearing and cleaning up' is your responsibility. Identify something specific He's done and thank Him for it.

READ: Romans 8:11-16
The Spirit of God, who raised Jesus from the dead, lives in you. (NLT)

How would you feel if your favourite celebrity or heroine decided they wanted to move in with you? I imagine you'd think it was pretty cool. How incredible is it then to have the Eternal and All-Powerful One living inside you? He couldn't come any closer and the fact He's chosen your heart as His home is proof of the intimate relationship He wants with you. The Holy Spirit makes what He touches holy, so His presence in you is also proof you've been forgiven and made new. You are holy and you are deeply loved. Take a moment to let that sink in again.

Some have turned following Jesus into a process of learning lots of principles and formulas to ensure we do life His way. Principles can be really helpful. But Paul says here that the Holy Spirit is in us to lead us into life through our relationship with Him. Not by handing us rules. It's the difference between using Google maps to get to your destination, or having a great passenger in the car with you who knows the way. We have access to Jesus and He has access to us as if He were physically by our side. Being led through life by the Holy Spirit (v14) results from a close relationship with Him.

Each day we have a choice: to live led by our old ways and habits (v 12) which we don't have to anymore, or to live led by the Spirit. The more we know Him, pay attention to Him, enjoy Him, learn how He works and listen to His voice, the more we're led by Him. The Holy Spirit continually reminds us who we are and that we belong to the Father (v16). He has so much to say to us and show us. Let's make it our goal to grow our relationship with Him. Let's become increasingly aware of His presence in us, and all the potential for life that He brings.

PAUSE
Why not set a few alarms on your phone to go off at certain times today. Each time one goes off, stop what you're doing for 3 minutes, take a deep breath, be still and turn your thoughts to the Holy Spirit living in you. Ask Him to make you more sensitive to His presence and ask Him to help you get to know Him better.

READ: Galatians 5:16-25
But the Holy Spirit produces this kind of fruit in our lives: love, joy, peace, patience, kindness, goodness, faithfulness, gentleness, and self-control. (NLT)

Every day is full of opportunities. Many things bid for our time, attention and energy. But wherever we have to go and whoever we have to see, each day offers us chance after chance to meet with Jesus. To love Him, learn from Him and do life with Him. Because He is in us. Fullness of life flows from the heart. Because He's in our heart, we hear the Holy Spirit speaking within us. He fills our heart with His peace and He heals and frees it. He directs our heart and shapes it with His love. Life as a follower of Jesus is a life lived from the inside out, because the inside is where He's chosen to live.

When I read this list of fruit that His activity in my heart produces, it makes me drool! I want more of all of those. (My family and friends want me to have more too!). But none of these characteristics are produced by trying hard. If you've tried, like me, to change a habit, or have a go with some new resolutions, you'll know they last for a bit but rarely for long. The great news is that the Holy Spirit has been tasked with producing this in us Himself. An increase in our joy, a growing peace, a greater kindness, the ability to control our fear rather than letting it control us. They are all the results of inviting the Holy Spirit into the everyday moments of our every day and doing them with Him, rather than without Him.

We don't have to hide anything from Him. We can't. He is in us. He expects us to ask Him for the power, grace and strength we need because Heaven is within us. He expects us to expect Him to speak to us during the day. Invite Him to show up in unexpected moments, as He did with the disciples. Tell Him your desires, share your thoughts and feelings, and listen for His. Listen to the internal promptings that come when you whisper a prayer or turn your thoughts to Him. Do your day with Him. He is in you. Always.

PRAY

Lord Jesus, I want to do life today with You not without You. I give you my life today and ask You to teach me to live today Your way. Help me to listen for Your voice, help me to notice Your presence. Help me to remember to share my moments with You, especially the highs and the lows. Thank You that You are in me, and that I have access to You and You have access to me.

READ: John 2:13-21
But when Jesus said 'this temple,' He meant His own body. (NLT)

Jesus messed with people's heads in various ways, and when He began to talk about the temple, it was no different. Up until He appeared, God's children had to go to the physical temple to meet with Him. The temple building was the place where Heaven touched earth. His presence was accessible to believers, but only in a certain way, in a certain place. Because of the problem of sin. In this passage, when Jesus talks about the temple, the people naturally assume He's referring to the building. But He isn't. He's talking about Himself.

Don't we all love an upgrade? Jesus introduced an upgrade on the physical temple. Because He was free from sin, He could be full of the presence of God. Therefore, He was the 'place' where people could meet with God. The temple got legs. Wherever He went, ordinary men and women were powerfully touched and met with the Father through Him. You are now a pop-up temple. Of the Holy Spirit. You also carry around the presence and life of Jesus inside you because the Holy Spirit is in you. That means you're a 'place' where others can encounter Him. People need an encounter with God. You are the answer. Jesus wants to speak to people and touch them with His love and power. Through you.

This is our assignment as it was Jesus' assignment; to be a 'place' of encounter for the person in front of us. For this to be a reality, we have to believe it. You need to say about yourself, 'I have a spirit of power, I have a spirit of love and I have a disciplined mind' (2 Tim 1:7). When you believe you're a temple, you believe Jesus wants others to meet Him through you. You expect Him to set up divine appointments and assignments for you. And you ask Him to open your eyes to them. You don't need special qualifications, only the presence of the Special One within you.

PONDER
Have you ever thought of yourself as a 'place' where others can have an encounter with Jesus? Declare: 'I have a spirit of power, I have a spirit of love and I have a disciplined mind.'

PRAY
Talk to the Holy Spirit about what this raises for you. Ask Him to open your eyes to the appointments He has set up for you today.

RE-VISIT: Day 2

PUSH IN

Imagine your heart as a home. Ask the Holy Spirit to show you what work He wants to do, or is doing in it at the moment. You might want to ask Him if there's a particular room He wants to work in, any cupboards He wants to clear out, any extension He wants to build or anything else. Offer Him your imagination and ask Him to speak to you specifically.

Then ask Him to show you how He wants you to work with Him and what He wants you to do.

RE-READ: 1 Corinthians 6:19-20

Have you forgotten that your body is now the sacred temple of the Spirit of Holiness who lives in you? You don't belong to yourself any longer, for the gift of God, the Holy Spirit, lives inside your sanctuary. You were God's expensive purchase, paid for with tears of blood, so by all means, then, use your body to bring glory to God! (TPT)

PUSH IN

Read these two verses through a couple of times, slowly. Hear Paul speaking them to you. Spend a few moments thinking about them and ask the Holy Spirit what He wants to say to you today through them.

Then jot down what He says, and the other things He's been saying to you this week about being His temple. Try and be as specific as you can.

READ: 1 Peter 1:3-9
Your faith...is being tested as fire tests gold and purifies it... (NLT)

The tough stuff in your life may squeeze you, but it's not meant to squash you. In God's hands, it's never intended to stifle you but to strengthen you. The Father wants to enlarge our hearts, expand our relationship with Him and extend our influence for Him. But sometimes He does so by using the tough circumstances in our lives instead of changing them as quickly as we'd like.

God says He's a refiner. A refiner is committed to purifying something. He removes the stuff that reduces the quality and value of whatever He's refining. What does God refine? Our faith. Our willingness to trust Him. Our confidence in His love and our conviction He's always working for our good, especially when what's going on around us could make us question it. Questioning is not wrong, but confidence in Him is better. Confidence in Him releases life in us and life through us.

These verses say our faith is more precious than gold (v7). Have you ever thought about your faith like that? Gold is a highly expensive metal, worth masses all over the world. It's retained its value over time, unlike many other things, partly because it's impossible to destroy. You are worth so much to the Father that Jesus paid the highest price for you. But your faith, your capacity to trust the Father in every situation, is also extremely valuable to Him. Our confidence in who He is, and what we can't see yet, is more precious than the priciest gold because it defines our relationship with Him.

Fire is what refines gold; trials and troubles are the 'fire' that God uses (not causes) to refine our trust. Gold emerges from fire stronger and more valuable, and God intends the same for us. He intends for us to emerge stronger from the heat of hardship. If you're facing trials or troubles right now, remember that the Father is using them. To increase your faith and strengthen your heart. Surrender to His work in you again today.

PONDER
Why do you think your capacity to trust God in all situations is so valuable to Him?

PRAY
Put your hand on your heart and invite Him to increase your faith so you experience more of Him.

READ: Malachi 3:3-4
He will sit as a refiner and purifier of silver...

Have you ever asked, 'God, where are You?' or, 'God, where were You?' or, 'God, why did You abandon me?' If you have, as I have, then be reassured that we're joined by almost everyone who has ever chosen to follow Jesus. Even Jesus asked this same question as He hung on the cross. The 'fire' of trials and trouble has a habit of causing us to conclude the Father has packed His bags and left us to it.

Malachi says God 'sits as a refiner.' In ancient times, a refiner sat by a fire. He put his gold or silver into a crucible and put the crucible into the fire. He'd watch the metal melt and the impurities in it rise to the surface as the heat increased. With great skill and patience, he then skimmed off that dross and repeated the process. The more dross he removed, the more valuable and strong the metal became. But it was a slow process.

What's in us comes out of us in the fire. Trials and troubles don't cause us to become someone we're not, or to behave in a way that's 'not me!' They produce heat on our hearts which causes the dross in us to rise to the surface. We can see it in our thinking, our reactions and our speech. Have you noticed how our fears and insecurities, our doubts and dependencies become more obvious when we're under pressure? Our unhealthy desires or motives, our wrong beliefs or wrong attitudes are suddenly visible to us, and often to others! The Father wants to deal with this dross, and He gives us a choice in this moment of opportunity: do we suppress it, excuse it, and blame it on the fire? Or do we take note of it, own it and invite Him to deal with it?

The refiner 'sits' because he can't leave the crucible for one moment. He controls the temperature and the time while the metal's in the fire. Otherwise the process would fail. The refiner takes great care with his gold, and the Father takes great care with you.

PONDER
What are you struggling with at the moment? Is it impacting your relationship with the Father?

PRAY
Be still before God. Ask the Holy Spirit to show you what He is wanting to teach you in your struggle. Ask Him to help you respond in obedience to His gentle promptings.

READ: Psalm 66:8-20
He trained us first, passed us like silver through refining fires. (MSG)

A few years ago, God encouraged a friend of mine to host a conference in Addis Ababa. To gather, encourage and equip women from across the nation. Fortunately, she invited some friends to join her! Twelve of us, who knew her but not each other, flew in from six different nations. We spent an amazing week with each other and the beautiful women of Ethiopia. And God moved powerfully.

The women on the team inspired me; many possessed a gentle strength and a radiant beauty that shone from a deep confidence in God. It was obvious in their words and their faces. Every one had stories from the fire. Life had assaulted each heart, but the Father had also attended to every one. He had tenderly and skilfully replaced ashes with beauty, mourning with dancing and despair with hope. They'd let the Refiner do His work in them. They each had a bigger heart, a deeper compassion, and made a greater impact on other lives as a result. Treasure had replaced tears. Trouble hadn't defined them, it had refined them.

We'll only let Jesus tend to your heart in the fire if we trust Him. Often, the fire comes as deep pain. If we believe He wants us in pain or doesn't care about our pain, we misunderstand Him. Pain is not His plan for us. Remember, there will be no pain in Heaven, and Jesus wept with others as He saw their pain. Pain is the product of a broken world, not the plan of a perfect Father. But He redeems pain. He promises to use it for our good. The Refiner will let nothing in this life, however awful, be wasted. If we trust Him. He wants to put it to work for our benefit. But we have to open up our hearts to Him and let Him meet us in the fire.

PONDER
Think about the time when Jesus wept as He stood by Lazarus' tomb. What does that tell you about His heart for people in pain? Can you think of a time when He has used pain for your good?

PRAY
Ask God to give you a bigger heart, a deeper compassion and to increase your impact as a result of every painful situation that you face. Thank Him that He doesn't waste anything.

READ: Isaiah 43:1-5(a)
When you walk through fire, you will not be burned, nor will the flames hurt you. (NLT)

Sometimes you have to go through stuff to grow. A story we had to read endlessly (and act out) to our kids was, 'We're Going On A Bear Hunt.' It's about a family hunting a bear (no surprise). On their journey they face many challenges, including a forest, a river, a storm and some thick mud. Each time they're confronted by one, they say to each other, 'We can't go over it, we can't go under it. Oh no – we've got to go through it.'

God says to us, 'When you walk through fire', not 'if'. It's a certainty, so let's not forget it. Sometimes He lets us go through fire instead of taking us round it, over it, under it or putting it out altogether. Why would He do that? Because He's promised it won't burn us. The flames won't hurt us. Hard as this is, I've had to accept that there are times when the Father knows fire is more beneficial for me than no fire. What He does *in* us is more important than what happens *to* us. The enemy wants us to believe that fire will destroy us, or that it proves God isn't good. But since He's a Refiner, God promises that fire can put power into our spiritual lives. It won't destroy us, but it will destroy what's in us that holds us back.

If the heat is on and you're going through it, keep going friend. It will pass. You may not see what your trials are accomplishing, but one day you will. I know my faith has grown most through fire. I'm learning to expect that whatever happens to me, the Father will use it to release blessing in me. I'm learning to look for what He is doing, not at what's happening; for what is going on inside me, not at what is going on around me. Moments can change our lives, but only God can change our hearts. Fire will not harm you and it won't hurt your future if you trust Him. He promises He's watching over you. Press in to that today.

PONDER
Speak this verse over yourself three times. Try putting the emphasis on a different word each time. What stands out to you the most?

PRAY
Ask God to bless someone you know who is going through the fire at the moment. Pray for them as you feel led. Why not contact them today to encourage them?

READ: Acts 16:19-25

About midnight, Paul and Silas were praying and singing hymns to God...

Have you noticed how when the heat is on, it's easier to focus on the flames than the Father. To question His goodness rather than depend on His grace. To feel His distance rather than know His presence? How can we stay connected and close to Him when the pressure's on?

There are many ways to go through tough stuff. Kicking, screaming, complaining, despairing, doubting, or fearing are natural ways to choose. Paul's recommendation to the Thessalonians is supernatural, but today's verses show him living it out while he's in the fire. He says, 'Rejoice always, pray continually and give thanks in *all* circumstances for this is God's will for you' (1 Thess 5:17-18). Why is it God's will for us when we're going through fire? Because praying, and giving thanks especially, do three things:

1. They connect us to His presence. The Bible says thanking God is like a doorway into His presence. Friend, He never leaves us, but a sense of His nearness does when we focus on the flames. When we decide to thank Him not *for*, but *despite* what's going on, we draw closer to Him. As we do, we become more aware of Him with us.

2. They connect us to His promises. Thanking God is like switching on a torch at night. It helps us see the things He's promised and the things He's already done. These can get lost in the fire.

3. They connect us to His power. Psalm 50 says a sacrifice of thanks (which is what it is when we don't *feel* like being thankful) opens the way for God to move; in our hearts *and* in our situations.

'Pray continually' is an encouragement to be honest about our present reality. 'Give thanks' is an encouragement to trust in His bigger reality for us. It's an act of faith that helps us focus on the Father, not the flames. It's not a natural choice to make, but the one that keeps us open to His supernatural grace. Don't you need that in the fire? I know I do!

PRAY

Spend some time thanking the Father. Thank Him for things He's done for you, for what He's promised you and for who He is to you.

READ: Luke 24:1-11

As two of Jesus' friends walked down the road to Emmaus on that first Easter morning, they were completely unaware He was with them. I'm sure it was the 'fire' of what had been going on a few days earlier that had prevented them from recognising His presence with them. They were distraught, confused, afraid and probably disillusioned. Jesus had to open their eyes so they could see Him in their midst.

PUSH IN

Pick a situation that's going on in your life right now. Perhaps it's one you've been talking to a friend about like these guys did. Imagine Jesus sitting with you now as you chat. Ask Him where He is in your situation, what He wants to say to you and what He wants to show you.

Write down anything He says to you.

RE-VISIT: Day 2

PUSH IN

Grab some paper or use the space below. Make a list of some of the 'dross' that comes up in your heart when you're under pressure or in a 'hot' situation. The following may help you to identify it:

- Where do you turn for comfort?
- What habits do you resort to?
- What kind of thing comes out of your mouth?
- What feelings surface in your heart?
- What assumptions do you make about God?
- What assumptions do you make about yourself?

Talk to God about what becomes visible when you're stressed. Own it, don't excuse it. Confess it without explaining it away, acknowledging it's in you. Thank Him that He's forgiven you, that He's committed to blessing your heart and invite Him to 'skim' off the dross. Ask Him what He wants to get hold of and how He wants to do it. Ask Him what truth He wants to remind you of today.

READ: Matthew 5:13-16
You are the salt of the earth.

Every time I put a meal on the table and serve the food onto the plates, the first thing my family does is reach for the salt. It doesn't matter what I've prepared, how amazing it looks, or how good I think it'll taste, one by one they go for the salt. For them, it makes all the difference.

As God's daughter, you're the salt of the earth. You are the seasoning the world needs. All over the globe, salt is used for all kinds of things. It adds flavour to food and effectiveness to cleaning products. It protects roads from icing over and meat from going off. It's not like saffron that's fairly rare and rarely used, or like sugar that wrecks teeth and waistlines. It has an edge to it. Salt is powerful and necessary. History records wars that have been fought over it! We could say a lot about salt, but its most important feature is: it makes a difference. It's valuable because it's essential, bringing transformation wherever it's scattered.

Jesus says, 'You are the salt of the earth.' Not, 'You might be salt one day when you're more together.' Or, 'You would have been salt if you'd lived a different life.' You are salt. Today. You have influence. You are a difference maker. Most people think influence is reserved for the elite or the experienced, for the famous or those with tons of followers. But in God's kingdom, those who make the difference He'd make are those who walk with Him, empowered by His Spirit. The only thing we need is His presence in us. Jesus doesn't tell us how to become salt, he warns us to beware of losing our flavour (which means it's possible). Over the coming days, we'll look at how that can happen. But the first way is by forgetting who we are. According to Jesus, you, friend, are what the world needs. He's appointed you to be a difference maker. Remember that today. Wherever you go, bring life to those He puts in front of you.

PONDER
Spend a few moments reflecting on this verse. Hear Jesus say it to you. Think about the transformation He has called you to bring to the lives around you as you walk with Him.

PRAY
Ask the Holy Spirit to show you the plans He has for you today. Ask Him to show you how you are to be salt.

READ: Matthew 14:13-21
'We have here only five loaves of bread and two fish,' they answered.

Salt is small. A few small grains on a big piece of steak, and somehow it makes a disproportionate difference to how the meat tastes. Jesus chose his words carefully and deliberately. And what salt tells us is we don't need to be bigwigs to make a big difference. It's not us that brings the 'big' to the table, but Him. I love that! He does the multiplying.

The young boy who had those five pieces of bread and two bits of fish in his bag that morning had no idea he'd impact so many stomachs that day. He made an extraordinary difference with a small contribution because in the hands of Jesus, small contributions become super-sized. We're told, 'Don't despise the small things' (Zech 4:10). Why? Because our human perspective can write off what Heaven wants to do. A human perspective says, 'What difference will a small picnic make?' (v 17).

No matter how small or insignificant you may feel, or how little you think you have to offer, God has set you up: to be the difference in the lives around you and the world He's put you in. Not by being big, or having a big plan, but by being big-hearted enough to offer what you have and who you are. Big dreams begin with small picnics. Your picnic may look like a word of hope, a spare room, a financial gift or an act of kindness. It may be praying a prayer, offering your skill set, lending a hand or taking a small risk. He'll do the rest. You don't know where He'll lead you, friend, but don't despise small because you'd prefer spectacular. Small is the Father's raw material. When we despise small things and small beginnings, we miss out on the 'big' God wants to add to them. We miss the difference they'll make and where they'll lead. Give what you've got and expect Jesus to multiply it.

PONDER
What do you have in your hand? What is the equivalent of your picnic that you could overlook or despise because it seems too small to make a difference?

PRAY
Thank Jesus that He's called you as a difference maker. Ask Him to help you take small things seriously, but also to increase your expectation that He will multiply what you offer.

READ: 1 Samuel 17:32-37
I have done this to both lions and bears... (TLB)

We all go through dry seasons spiritually. Times when we feel hidden, when no one really knows what we're going through or seems to care. Times when we feel nothing is happening. Times when God feels distant, as if He's gone for a walk on His own! It may be connected to our circumstances, or it may not be. We may feel it in our place of work or our home, our church or our relationships. Or we may just feel it in our heart. But alone is how we feel. Dry. Disorientated. And invisible.

If the psalms are a window into David's soul, he was no different. He too experienced spiritually dry times even though he was a difference maker and a history maker. The two are connected. The way David lived in the hidden place prepared him for greater influence in the public space. We love the triumphant moment David's small stone slayed a super-sized Goliath, but it did so because of all the times he'd practised on the lion and the bear. He'd worked and walked with God when no one was watching. Taking care of his father's sheep was a lonely, unrewarding existence. But he made a difference where he was, to his sheep, and took on their predators. Later, he made a difference to a nation.

God knows you and He knows where to find you, as He did with David. Stay there! The temptation in the hidden place is to short-circuit the process He's using to prepare us for the next public space. Difference makers don't try and escape the dry place for a more comfortable space. They submit to His work and let Him have His way. David learned to throw stones, look after sheep and submit to his Heavenly Father when no one was watching. He was ready when the moment arrived where everyone was watching. If you feel like you're out on a hillside or in a hidden place, trust God and His timing for your life. And get good at throwing stones.

PONDER
Do you trust God knows you and knows where you are? What bears and lions are you learning to deal with right now?

PRAY
Spend time praising the Father who sees you, knows you and has a plan for you.

READ: Mark 12:41-44
Then He saw a poor widow put in two pennies. (MSG)

Don't listen to the whispers of the culture that say we're defined by what we own and what we've achieved. Your worth, friend, is not determined by how many followers you have or how you look. Status doesn't reflect significance. Let me remind you again today this is not kingdom truth. In years to come, future generations will be unaffected by the effort you put in to your appearance (even on social media), by what you accumulated, or by what you achieved. They will be more impacted by what you gave.

We can lose our saltiness when we forget that legacy is determined more by the level of our sacrifice than the level of our achievement. I know, sacrifice isn't a popular word. But it's a powerful one. Different people gave different sums of money that day. The woman Jesus spotlighted, to inspire millions to generosity for thousands of years to come, gave the least in money terms. But she gave the most sacrificially. Her two pennies really cost her. Difference makers are givers, not takers.

Sacrifices come in all shapes and sizes. From staying at home to care for a family member, to talking to the person that no one is talking to (when you'd rather talk to someone else!). From giving up a picnic and going hungry, to giving up your home and moving overseas. From spending time with Jesus when you've got too much to do, to staying single when you don't have God's peace about a relationship. From speaking up when you're afraid, to staying silent when you'd rather say your bit. Sacrifice, however big or small, is the flavour of the kingdom and its a magnet for the favour of God. It attracts Heaven's multiplication factor. It doesn't flow from duty but from desire, because it's motivated by love. That's why He sacrificed His life for you. Because He loves you.

PONDER
Is there something you're doing at the moment that you find hard, but you're doing it because you love Jesus?

PRAY
Talk to Him about it. Let Him remind you that you're making a difference in eternity because of what it's costing you. Ask Him for strength to keep going.

READ: John 12:42-43

When push came to shove they cared more for human approval than for God's glory. (MSG)

Approval is a powerful thing. It makes us feel valued and accepted and contributes to our sense of well-being. We need it because we don't want to be rejected, and rejection comes with disapproval. But our need for approval can become a roadblock to the plans and purposes of the Father, depending on where we look for it. We find approval in two places; other people and Jesus. When we want to please others more than we want to please Jesus, we compromise our ability to make a difference.

If Noah cared most about the approval of his friends, he wouldn't have built an ark. If Esther cared most about the approval of the king, she wouldn't have saved a nation. If David cared most about the approval of his brothers, he wouldn't have taken on Goliath. If Mary cared most about the approval of her family, she wouldn't have carried the Messiah. If Jesus cared most about the approval of men, He wouldn't have been crucified. They all cared more about pleasing God. In this little passage, many leaders believed in Jesus. But they didn't make a difference with their lives because they lived for the affirmation of others.

Friend, let's acknowledge the fear of rejection or ridicule is powerful. If we give in to it, it will derail our potential as difference makers. It silences us about our faith, stops us from standing up for what matters to Him, and prevents us saying yes to Him when we might look foolish. There will always be people (and an enemy) who have other agendas for us but we are not called to make them happy. So let's not spend our days trying to do so. Please Jesus. That's where overcoming the fear of man begins. Live for the Father's 'well done', and you'll live as a difference maker.

PONDER
Can you think of a time when you could have stood up for your faith, or what is right? How did your desire for approval influence your response?

PRAY
Ask Jesus to grow your desire to please Him and to give you courage to face the disapproval of others.

READ: Matthew 5:3-11

To make a difference we have to *be* different. The world wants to keep us shaped into its mould. Jesus is shaping us into His. He says being shaped into His mould will cause us a bit of trouble (v11), but otherwise, salt loses its flavour.

PUSH IN
– List the qualities in this passage that describe difference makers (they precede His comments about salt).

– Review the list: are there any qualities that surprise you?

– What would you have put on the list that isn't there?

– Identify which quality you'd like to see more of in your own life and ask Jesus to grow it in you. Ask Him if there is anything He wants you to do.

PUSH IN

– Declare this over yourself: 'I am a difference maker because I am the salt of the world.'

– Summarise what you sense the Holy Spirit has been saying to you this week about being a difference maker.

READ: Zephaniah 3:16-17
The Lord your God is with you, the Mighty Warrior who saves.

'Why don't you pray him out?' That was the suggestion made to a friend who confided in someone about her tricky boss. The boss was a difficult character and proving challenging to work for. But he didn't look like he'd be going anywhere anytime soon as he'd been at the company for 12 years. So my friend prayed; that God would move him on somewhere else. A few months later, he left the company for a better job!

God is our loving Father who's neither distant nor disinterested in our daily battles. He's not unmoved and unresponsive like an uncaring acquaintance. Quite the opposite – He's a warrior and a mighty one at that! And He loves to use His strength for our good, in big ways and small. My friend experienced this in a minor but fresh way when God fought for her in her workplace. Instead of turning her boss into her enemy (as someone to fight) for making her life difficult, she turned to the Warrior to fight for her instead. She prayed, and continued to do her best for the guy in charge. In turning to God, she discovered He could bring about an outcome that was good for everyone.

Turning to God to fight for us is so often a last resort not a first resort, have you noticed that? Perhaps we don't believe He'll fight for us, or we think we'll do better job. But the Bible says God is with us, and He's a warrior who wants to contend for us. Prayer is the way we let go so He can have a go. Whatever battles you're up against, whether they're internal or external ones, remember the Father is bigger than those battles. Trust Him to fight them for you and resist taking matters into your own hands. Instead, put them into His. On your knees. Keep loving those around you and let Him amaze you, like He did my friend, with what He does for you.

PONDER
Do you tend to see the Father as distant and disinterested when it comes to your battles? Or do you see Him as present and proactive, wanting to intervene on your behalf?

PRAY
Hear the Holy Spirit speak the words above to your heart. Confess any lie you've believed about His desire to fight for you and thank Him that this promise is true for you in every situation.

READ: Exodus 14:10-14
The Lord Himself will fight for you. Just stay calm. (NLT)

Peace or panic? That's the choice we face whenever we face pressure that overwhelms us. In this story, as the pressure builds and the Egyptians approach, the Israelites choose panic. Their panic comes because they're not confident the Father will fight for them. They turn on Moses and blame him for their scenario (blame is a close relative of panic) believing God is going to let them die. Why didn't they assume He would look after them as He had done before? Why did they assume He'd leave them to fend for themselves and suffer the consequences?

Moses tells them to chill out because God will rise up and fight for them. In the next chapter, on the other side of the Red Sea, they're singing about it. God asks us to trust He'll fight for us no matter what we're facing. If I'd been there, I might have told Moses, 'Your suggestion that everyone stays calm with a powerful army hot on their heels is a tad unrealistic'. But the Father expects a supernatural response from a simple people who have a supernatural God on their side.

When we believe God will fight for us, fretting fades. When I feel my heart-rate rising or I wake up in the middle of the night panicking, I try to remind myself I have a choice: to remember my Father is a Warrior who's promised to come through for me, or to assume He won't. The battle with the thing I'm panicking about is His battle. The battle to trust He'll fight it is mine. Peace is not an easy choice to make when we're under pressure. But let's be more determined to fight for it, friend. Why give in to panic when He says we have power to choose peace? Remember the Warrior of Heaven is on your side. Whatever your pressure points, when panic is stirred up, learn to wield this promise as a powerful weapon. It's designed to protect your peace and protect others from your panic!

PONDER
What makes you panic and what happens when you do? What behaviour comes next? What difference would believing God will fight for you make? Learn this verse.

PRAY
Ask the Holy Spirit to grow your confidence in this promise and the heart of Jesus to fight for you, so you can live in His peace and stay calm.

READ: Judges 7:2-15
You have too large an army with you, I can't turn Midian over to them like this – they'll take all the credit... (MSG)

If God Himself is a warrior and fights for us, what do we do? Do we put up our feet and put on a box set until He calls us to let us know He's done? Obviously, the Father doesn't work like that! The Israelites had been crying out for Him to free them from the Midianites who were oppressing them. Although God is a Warrior and had promised to do so, He works with human warriors. So He called Gideon to join the battle. Gideon had to turn off the box set and play his part.

There are different battles to fight. It might be fighting temptation, a toxic mindset, or fear. It might be fighting for a marriage, for your faith, for justice, for freedom or for a breakthrough. Whatever it is, God calls you a warrior and He calls you to fight. But He also says, 'I'll fight for you.' It's a partnership. The battles He's called us to fight and win are ones we could never get victory in without His help. He wants to give us ground for His kingdom. He has big expectations of what we can do with Him, and what He can do with us. Any time we assess our ability, our resources and our plans and expect to succeed, our battle isn't big enough. And it's therefore unlikely to be one He's called us to fight.

Not only did Gideon think he couldn't defeat the Midianites, God told him his army was too big. He asked him to go into battle against 135,000 men with only 300 of his own. Why? Because the battle needed to be fought the Father's way. And His way is rarely with human strength. God's battles aren't won with clever words or cunning strategies, or with any other strength or power we can muster up. If you're fighting and you're exhausted or you don't seem to be seeing much change, perhaps you need to come to the Father. Ask Him how He's asking you to play your part, so He can play His bigger part.

PONDER
Is there a battle that you're fighting at the moment that you need to invite Jesus into again?

PRAY
Ask Him what He wants you to do so He can fight for you. Surrender the battle to Him.

READ: 2 Chronicles 20:1-4, 14-22
You won't need to fight in this battle. Just stand strong in your places, and you will see the Lord save you. (NCV)

There will always be problems, and there will always be battles. Jesus made sure we knew that when He said we'd have trouble in this world. But He went on to say He'd overcome the trouble. In other words, trouble is no longer the last word. If we trust Jesus as a Warrior, it shows up in our response to trouble. Jehoshaphat was afraid because of the news he'd just heard, but instead of doing a runner in fear, He ran to God for help (v3). He knew He was a Warrior and would want to fight for them.

As Jehoshaphat prayed, the strategy God gave him was to be still. But it wasn't a 'do nothing' stillness. They needed to face their enemy, but at the same time trust that God was moving (v20). Jehoshaphat went on to remind the people that trust would enable them to 'stand strong in their places'. It would stop them doing things their way – on this occasion, running away in fear. To drill down into their determination to trust Him, they began to praise God, declaring how they believed Him to be good and faithful. As they did, God moved as He'd promised, and gave them victory.

We must pray about our battles, but we must also believe God is moving. We don't wait to see what He's doing *before* we believe. These men had to trust in their hearts, stand firm in their faith *and* praise Him with their lips before they saw anything with their eyes. Not your everyday battle strategy. But in the kingdom, believing comes before seeing. And what we believe shows up in our words. Which is why their praise was so significant. The Father wants to fight for you. Always. Whatever the specific strategy He gives you for your part, it will always involve believing and praising before seeing.

PONDER
Is there a breakthrough you're praying to see?

PRAY
Spend some time praising God in faith that He is fighting, that He is faithful and good, and that He is working even though you can't see what He is doing.

READ: Revelation 19:11-14
The name of the One riding it was Faithful and True, and with pure righteousness He judges and rides to battle. (TPT)

Have you noticed how most pictures of Jesus don't depict Him as a warrior? Most of the time He's either carrying a lamb or looking like He belongs in a library! I'm convinced if He had Instagram, the pictures of Him would look nothing like the images we're used to. Revelation paints a very different picture of Him riding into battle on a white horse, leading the armies of Heaven. Contrary to how He's often portrayed, He's a Warrior King. There is so much to fight for.

When Jesus was born in Bethlehem, He wasn't just born into a sleepy little town but into enemy territory. The enemy was after Him from Day One. He came to fight for you and me, to rescue us from the kingdom of darkness. He came to release us from the power of sin, to defeat the powers of darkness in our life and to bring us into relationship with the Father. In the garden of Gethsemane, He fought His fear of the horrific crucifixion that awaited Him, so He could win the battle with death that lay ahead of Him. So fierce was His battle that He sweated blood before He shed His blood. Jesus fought for your freedom and for your heart.

Having fought for you with His life, He will not leave you high and dry, now or ever. Trouble comes and when it does, it's tempting to ask, 'Why is this happening?' 'Have I done something wrong?' 'Is God mad at me or upset with me?' 'Why doesn't He answer my prayers?' It's important to be honest with Jesus and to talk to Him about everything. Vulnerability fuels intimacy. But remember, whatever you're facing, He hasn't stopped fighting for you. He is Faithful. He knows how to deliver you. He made plans to do what it takes before you prayed your first prayer. Keep praying, keep trusting and keep doing what He tells you – He *will* come through for you.

PAUSE
Reflect on how Jesus fought for you at the cross. Picture Him as the warrior on the white horse. Invite the Holy Spirit to speak to you about Him as you do so. Then turn your thoughts into thanks.

READ: Psalm 40

This is one of David's prayers to God when he was desperate for God to fight for Him as he faced some sort of trouble.

PUSH IN

– Where does the balance lie in this prayer between reminding himself of past victories that God had won for him, honesty about his present experience and feelings, specific requests he makes and declarations of his confidence in God?

– What could you learn from the way David prays here?

Talk to Jesus.

READ: Exodus 2:11-14, 3:1-10

Moses wanted to fight the Egyptian oppression of his people, the Hebrews. One day he did so, in his own strength. He didn't wait for God's timing or instruction, so ended up needing to run for his life. As a result, he spent many, many years in the desert, living as a shepherd.

God, too, wanted to fight the Egyptian oppression of His people. When the time was right, He rose up to fight for them. But He needed a human partner to carry out His purposes on the ground. So He approached Moses, because Moses still shared the same desire to see the Hebrews set free.

PUSH IN
– Is there some kind of battle you have a heart to fight, to see God's kingdom come in some way for a particular group of people?

– If so, talk to the Father about it. Tell Him your desires and what's on your heart and invite Him to involve you. Offer yourself to be His partner on the ground. Surrender to Him and ask Him to make it clear what He's asking you to do. Write down any thoughts that come to mind as you pray. Ask Him to give you patience to do things His way, in His timing, but commit to praying about what He's shown you, and anything He's asked you to do straight away.

READ: John 15:9-15
I no longer call you slaves...now you are My friends... (NLT)

'Words are easy, like the wind; faithful friends are hard to find.' Those are the words of William Shakespeare. Is that your experience? Quotes about friendship are everywhere, from greetings cards to fridge magnets. Because friendship matters. It's a precious gift. We need friends and life is better with friends. They're an antidote to loneliness, they make the bad times more bearable and the good times more beautiful. Life was meant to be shared and a good friend is someone who'll share yours with you – the good, the bad and the ugly!

The Author of friendship doesn't need friends like we do, but Jesus wants friends. He may be the King of kings, but He longs for friendship like everyone else. The night before He died He told His disciples; 'You guys are my friends.' Imagine that. He knows them inside out, their selfish tendencies, their super-sized egos and their inability to love Him the way He loved them. But He still says, 'You're my friends.' He says the same to you. His call to relationship is an invitation to friendship.

Jesus not only loves you, He really likes you. He likes His friends and loves to spend time with them. He likes to hear what's on your heart. He wants to hear your voice. He loves to share your life and share His life with you. He calls us His friend not because we're perfect or because we're a good friend back, but because He likes us. Even though we still let Him down and want things our own way sometimes, He's not put off! He's patient and kind and is the best friend we could ever have. He says to you today, 'You're My friend.' When you come to Him, remember you're spending time with the One who enjoys spending time with you.

PONDER
Spend a few moments thinking about Jesus' desire for friendship with you. What does it mean for you to be a friend of Jesus? Do you believe He likes you?

PRAY
Thank Jesus He calls you His friend. Ask the Holy Spirit to show you how much Jesus likes you. Talk to Him today as you would talk to a friend, and tell Him what's on your heart.

READ: Psalm 25:12-15
God-friendship is for God-worshippers; they are the ones He confides in... (MSG)

God has always wanted friends. Friendship was His idea in the first place. In pre-apple days, before Adam and Eve withdrew from Him, God used to walk and talk with them as His friends. Have you ever wondered what they talked about? What they laughed about? What experiences they shared together? Abraham, a bit later on, is described as 'a friend of God', and Exodus 33:11 tells us, 'The Lord would speak to Moses face to face, as one speaks to a friend'. His heart is for friendship and He wants to grow His friendship with you.

One of the many dimensions of friendship is sharing our heart. God is no different – He wants to share His heart with His friends. This psalm, written by God's friend David, says He confides in His friends. Stop and think about that for a minute. The Creator of the universe wants to tell His friends what matters to Him, just like you do. He wants to let them in to what He's doing and what's on His heart. I know I choose to open my heart and share my life with my pals, but the fact that God wants to do the same messes with my head a bit!

The friends of mine that want to confide in me don't get very far when I'm too busy to make time, too distracted to pay attention, or too keen to keep talking about what I want to talk about. I have to be ready to listen and willing to ask. Jesus confided a huge amount in His disciples. He told them about things He was planning to do. He was open with them about how He felt. He told them about the plans He had for them, and He told them what was going to happen in this world. He shared His heart with them and wants to do the same with you. He wants to confide in you about what He cares about, what He's doing and what He wants to do. In your world and beyond. Has He got your time and attention?

PONDER
Ask Jesus to confide in you what He wants to do in your home, your workplace or your community (pick one). Listen and pay attention to what 'pops into' your mind. Note it down.

PRAY
Ask Him how He wants you to pray about what He's shown you and then go for it.

READ: Exodus 32:1-14
So the Lord changed His mind... (NLT)

God is interested in your input, did you know that? One of my favourite things to do is sit in a coffee shop with a friend and have a heart to heart over a mug of something hot! One of the Father's precious gifts to me is people I care about who I can share my personal highs and lows with and get input and perspective from. He is no different. He enjoys spending time with His friends and takes what His friends say to heart.

As we've seen, Exodus 33:11 describes Moses as a friend of God. In this previous chapter, we eavesdrop on an unusual conversation between them. It reveals something extraordinary about God's friends; they have influence with Him. It's one thing to have influence in the world on His behalf and use it to make a lasting, life-changing difference. It's another to have influence with the Father Himself. But in this passage, God is sharing His broken heart. The people He loves and has just rescued have given their hearts to another god, committing spiritual adultery. He tells his friend Moses what He plans to do, and Moses tells Him what he thinks! Moses thinks He should do something else. And after a long chat (aka prayer), God changes His mind.

All kinds of people debate long and hard whether God can be God, know everything, and also change His mind. The deeper truth here is that He's chosen to let His friends influence Him. He cares what His friends think. He cares what you think. Moses cared deeply about the future of the Israelites. He wanted the Father to save them, although they didn't deserve it. It's important to care enough other about people's futures that we talk to God about them. We need to be serious about it, like Moses was. God wants to remind you today that as His friend, you have influence with Him. What a privilege. What are you doing with it?

PONDER
Whose futures do you want to see changed by the mercy of God and His sovereign intervention?

PRAY
Spend time praying for the people/community you've identified and talk to God as His friend.

READ: John 15:14-16
You are My friends if you do what I command. (NLT)

Do you have people who speak into your life? I hope so for your sake! I have a handful of friends who care enough about me to help me out when I'm up the creek without a paddle. But they're also friends who love me enough to tell me stuff. Like when I need to give something up because it's harming me; like when I need to take something up that will do me good; like when I need to hold out, step up or push on. I'm so thankful for their commitment to me.

Obedience is important in our relationship with the Father. Jesus says that doing what He says is a mark of friendship. We don't do what He says so He'll like us more, He already likes us. We do what He says *as evidence* of our love and trust that He's a friend who wants the best for us. I hope you listen to your friends if they're good friends. Doing what they suggest is proof they're people we trust. If we don't respond to what Jesus asks us to do, it's not much of a friendship!

The enemy has always tried to persuade God's friends that doing what He asks will mean we'll lose out; that we should be wary of close friendship with Him because of what He might want from us. That's why we sometimes find putting His words into practice such a challenge. We can hear the enemy whispering, 'You'll end up worse off'. Why do you think he lies to us like that? Because he knows that if we're a friend of Jesus and we do what He tells us, we'll live a life of peace and power. Friend, Jesus shares all He has with His friends which means He shares all that He has with you. Focus on being a good friend and letting Him be a friend to you and you'll find yourself wanting to do what He says.

PONDER
Have you fallen for the lie that you will be worse off if you obey Jesus? What is Jesus asking you to do today as His friend? Invite Him to speak to you and then wait.

PRAY
Pray about what He's shown you and ask the Holy Spirit to give you grace to obey Him.

READ: Matthew 11:1-6
And blessed is (s)he who is not offended because of Me. (NKJV)

Offence is a threat to relationship. Proverbs 11:19 says something strong: 'An offended friend is harder to win back than a fortified city.' Really? Fortified cities are easier to take? If I lived on a desert island I might have my questions about that statement. But I don't, and I've seen close friendships disintegrate because of offence. I've also wrestled with the destructive power of it in my own heart too.

Offence has this strong urge to pull us away from whoever offended us. Whether they said something, did something or didn't do something. In this passage, Jesus is talking to John's disciples. John (Jesus' cousin and friend) is in prison and sends some of his followers to ask Jesus if He really is who He says He is. I imagine John is wondering why Jesus hasn't set him free, since He'd said, 'I've come to set prisoners free' (Luke 4:18). Jesus says, 'Tell John, Yes I am, and what I've been doing proves it; and if you don't get offended by Me you'll be blessed.'

Perhaps Jesus knew John might get offended. He hadn't intervened how John would have wanted. We're not told. But Jesus does tell us we can get offended at Him. That offence, if we hold on to it, will spoil our friendship with Him. Friend, when we hold offence in our heart towards God because He hasn't done something we were hoping He would do, our friendship with Jesus suffers. We'll be tempted to pull back from Him as our offence grows into a wall between us. He is always good and He is always for us, but even as His friends, we'll never fully understand His ways this side of the grave. Resolve not to let offence rob you of the blessing of His friendship and His presence.

PONDER
Ask the Holy Spirit to show you if there is any offence in your heart towards God.

PRAY
Let go of any offence He's shown you. Confess it and give it to Him. Tell Him you don't want it anymore. Ask Him to increase your trust in His love when you don't understand what He's doing or not doing.

READ: John 15:14-15
**You show that you are My intimate friends when you obey all that
I command you.** (TPT)

PUSH IN

Jesus calls you His intimate friend. He loves friendship. Review your friendship with Him today.

– Is there anything you need to apologise to Him for? Is there anything you've done to damage your friendship with Him? If yes, confess it now and then hear Him tell you He forgives you.

– Is there any area in your life where you're ignoring what He's been asking you to do and living in disobedience? Ask the Holy Spirit to show you, and be honest with yourself and Him.

Whatever He's asking you to do or stop doing, it's not because He's mean, it's because He loves you and knows the way to release more life and love into your heart. Talk to Him about what He's shown you. Ask Him to help you take a step forward in obedience today, trusting His heart for you. Ask Him to show you what else you might need to do to help you succeed. Is there someone you need to enlist to help you? Something else you need to put in place? As your friend, He'll help you do what He's asking you to do.

PUSH IN

Grab a bit of paper or use the space below and spend a few moments writing down what it means to you to be called a friend of Jesus. What desires do you have for your friendship? What do you enjoy about it? What do you like doing with Him as your friend? Is there a part of your life you keep out of your friendship with Him? What have you learned about His heart? How could you be a better friend to Him?

Thank Him that He calls you His friend; talk to Him as your friend today.

READ: Psalm 85:1-7

Now restore us again, O God of our salvation. (NLT)

In this world, things get damaged and broken. In my home this week, there's a ripped pair of suit trousers (ripped in a rather challenging place) and a bike chain awaiting attention. Both have taken a battering. Last week it was the clutch that broke – much more serious and expensive. The week before, it was a tooth that needed fixing.

Some things are easily replaced, like a pair of trousers or a bike. A clutch is more costly. But many things can't be replaced when they get lost or broken. Like a friendship with a precious history, a bank balance, a business venture or a heart. God's not in the business of replacing but restoring. He doesn't just write off what's been stolen or broken in your life and say, 'Let's just start again.' Intrinsic to the word restored is putting something back into its original condition. Like resetting a phone to factory settings. The Father is set on hitting reset on all things. From hearts to hope, money to marriages, faith to family and from your peace to your passion for Jesus. You name it, He has a heart to restore it.

When you're facing loss or feeling broken or burnt out, do you expect the Father to restore you? When you look at others and their lives, or when you look at your community, do you expect the same thing? In this psalm, God's people are asking Him to hit the reset button on them and their relationship with Him. They're praying this because they know He's the Restorer. He'd already restored their fortunes (v1) and they were asking for more. The Bible is stuffed full of promises about restoration. God wants His daughters to know His heart on this, so we pray like these people. He wants us believing for, contending for, and expecting to see His restoration in our lives and the lives of others. In our communities and in our nation. Hear Him tell you today, 'I want to restore what you've lost, what's been stolen from you, and what's been broken in your life.'

PONDER
Have you experienced God's restoration in your life in some way? If so, how did it come about?

PRAY
Thank the Father that He is a Restorer and ask Him to grow your expectation of restoration today.

READ: Genesis 41:37-52

He dressed him in fine linen clothing and hung a gold chain around his neck.
(NLT)

If the story of Joseph had a backing track to it, this moment would be set to a dramatic crescendo. Thirteen years after Joseph had his cloak ripped off by his brothers, God raised him up to a place of honour and power. Having been sold into slavery and then falsely imprisoned, it was a position he could never have reached on his own. The moment the 'fine linen clothing' was placed on his shoulders was a freeze frame one for Joseph. Surely, it was a reminder to Him that his Heavenly Father loves restoration.

God is a Restorer, but restoration is a process. I love the instant stories of restoration – seeing a body restored in a moment is exciting. But whether it's restoring a heart, a relationship, a dream, a life, or anything in between, it's usually a process. And a process takes time. For Joseph it was many years. Years during which he would have wrestled with hope, wondering, 'How can God possibly give me back a future, a purpose, and a position of honour and influence? Will He restore my broken family relationships?' (which happens a few chapters on). Do you think he gave the restoration of his gorgeous garment a second thought?

If you're praying, waiting and believing for God to bring restoration in your life in some way, keep trusting. He's at work, if you're on your knees. Don't fall for the lie that because it hasn't happened, it's not going to. No one could have figured out how He'd do it in Joseph's life, but that didn't stop the Father from working, or Joseph from trusting. Don't try and work it out, work with Him. Pray and obey what He's asking you to do right now. But expect Him to bring restoration to you in His timing. Because that is His heart for you.

PONDER

Is there anything you've believed God can't restore? Which bit of Joseph's story do you find most encouraging? Do you ask God to bring restoration when you experience loss or wounding?

PRAY

Talk to God about it and ask Him to speak to you. Then declare: 'I do not need to be afraid of loss, because You are the Restorer.'

READ: Job 42:7-10
After Job had interceded for his friends, God restored his fortune. (MSG)

Certain heart attitudes position us for God's restoring work in our lives. One of the most significant is forgiveness. Job lost a lot of things in a short space of time, including family members, his business and his reputation. He ended up with a broken heart. Having been mightily blessed by God, he went through a season of extreme difficulty and pain. His story is told in the book named after him.

When we experience loss or pain, there is often someone to have a go at. Either another person or ourselves. Perhaps they caused the trouble in the first place, or maybe they made it worse. Knowingly or unknowingly. Job got it on all sides. Not only did he experience terrible tragedy, his friends then added to it. Instead of bringing comfort and being kind as he struggled to cope, they told him his trouble was his fault. They then gave Job unwanted advice about what he should do next. He could have blamed them in his pain and I wouldn't have blamed him!

If you're longing to see something restored in your own life, whether that's your heart, a relationship, your fortunes, your dream or an opportunity, remember this: certain things can prevent God moving how He wants. We can prefer revenge, or pray for restoration, but we can't have both. Job had to forgive his friends for the way they'd wounded him before God could move. God told him, 'Pray for them so I can bless them.' I bet He'd said the same to Joseph! It's a top tactic to make sure we're not holding resentment towards someone in our life. Only after Job prayed was restoration released into his life. God gave him back twice as much as he'd had before. For the door to restoration to open, friend, we need to let go of unforgiveness. Even if it's connected to the loss or damage we've experienced. You may need to forgive others. You may need to forgive yourself. But take a leaf out of Job's book. Don't let unforgiveness rob you of the miracle of restoration.

PAUSE
Ask the Holy Spirit to show you if there is someone you need to forgive and pray for. Ask Him to help you let go of your desire to see them suffer somehow for the pain they've caused you. Invite God to heal your pain and ask Him to bless the person that has hurt you.

READ: Zechariah 9:12

**Return to your fortress, you prisoners of hope; even now I announce that
I will restore twice as much to you.**

When we know God as the Restorer, we get an upgrade on our peace. Recently, my son lost a lot of money because someone made a mistake. But he knows the Father as his Restorer. So before he'd told us what had happened, he'd begun asking God to restore that money to him. And more. Over the next few weeks, God did. Miraculously. He ended up with more in his pocket than before. My son wasn't surprised. And in the meantime, he'd been free. Free from anxiety and anger, and any other emotion the original event could have stirred up.

This is God's promise; to restore more than before. Sometimes in quality, sometimes in quantity. Things get messed up or go wrong. People make mistakes. I make mistakes. Lost opportunities, broken relationships, shattered dreams, wasted years, bad choices, and all kinds of injustices may be part of our life story. But in each scenario, God makes this promise to His girls. If we take it (i.e. believe it), we won't live in fear, or despair, or regret or bitterness. We don't have to worry about what might go wrong, who'll pay, or how we'll recover. It's not a naïve perspective but an incredible commitment to surround us with hope if we run with it.

When we expect the Father to be who He's promised to be, hope (rather than anything else) is what rises in us in the face of trouble. Kingdom hope doesn't rely on human ability to make things better or sort things out. And it doesn't give in to resignation either. Kingdom hope prays faith-filled prayers, asking God to restore double for our trouble. If He has said it, then we're to expect Him to do it. Let's take Him at His word, and let's see trouble (when it comes) as an opportunity for Him to bless us, or others, with more than was there before.

PONDER
How do you respond to this promise? Commit it to memory. See if you can remember it during the day.

PRAY
Ask the Holy Spirit to help you see trouble, not as coming from the Father, but as an opportunity for Him to bless you even more than before.

READ: John 21:15-19
Peter was hurt because Jesus asked him the third time, 'Do you love me?'

We make mistakes and messes in life and get things wrong, but God's heart is to restore all things, top of the list being His children. Peter was hiding in shame. He was ashamed of denying Jesus after insisting he wouldn't. He was ashamed fear had got the better of him and he was disappointed in who he thought he was. Know that feeling? So he gave up and went fishing. But Jesus got up and went after him.

Failure isn't final, but it does need dealing with. Otherwise, its legacy takes a toll on both our hearts and our identity. Jesus deals with us kindly and with compassion, as He did with Peter. He doesn't condemn us, but He does convict us. He doesn't push our failures under the carpet, blaming them on something else going on. We might do that, but He puts His finger on our sin and makes us confront it. Coming clean always precedes restoration.

We have an incredible power to excuse and explain away our actions, have you noticed that? But Jesus won't collude with our self defence. Because it traps us in shame. Forgiveness releases us. But we only experience forgiveness when we own our stuff. Peter thought His love for Jesus was strong enough to mean he wouldn't turn his back on Him (Matt 26:35). It wasn't. But he hadn't admitted it to himself or Jesus. So Jesus helped him. Three questions later, Peter confesses he doesn't love Jesus like he thought. Friend, failure doesn't disqualify us, but shame does. Jesus lifts off Peter's shame in this honest moment, by repeating the assignment He'd given him. 'Go, feed My sheep, Peter. I still choose you. I haven't changed My mind about you.' The Father can handle your weakness and your failure. Be honest with yourself and with Him. And be honest with someone else you trust. Someone who won't excuse your failure but will accept you and love you anyway. That's where His restoration begins.

PAUSE
What weakness or failure are you ashamed about that you would change if you could? Talk to Jesus about it. Thank Him that your weakness and failures don't define you and are never final. Thank Him He wants to restore you. Ask Him to do so and to speak to your heart. Ask Him to show you anyone else He wants you to be honest about it with.

PUSH IN

Read through these verses and pick one that stands out to you:

'He *restores* my soul'   (Ps 23:3)

'*Restore* to me the joy of your salvation'   (Ps 51:12)

'Though you have made me see troubles, you will *restore* my life again'   (Ps 71:20)

'I will *restore* to you the years the locusts have eaten'   (Joel 2:25)

'*Restore* us to Yourself, Oh Lord that we may return'   (Lam 5:21)

'The Lord their God will care for them, He will *restore* their fortunes'   (Zeph 2:7)

'Return to your fortress, you prisoners of hope; even now I announce that I will *restore* twice as much to you'   (Zech 9:12)

'And the God of all grace...after you have suffered a little while, will Himself *restore* you and make you strong...'   (1 Pet 5:10)

– Memorise the verse you picked, and as you do, ask the Father to speak to you through it. Ask Him to give you fresh revelation about His heart, for you and for others.

– Ask Him to show you someone who needs to be reminded today that He is the Restorer. Message them one of these verses to encourage them.

READ: Revelation 21:5

And the One sitting on the throne said, 'Look, I am making everything new!' And then He said to me, 'Write this down, for what I tell you is trustworthy and true.' (NLT)

This is the heart and work of the Father, Jesus and the Holy Spirit: making all things new. Not replacing, not repairing, but restoring. They love to restore people to relationship with Jesus, and to restore individuals. And they delight in restoring relationships, families, businesses, prospects, communities and more. It's so important to Jesus, He told John to write it down! It's the heartbeat of the kingdom and it's the story of God.

PUSH IN

– Spend a few moments reflecting on this verse and back over this week. What has Jesus been showing you? Summarise it in two or three sentences.

– Is there a lie you've believed about the Father in this area that you need to confess and stop agreeing with? Ask Him to show you.

– Ask Him to show you where He wants to involve you in His restoring work in the lives of others.

READ: Acts 1:1-11
You will be My witnesses... (NCV)

Have you ever tried something because someone else recommended it to you? We went to a holiday destination a few years ago because several friends raved about it. They'd been there, and their description of it and the stories of their experiences meant we just had to try it for ourselves! We had a fabulous holiday (we'd love to go back one day) and now recommend it to others as a place to visit.

Witnesses are people who have seen or experienced something themselves. They're not the people who've seen the holiday destination on the internet, they're the ones who've actually been there. When Jesus came back to life, He appeared to over 500 people after His resurrection, giving them the chance to believe in Him before He went back to Heaven. Those people were His first witnesses. They saw Him and experienced Him *alive*. Can you imagine? He told them to tell other people He was alive, so they too could know Him and have a relationship with Him. That's the chief reason people are still meeting Him today. Because witnesses are still at work.

Jesus has adopted you as His daughter and appointed you as His witness. It's not something you do, it's someone you are. You've been impacted by His love and you've experienced His goodness. You've heard His voice and you know He's alive. You're His witness in this world for the sake of others. He's positioned you and wants to use you right where you are. Those who don't know He's alive stand a chance of believing in Him, meeting Him and knowing the One who died for them when witnesses speak up. That's you.

PONDER
Who was a witness to you about Jesus being real? What made them a witness?

PRAY
Thank Jesus He sent a witness/witnesses to you. Thank Him for those people, and if they're still alive, ask Him to bless them today.

READ: John 4:39-42

Many of the Samaritans from that village committed themselves to Him because of the woman's witness. (MSG)

Who do you share your stories with? In the last 24 hours, I've caught up with two close friends, bumped into someone I know in a favourite shop, and been messaging a distant relative. Each time, the chat has included different-sized bits of our recent personal stories, whether small or significant. Sharing moments, updates or experiences and our response to them is all part of our interaction with others. Millions of us update stories on social media every day. You may not realise it, but we tell parts of our story all the time.

A witness is simply someone who tells stories. Their stories. Imagine a car accident witnessed by three different individuals standing in three different places. Each would have their unique take on events depending on where they were and what they saw. But each person's story would be valid and vital. As Jesus' witness, you have a unique and personal story to tell of your own relationship and experience with Him. It's valid and vital, and it's important you tell it.

This Samaritan woman is arguably Jesus' first witness. Many fellow villagers believed in Him because of her story, not because they met Him themselves. That came later. I love her exaggeration – 'He told me everything I ever did.' Not quite! But her encounter with Him changed everything for her. That was the story she shared with others, and it changed everything for them too. Don't diminish the value of your story, and the chapters in it. Others only get the chance to discover what God could do in their lives when they hear what He's done and is doing in yours.

PONDER

Do you believe your story (and its different parts) has value for others, and God wants to use it?

PRAY

Spend a few moments thanking God for your story with Him. Thank Him for how it began, and thank Him for what He's been doing in your life recently. Ask Him how the recent bits could become part of your witness this week.

READ: Acts 4:5-13
...they were astonished and took note that these men had been with Jesus.

The only qualification you need to be Jesus' witness is to know Him. Nothing else will disqualify you. No matter how old you are, what kind of past you have, how long you've been a believer or how much you've failed, you're qualified. You only need one quality: courage.

Peter and John started off life as fishermen. That was a profession that required you to be good with fish, not good with words! But Jesus doesn't choose the people our world would. Unsurprisingly, the people listening to Peter and John were surprised at what they said. They wanted to understand why their message was so powerful, but the answer wasn't found in the boy's skill set. They hadn't been on a training course on how to communicate. The answer was found in their hearts. They'd spent time with Jesus, they knew Him and they had a story to tell about His goodness to them. They also had the courage to tell it (v13).

Witnesses don't need skills, they need courage. The enemy wants to keep everyone away from the truth about Jesus, so he tries to get us to keep our mouths shut. He attempts to intimidate us into silence. Fear – of rejection, of being judged, of sounding like an idiot, of being misunderstood – is a weapon he uses against us much of the time. Friend, let that fear encourage you. Your story is worth telling. But the enemy wants it kept quiet. The Holy Spirit will always give you the courage you need to use your voice and tell your story. So remember to ask Him for it and depend on Him for it. You and I are God's Plan A for His good news to get out there. There is no Plan B.

PONDER
Where do you need courage? To take opportunities? To let others know you're a follower of Jesus? To let them know about some of your experiences with Him? With certain people more than others?

PRAY
Thank Jesus that He's given you His Holy Spirit and He lives in you. Ask Him to give you opportunities to open your mouth today, and courage where you need it.

READ: Acts 4:16-20
As for us, there's no question – we can't keep quiet about what we've seen and heard. (MSG)

Most people around you need encouraging. Most people you bump into need hope in some area of their lives. God wants to use you to bring life to them by sharing some of your experiences of Him. How has He impacted you, how has He helped you, how has He been good to you? When you tell parts of your story, explaining what He's taught you or how He makes a difference in your life, you're being His witness.

The word 'witness' makes me think of a courtroom. The witness has a very simple role. She isn't the judge deciding on an outcome, and she isn't the lawyer doing her best to persuade anybody. She just tells her experience. Isn't that a relief? As His witness, you're not responsible for persuading anybody or proving anything. A witness proclaims her version of the story. You don't have to be able to talk about Jesus in an articulate way or have a brilliant understanding of the Bible. You don't even need to be able to explain why He was crucified (although it's a good thing if you can). You're not His lawyer, and you're not the judge. You're called to tell what you've seen and heard. Peter and John just couldn't keep quiet about what they'd experienced. Is that true of you?

If you've ever felt responsible for how others might respond to you telling bits of your story, let that one go today. The Holy Spirit's job is to open eyes and hearts, yours is to open your mouth. Have you seen Him provide? Have you heard Him speak? Have you known His guidance? Have you experienced His peace? Has He been good to you? Have you seen Him work in somebody else's life? You have stories to tell, and there are all kinds of people waiting to hear them.

PONDER
Have you ever felt you needed to persuade people about Jesus?

PRAY
Ask Jesus to lead you to someone in the next 24 hours who needs to hear a bit of your story with God, because it will encourage them. Ask Him to provide an opening for you and give you courage to share it.

READ: Luke 5:12-16

Your cleansed and obedient life, not your words, will bear witness to what I have done. (MSG)

You've heard it said, 'Actions speak louder than words.' Jesus didn't say that, but He does say actions speak. Actions communicate messages just as words do. If I slam a door, my family know I'm cross without me saying anything! In this story, Jesus told the leper to be a witness through his actions, not his words. His quiet obedience in going to the priest, showing his skin and bringing the offering demanded by the law, would speak as powerfully about what God had done as telling his story.

You're His witness. He's positioned you where you are and you have a story to tell. But remember, your actions tell a story too – hopefully the same one! When my kids were young, they used to do a 'show and tell' slot at school. They had to tell their classmates about something they'd done or something they loved, but they also had to take in something to show about it. Witnesses show *and* tell. How we live tells a story.

When we put the needs of others above our own, we tell a story of a God who loves them. When we obey God's word, we tell a story about One who can be trusted. When we live gratefully, we tell a story about a generous Father. When we believe for miracles, we tell a story about One who is powerful. When we refuse to gossip, we tell a story about a God who protects others. When we do more than we could, not less than we could at work, we tell a story about a Father who gives His best. You get the idea. The leper had to tell his story, he couldn't help it, but he added the 'show' to his 'tell'. We are most effective when we do the same.

PONDER

Think about the people you see regularly, in different contexts. What actions or attitudes of yours might they say point to your relationship with Jesus?

PRAY

Thank Jesus for some of the ways He has shown you the Father's love. Ask Him to give you an opportunity to show His love to someone today.

READ: Acts 4:13
...they were astonished and took note that these men had been with Jesus.

The story you have to tell to this point in your life is the result of you having been with Jesus. He is the author of your story and He is still writing it.

PUSH IN

Grab a pen and some paper, use your phone or the space below, and spend the next five minutes writing out your story in headlines.

- Write down how He introduced Himself to you.
- Write down how your life began to change as you began to get to know Him.
- Write down some of the main things you have discovered about Him.
- Write down what difference He makes to your life on a daily basis.
- Write down what He is teaching you in this season of your life.
- Write down any particular moments / experiences that you've had that have been significant (if you haven't already included them).

Thank Him for your story and His work in your life. Get ready to share it!

RE-READ: Luke 5:14

Your cleansed and obedient life, not your words, will bear witness to what I have done. (MSG)

God has positioned you for His purposes amongst certain groups of people.

PUSH IN

Spend a few moments thinking about the different communities you are part of. Work, family, school, university, local neighbourhood, gym, online, etc.

Name each community before God, one at a time, and name some of the people you rub shoulders with.

– Thank Jesus that He's appointed you to be His witness in these places.

– Ask the Father to show you one thing you could do to be a more effective witness amongst them.

– Pray He would stir up a hunger for Jesus in these people. Pray He would open up doors of opportunity for you to share bits of your story with them and ask Him to give you the boldness to do so.

READ: 1 John 4:7-12
The one who doesn't love has yet to know God, for God is love. (TPT)

God is love. Three words that are so easy to say but which take more than a lifetime to grasp. John doesn't say God loves. Love is something God is, not something He does. Why's that important? Because if love is something the Father does, then He could stop loving. He could decide not to love you on your bad days or in your bad moments. Since He is love, He can't do that. Phew! He can't not love us just like the sun can't not shine. His love for you never changes and never stops. Everything He does, even His reshaping of you, is done out of love.

The challenge for every human on planet earth is that we've never met anyone who *is* love. Everyone we meet has an on and off switch to their love. And everyone we've ever known has had limits to their love, even when they were doing their best. That's because sin spoils love. Human love is conditional on something (i.e. we need to measure up) or limited by something (i.e. someone's own ability to love). The Father, Jesus, and the Holy Spirit love us in a way we've never experienced. We struggle to get our heads round it because not even the most loving people we know have loved us as fiercely and fully as they do.

To live in God's love, we have to let Him reset and keep resetting our human ideas about what He's like. When He came, many people didn't recognise Jesus as God because their human ideas got in the way. Our human ideas about His love get in the way too. The Holy Spirit teaches us how to live more fully in His extravagant, no-strings-attached love. And He has something to show us about it every day. Let's not underestimate how much we have to learn! Friend, never settle for an arm's-length relationship with God. Open yourself up again today to His passionate, affectionate love for you. Make knowing Him and His love for you the highest goal of your life. It changes everything.

PONDER
Have you ever acknowledged with God that the way He loves you is totally different to the way anyone else has ever loved you? If not, do so now.

PRAY
Ask the Holy Spirit to help you experience and feel the Father's affection for you today.

READ: Exodus 34:4-10

The Lord, the Lord, the compassionate and gracious God, slow to anger, abounding in love and faithfulness...

If someone asked you to describe yourself, what would you say? Moses wanted to know God better. Long before God showed the world what He was like by sending Jesus, His friend said to Him, 'Show me what You're really like.' So God walked in front of Moses. He didn't let Moses see His face, but Moses felt the weighty presence of his Maker right next to him. Wow! In that magic moment, God could have said, 'Hey Moses, I want you to remember this about Me: I'm a brilliant strategist, a powerful ruler and a creative genius.' But He didn't.

The words above are how He described Himself: as a lover. These are relationship words. They're heart qualities desiring intimacy, not abilities designed to impress. He's compassionate; He cares deeply about you and about all you go through. When you hurt, He feels your pain since He tied His heart to yours when He made you. When you struggle, He's right there with you. He faced what you face when He was here in skin. He's gracious; He doesn't treat you as you deserve. He's ridiculously kind. And He's slow to get angry; He is super patient with you. Patience isn't one of my strong suits. Whether it's on the roads, on the phone or on my laptop, having to wait for a car to move or a page to load doesn't bring out the best in me. But God is so patient, willing to wait and then wait some more for us to respond to His love and His promptings.

When we're in pain or in trouble, the enemy tries to blind us to God's deep love and affection for us. We need an alarm to go off to wake us up to that danger. If we let our limited perspectives in those moments draw conclusions about His love, they will be way off. They'll wound our hearts further and woo us away from His love. Wise up to that trap, friend. When the fog descends, walking by faith means trusting what you can't see. He is who He says He is. He *is* love. And He loves you.

PAUSE
Re-read this verse out loud, very slowly. Do it a few times. Notice which words stand out or impact you. Pray your thoughts back to God, whether that's asking Him a question or expressing your thanks and / or your longings to Him.

READ: Exodus 34:10-17
Don't worship any other god. God – His name is The Jealous One –
is a jealous God. (MSG)

Jealousy. It's not a feel-good word that gets a good press. We know that being jealous of someone or what they have is wrong. And we know we should wrestle jealousy to the ground in our own hearts (or at least ask Jesus to help us with it). But God says He's a jealous God, so why is He jealous if jealousy isn't a good thing?

Let's dig a bit. The Old Testament word translated as 'jealous' is only applied to God, not humans. His version of jealous is different. This word describes the idea of becoming very red. It refers to a face becoming red, not from intense exercise but from intense emotion and passion. God's jealousy isn't stirred up because He's insecure or selfish, it's the result of His red-hot love for us. He feels so strongly about us and wants the best for us. If you find it hard to get your head round 'jealous', try 'zealous'. They mean the same thing. God is a zealous lover.

The Father is zealous for us and wants an exclusive relationship with us. Because it's the best thing for us. He's clear in this passage that we're not to share our hearts with other gods. That might sound crazy because we don't deliberately worship other gods. But a god can be anything we devote so much time, affection, or energy (emotional or physical) to that it interferes with our relationship with Him. It's often something we refuse to give up or let go of because we think we can't live without it. How do we know if we worship another god? Ask Him. If we seriously want to know, He'll get serious and show us. As a jealous God, He won't tolerate or bless rivals that seduce your heart, whatever they are. You're too precious, friend. The truest thing about His heart for you is not disapproval or indifference, but zealous love that blazes like fire.

PONDER
Ask God to show you if He has a rival for your heart and if so, what/who it is; what would you find hard to give up if He asked you? Whatever comes to mind, ask Him what you should do about it.

PRAY
Hear Jesus speak the words in the verse above to you. They're His words. Confess the weakness of your love for Him and ask Him to grow in you a passionate, zealous love for Him.

READ: Hosea 2:14-23

I am now going to allure her; I will lead her into the wilderness and speak tenderly to her.

Do you know the tender love of the Father? The tender expression of the fierce love that burns in His heart for you? Hosea is one of my favourite books of the Bible. It paints a beautiful picture of God's love for His people. Hosea was a prophet who loved the Father. God asked him to marry an unfaithful woman who carried on being unfaithful once they were married. God told Hosea to keep forgiving her, keep loving her and keep pursuing her. Big ask! But the Father wanted Hosea to be a visual aid so His people could see the unbreakable nature of His own love.

God's heart for you is tender. No matter how far you've strayed, and how unfaithful to Him you may have been, His heart is always to draw you back again. He often does that in a desert place where He can talk to you. His people deserved stern words, but instead they heard tender ones. He hoped His affection would persuade them to live differently as He refused to control them with power. He does the same with you.

God spoke His tender words in the tough place of the wilderness, and it's still the place He reveals His heart to you. The wilderness represents an empty space. It's empty of the things that compete for our affection and clamour for our attention. God may lead you to a wilderness for a season in your life, as He did with Jesus. It may feel like a dry and barren place which is hard for you to be in. But expect Him to speak tenderly to you there. Jesus also regularly withdrew to a solitary, empty place (Mk 1:35) by choice, so He could hear His Father's loving words. In the natural realm, not much grows in the wilderness. In the spiritual realm, intimacy with God and dependency on Him grow there like nowhere else.

PONDER
Do you have a 'wilderness' place you go to, to be with God, or do you need to create one? What are the distractions that compete for your attention? How can you eliminate them?

PRAY
Thank God that He wants to speak tenderly to your heart. Tell Him you long to hear His voice. Ask the Holy Spirit to help you create a 'wilderness' place so you can grow closer to Jesus.

READ: Romans 12:9-13
Love must be sincere. Hate what is evil, cling to what is good.

Have you ever associated God with the word 'hate'? If so, have you ever thought about what He might hate? Sadly, some people seem to think the pain in the world is evidence that God hates people. Since He is love, He cannot hate people, but the enemy does. He hates what God loves. The Father loves all people. Whoever they are and whatever they've done. Jesus died for every human that ever lived, so they stood the chance of discovering the Father's love and forgiveness.

God is love, so some people think that means He can't hate. But hate is an outworking of love. You can't truly love someone without hating what hurts them. I hate cancer; my mother died of it. I hate it because of what it does to people I love. But that doesn't mean I hate those people! God hates sin. He loves everyone but hates the ungodly choices we make and things we do. Our culture tells us if we love someone, then we'll accept them *and* everything they do. But Jesus doesn't play by culture's rules. He is holy. He hates sin *because* He loves people. His love isn't a passive, chilled out, anything-goes kind of love. It's strong and pure and is against whatever damages or diminishes us.

The Bible is specific about some of the things God hates. Look them up some time. If we love Him, we'll love what He loves (as He commands in this passage) and we'll hate what He hates. When He confronts the attitudes or behaviours in us that compromise who He created us to be, let's not resist Him. When He challenges what compromises our ability to love Him or love others, let's not reject it. He's contending for our heart. And when He calls us to represent Him and confront those things around us or in our culture that damage or diminish others, let's be ready to rise up. But let's remember to do it in love.

PONDER
Have you ever thought about what God hates before? How do we love people without loving everything they do? Who is God asking you to love like this?

PRAY
Ask Jesus to teach you to love how He loves. Invite Him to wake you up where you've become indifferent to the things He hates.

READ: 1 Corinthians 13:4-8

Love is large and incredibly patient. Love is gentle and consistently kind to all. It refuses to be jealous when blessing comes to someone else. Love does not brag about one's achievements nor inflate its own importance. Love does not traffic in shame and disrespect, nor selfishly seek its own honour. Love is not easily irritated or quick to take offence. Love joyfully celebrates honesty and finds no delight in what is wrong. Love is a safe place of shelter, for it never stops believing the best for others. Love never takes failure as defeat, for it never gives up. Love never stops loving. (TPT)

PUSH IN

You may want to read these verses in another version or two.

– Start by asking the Holy Spirit to come and speak to you about the Father's heart for you.

– Re-read the verses above, replacing the word 'love' with 'the Father', so you let this passage describe Him, because He is love.

– Notice which phrases stand out to you as being either unfamiliar or difficult to get your head round.

– Pick one that stands out and ask the Holy Spirit to reveal to you any lie you've believed about the Father. As He does, confess it and ask Him to break its power over your heart. Ask Him to plant the truth in you today.

– Spend some time being still in His presence. Receive His love for you and let it fill your heart again. Then ask Him to help you love like this too. He has given you His Spirit to empower you to love others the way He loves you.

READ: John 3:16
For this is how God loved the world: He gave His one and only Son... (NLT)

Giving sacrificially is one of the main expressions of love.

PAUSE
– Spend some time thanking God for all that He has given you as an expression of His love for you, beginning with the gift of His Son.

– How could you give to Him today by giving to someone else, as an expression of your love for Him?

READ: Ephesians 6:10-18
Therefore, put on the full armour of God.

Once, while on holiday, I had a short-lived change of identity, much to the shock of my family. For a few hours, I became a white water rafter. I was kitted out with a big life jacket, a helmet and some other things to equip me for the excitement to come. A good job it was too; I ended up paying an unexpected visit into the water! Being prepared matters.

The equipment Paul talks about in this passage is needed by warriors. White water rafters wear one lot of stuff, warriors wear another. It's warriors who wear armour, take up shields, and carry swords. Swords and shields are useless in a boat, but crucial on a battlefield. Paul is talking to you. As God's daughter, you need His armour because you're a warrior. You may not feel like a warrior, and you may not look like one. But if you don't think like one, you're in trouble. Because we are in a battle.

Sometimes life is overwhelming and duvet days seem like the best option. Why? Because as Paul says, 'You have a very real enemy'. The battle is real. He's not a physical enemy, but a spiritual one. He's a thief. He's out to steal and destroy (Jn 10:10) your hope, your faith, your peace, your joy, your relationships, your identity and your impact in this world. Life on earth involves a string of battles and nothing will change that. But Jesus doesn't want you falling for lies like, 'It's just life', 'He's not good', 'Nothing will ever change', 'You're on your own' or 'You can't cope.' He doesn't want you curling up in fear or defeat, or hitting cruise control. Neither will lead you forwards. Friend, let me remind you today you're a warrior. Jesus calls you to rise up and fight, no matter how you feel. The reason you can is this: He is in you and He is for you.

PONDER

Do you see yourself as a warrior? What is going on in your life right now that's threatening your peace, your joy or your hope? Have you seen it as a spiritual battle or have you made other assumptions that Jesus wants to correct today?

PRAY

Ask the Father to show you what He wants you to learn about being a warrior this week. Hear Him tell you to put on your armour. Ask Him to help you rise up and fight.

READ: Colossians 2:13-15
In this way, He disarmed the spiritual rulers and authorities. He shamed them publicly by his victory over them on the cross. (NLT)

You live on a battlefield. You can ignore the reality of the spiritual world or embrace it. But in His word, God makes it clear that the constant backdrop to human history is the battle between the kingdom of darkness and the kingdom of Heaven. Between Himself and Satan. Until we accept this, we misinterpret most of life. He's set you up to win as His daughter. He who is in you is greater than he who's in the world (1 Jn 4:4). But if you're ill informed, you're ill prepared.

The major battlefield in life is between our ears. The enemy was defeated at the cross but is not yet destroyed. He has limited weapons but a loud voice. He knows our true identity and is set against us. He wants to draw us away from the Father and keep us from the strength and life God has for us. His number one tactic is to use his voice to whisper lies to us, because the voice we follow shapes our future. You hear the whispers as thoughts in your mind: 'You're no good'. 'God doesn't love you.' 'That won't harm'. 'This is all there is.' 'Prayer doesn't work'. These thoughts aren't your thoughts, they're his lies. If he can get you to believe them, and even better, continue lying to yourself, then he can steer your life.

Don't let this worry you, friend, let it wake you up. Warriors pay attention to the thoughts in their minds. They don't accept that every thought is true, or originates from them. So recognise you can *choose* which thoughts to listen to, or accept, or agree with. Police them. God says, 'Take captive every thought' (2 Cor 10:5). Some stuff that you hear between your ears needs to be confronted and captured so you can walk on in freedom and faith. But only you, mighty warrior, have the power to do that.

PONDER
Do you 'police' your thinking or do you accept every thought you have as being true and being from you? What would confronting and capturing a thought look like for you?

PRAY
Put your hands on your head; ask Jesus to help you as you commit to win the war in your mind.

READ: Joshua 1:1-9

Do not be afraid or discouraged. For the Lord your God is with you wherever you go. (NLT)

Two of our biggest battles are against fear and discouragement, have you noticed that? They have the power to flatten our faith and immobilise us. I love the story of Joshua; we named one of our sons after this amazing warrior. God gives him a pep talk, Father-to-son kind of thing. 'Son, it's time for you to take hold of what I've promised you. I'll give you everything you go after. I won't leave you or give up on you, but you've got to be brave and strong. So fight your discouragement and your fear.'

I love this! Even our hero Joshua could get discouraged and fearful like me. He too could let his circumstances and his thoughts about them delete his hope and courage. He was likely (like me) to think, 'I can't do it', or 'What if...'. God orders him to fight those thoughts and feelings instead of giving in to them, and He gives the same order to us. If the Father says we can do it, then we can, no matter how hard it is.

Fear and/or discouragement usually stand in the way of where God is taking us. The enemy personalises his attacks on us, often through our circumstances, have you noticed that? He knows how to wind *you* up and get *you* down. He knows *your* weak spots. He knows how to get *you* to step back or give in. Remember that warriors see discouragement and fear as enemies. Instead of letting them dictate whether you speak up, step up, keep going, keep giving, keep praying, keep trusting or keep loving, learn to see them differently. Let discouragement and fear remind you that God's plan for you is right in front of you. The enemy wants to hold you back. The Father wants to give you ground. Decide again today to take on your fear and discouragement so they don't take you out.

PONDER

What is causing you to be afraid or discouraged at the moment? Decide again not to give in to fear or discouragement today. What could you do (that you're afraid of or feel discouraged from doing) so you actively take a step forward?

PRAY

Confess your fear or discouragement to Jesus. Ask Him to help you take that step today.

READ: Ephesians 6:12-13

For we are not fighting against flesh-and-blood enemies, but against evil rulers and authorities of the unseen world... (NLT)

Don't get caught up fighting the wrong battles. What Paul says here is a powerful reminder I need on repeat, as it's the opposite of what my culture or my feelings tell me! Our enemy is not the boss at work, or the family member making life a misery. It's not the colleague who criticised us, the leader whose decisions affect us or the person who disagrees with us and stands in our way. Our enemy is spiritual and 'unseen', not human. But he tricks us onto the wrong battleground. We fight the real battle in the invisible realm. As we do our bit, God does His, and brings the victory we're contending for.

I've watched too many daughters of God neglect the invisible battle. I've watched as friends have got stuck, blaming others for their pain rather than fighting the invisible enemy of bitterness that sucks the life out of them. I've seen others ignore the enemy of jealousy, justify an alliance with anger, become friends with anxiety or overlook the danger of offence. Friend, unless we commit to fighting these and other enemies of our hearts, we'll end up in the quicksand of resignation, disillusionment or cynicism. And faith can't grow there. People aren't our problem, powers and principalities are.

The Father calls you a warrior. His Spirit in you empowers you to fight for your heart, your relationship with Him and for others. Have you ever felt like giving up on God? Have you ever struggled to trust Him? Have you ever failed to make time to spend with the One who loves you more than any other? Have you ever given in to temptation? Have you ever given in to despair or pride or apathy? It's not because you're a failure, but because you're a fighter. Warriors face all kinds of battles. We lose some along the way. But make sure you fight the right ones.

PAUSE
Learn the verse above. As you commit it to memory, what stands out to you most? Is there a flesh and blood enemy that you need to stop fighting?

PRAY
Talk to Jesus using this verse as a springboard.

READ: Ephesians 6:17-18

God's word is an indispensable weapon. In the same way, prayer is essential in this ongoing warfare. (MSG)

Would you ever go to the beach on a sweltering day in your overcoat, scarf and stilettos, and without your sun cream, towel and bikini (or swimsuit)? I'm sure you wouldn't. If you did, the crowds would have a laugh, and you'd have a shocker as you'd be ridiculously ill-equipped. But spiritually, that's often how we approach the situations we face in life.

The Father has given us the weapons we need to be effective in the battles in life. Our two most powerful ones are the (s)word of God and our prayers. If the true battle is spiritual and therefore won in the spiritual realm, we need weapons of spiritual power. Human solutions like hatching a plan or hurling emotions might seem more effective in the moment. But prayer, and trusting the promises and proclamations of God, before we move into action, will always win more battles. Together they're an unrivalled power-force. So the enemy works hard to stop us praying, keep us out of God's word, and keep God's word out of us.

Whatever your battle, find a promise or a truth in the Bible that applies to what you're facing. Write it down and learn it. Declare His word over your circumstance and over yourself, over and over. Remember, the power of life is in your tongue (Pr 18:21). When you make His word your own by proclaiming it, it's as if God is speaking. And when He speaks, things happen. And pray into it and keep praying. The Message version says, 'Pray hard and pray long'. Don't you love that? That's not long prayers but pray long enough – let's not quit too soon. When we put our trust in the Father's weapons and wield them instead of our own, we pick a fight with the enemy. And when we do that, we make way for God to move in power and accomplish what we never could.

PONDER

Do you think of the word of God as a weapon? How often do you declare it over the situations you are praying for, and over your own heart and mind? Do you believe it is powerful?

PRAY

Thank God, using the verse above. Thank Him He's given you His word, and the ability to pray, as two powerful weapons. Ask Him to teach you to use them more effectively.

READ: 2 Corinthians 10:3-4

We are human, but we don't wage war as humans do. We use God's mighty weapons, not worldly weapons, to knock down the strongholds of human reasoning and to destroy false arguments. (NLT)

To knock down strongholds of human reasoning (repeated, relentless thought processes) we need to police our thoughts in order to deal with them. We cannot conquer what we won't confront.

PUSH IN

– Identify some of the most recurrent toxic thoughts you have about yourself, your circumstances or your future (especially the ones you've had this week). Ask the Holy Spirit to show you what they are if you don't know already.

– Alongside each one, ask the Holy Spirit to show you what His truth is. Write it down.

– Go through each one and ask for His forgiveness for listening to the enemy's lies (anything that opposes God's truth is a lie) and declare in faith the truth He has shown you. Do it out loud and write it down.

Ask the Holy Spirit to help you to begin to do this regularly to win the war in your head. Ask Him to help you police your thoughts and thank Him that He has empowered you to win this battle.

READ: Judges 4:1-24
...the Lord's victory over Sisera will be at the hands of a woman. (NLT)

Here are two awesome warrior women engaging in battle. Don't get hung up on the battle details from thousands of years ago, hang on to the headline – victory came through the hands of a woman. In this story two women were working together: Deborah, who was fighting an enemy at a national level, and Jael, who fought an enemy in her own home. Both are significant.

As a daughter of God, you've been called to fight for His kingdom in your life and in the lives of those around you. Fighting to see people set free (physically, spiritually or emotionally); fighting to see hearts and bodies healed; fighting to see relationships restored, people cared for, families strengthened, communities prospering, nations changed, people equipped for life and introduced to the love of God.

For some of us that will be on a national scale, for some of us that will be on a local scale and for some of us the most significant battles we'll fight will be under our own roof for the sake of our families.

PUSH IN
– Remembering that your battles as a New Testament daughter are never against flesh and blood, can you identify how God has called you to fight for others or who He's called you to fight for? Ask Him to show you if this is something you're not sure about.

– Ask Him to show you what He's calling you to do and how He wants you to pray.

– Deborah and Jael fought together as battle buddies, encouraging and supporting one another. Do you have a battle buddy to pray with who you can encourage, and be encouraged by? If not, ask the Holy Spirit to bring you one. Be courageous and ask them when God shows you who it might be.

READ: Psalm 94:1-7
Judge of the earth, take Your stand... (MSG)

God is always a loving father, Jesus makes that clear. But how can a gracious father also be a judge? Have you ever wondered that? How can a kind father judge people? Why would He want to? And where does that leave me?

Let's flip this on its head for a moment. Think about a time when you were treated unfairly, betrayed, or wounded. Or when you watched someone you love cheated or abused. You know what it's like to want a wrong put right, to shout, 'It's not fair.' You know what you feel about injustice against yourself or others. We don't always handle our woundedness well, but that longing for justice comes from a deep place in us. It rises because we're made in the image of the Father. God is passionate about justice and His kids being treated right. We want the same for ourselves and for others too. But justice isn't possible without a judge. A judge rules on what's right and what's wrong and makes sure justice happens. God has to be a judge for there to be ultimate justice.

Imagine if the Father was indifferent about the injustices in your life. Imagine if He wasn't bothered about the injustices in others' lives. Or imagine if He did care, but had no power to do anything about them so we all had to put up with being wronged forever. God's heart for justice is part of His love and kindness. Psalm 94 says He's judge of the whole earth, meaning He makes judgements and will deliver justice in all kinds of ways. It's an expression of His goodness. God is a judge. And because He is, He's able to fulfil His loving commitment to you that He will not overlook the injustices in your life. And He will not waste them.

PONDER
Have you ever accused God of being unfair or unjust with you?

PRAY
Think of an injustice/unfair situation that you're struggling with or someone else is facing. Thank God He's a good judge and that He cares about the situation and how you or the other person feels. Thank Him that He won't let it be wasted. Talk to Him about what you want Him to do. Then hand it to Him and trust Him to work out His justice for you or that other person today.

READ: 1 John 4:16-19
Such love has no fear, because perfect love expels all fear. (NLT)

'Does God judge me?' You know what it's like to feel judged by others, but what about by God? Are you convinced about the answer to that question? The Father wants you to be sure as it changes your relationship with Him. The fear John talks about here is the fear of punishment (v18). And punishment comes to those who've been declared 'guilty'.

As a good judge, God has to judge us. Scary. He cares deeply about all the ways we've been hurt and wronged. But there's another side to that; He also cares about the ways we've wronged others and disobeyed Him. If He ignored the way we've wounded and treated others (either by what we have done or what we haven't done) but cared about the way we've been wounded or treated ourselves, He'd be biased and unfair. But as a good judge and perfect father to everyone, He's not.

Does that mean He judges us and punishes us each time we get it wrong? Of course not! He did that at the cross. Once and for ever. Justice had to be done, because God is fair. He declared us 'guilty' because we were. But then Jesus stepped forward and volunteered to stand in for us, taking our sentence as if it was His. He got our punishment and paid what we owed, so we got mercy and went free. He chose the greatest injustice ever so the Father could say over us, 'Not guilty.'

'Does God judge me?' Yes – He judged Jesus guilty and judged you not guilty. That's your defence against the lies and accusations of the enemy about who you are. Point to and trust His work on the cross. You're loved, forgiven, freed and favoured. Have you accepted it? Seize this truth again today, friend, and keep declaring it over yourself until it sinks in.

PONDER
Are you fearful about God's judgement of you in any way? If so, be honest with yourself about what you fear being judged for.

PRAY
Thank God in faith that He's forgiven you for whatever you've identified. Receive His forgiveness. Thank Him that He declared you 'not guilty' at the cross and that's His word over you. Hear Him speaking that over you again today. Spend some time adoring Jesus for taking your place.

READ: Matthew 18:21-35
...forgive your brother or sister from your heart. (NLT)

Have you ever stood in a courtroom? I've never been in a real one but I've often been in an imaginary one and sat in the judge's seat rehearsing my judgements! If God is the judge, then we are not. And yet how often do we play judge and decide what treatment other people deserve, especially those who've wounded us?

The first judge in this story was the master. He represents God and calls time on the servant's debt– 'pay up or go to prison.' The amount the guy owed was enormous; about 200,000 years worth of salary! He'd never repay it, so begged for mercy. The kind judge wrote it off, taking the hit himself. But then this servant turned judge on a colleague who owed him just four month's wages. He sent the guy to jail because he couldn't pay.

When we refuse to forgive someone for what they've done to us, however big or small, we're playing judge. We're demanding justice, insisting they pay for what they've done. Unforgiveness is usually justified; literally, it's the result of an injustice and we can justify it to anyone who'll listen! God's people are now being fed lies that forgiveness can only happen once there is justice. Don't fall for it, friend. It's not what Jesus says. He says if we've escaped justice with God (like the servant) but demand it for others, we end up in a prison (v34), tortured by bitterness and resentment and unable to experience God's favour.

I've had to work super hard on forgiveness. I've been the victim of some big and painful injustices. But God is the judge. He cares about what's happened, but He'll do a better job of judging than I will. He promises me justice, but for that to happen, I have to let Him do His job instead of doing it for Him. My job is to work at forgiving. It's your job too, however hard it is. That prison just isn't worth it.

PRAY

Ask the Holy Spirit 'Is there anyone I need to forgive today?' Tell the Father how you feel about what's happened to you. Thank Him He's the judge and you're not. Say, 'Lord please forgive me for trying to do Your job as judge. Please do the judging from now on.' Ask Him to help you forgive that person and trust that He'll deal with them so you don't have to. Ask Him to free you from any bitterness, resentment or judgement that has trapped you.

READ: Hebrews 12:5-11
No discipline seems pleasant at the time but painful.

One day when one of my sons was little, he refused to put on his shoes. I tried my best to encourage him it would be a good idea, but he wasn't having any of it. And I wasn't going to force him. He knew what he wanted, and he was going to get it! As we walked to the car (a way down the street) in the pouring rain, he didn't like it one bit. His feet got cold, wet and dirty. But he learned to trust his mum a bit more that day!

God disciplines us when we need it. Not much happens without discipline. No trophies get lifted, no habits get broken, no ground gets taken. The Bible says God's discipline is a sign we're His treasured children. Any parent who wants the best for their kids teaches them how to live and puts boundaries in place for them. But those lessons or boundaries aren't normally fun, are they? Another word for discipline is training. God trains us to trust Him, because the more we trust His love, the further we'll go and the freer we'll become. True freedom isn't the absence of responsibility or consequences. It's freedom from the inner stuff that grinds us down – like fear, anxiety, guilt, despair, insecurity, jealousy, anger and shame. Yes please!

Discipline doesn't feel good, so it's easy to confuse it with judgement. Have you fallen for the lie that 'life is hard so God is punishing me'? Remember, Jesus took your punishment. Life is hard because the world is broken, and broken people live in it. But the Father doesn't let anything go to waste. He takes the hardship and puts it to work for our good; to train us, shape us and prepare us for what He's next for us. So work with Him, don't withdraw from Him. He couldn't love you any more than He already does. Let His discipline remind you you're His beloved child (v6).

PONDER
Is there a difficulty in your life that God wants to grow you through? Have you questioned His love for you because of it?

PRAY
Ask Him 'Lord, what are You wanting to grow in me?' Be still for a few moments and listen for what He may say to you. Thank Him that He uses all things for good and that He wants the best for you. Decide to trust Him again today, and specifically, that He is working for your good.

READ: 2 Corinthians 5:5-10
For we must all stand before Christ to be judged. (NLT)

I'm sure you have all kinds of dates in your diary. Perhaps some of them are things you're looking forward to like a spa day, a friend's wedding, a birthday celebration, or a holiday. Maybe there are other dates you're looking forward to less: a meeting at work, a hospital appointment, or a funeral. God has a date in His diary that's been in it since time began. It's a day when He will judge the world with justice. It is not a scare tactic, just a reality. And He's kind enough to give us a heads up about it.

On that day, we will each stand before Jesus to be judged. 'But I thought you said God doesn't judge us?' He doesn't. But He's given authority to Jesus to judge (on that day) what each of us has done with His offer of forgiveness, salvation and life. Did we accept it or did we reject it? He's the same yesterday, today and always, so we know His judgement will be loving and perfect, even though we don't fully understand it. But we don't need to fear because we know He won't spring any surprises on us. Nothing about it will cause us to say, 'But that's not fair.'

This passage says He'll look at how we've lived as His daughters and what we've done with His offer of relationship. Why? Because He's a generous God and He rewards faithfulness and obedience. There is life in eternity for you if you've accepted His forgiveness, trust His love and walk with Him. But then He will also reward all the other decisions and choices you made because you loved and trusted Him. So each time you obey a challenging command, forgive a difficult person, resist temptation, surrender your way for His way or keep going when you feel like giving up, remember this: it doesn't go unnoticed or unrewarded. You can't do anything to make Him love you more than He already does, but on 'that' day He will richly reward your love for Him.

PAUSE
Take a deep breath, invite Jesus to draw near to you and spend a few moments in complete silence, focusing on His love for you. Note where your thoughts go. After a bit, turn your thoughts into prayer and praise.

READ: Hebrews 4:15-16

We are encouraged to approach God's throne with boldness and confidence. Jesus offers us mercy and grace every day, but we only get to receive it if we come to Him boldly, confident that He judged Jesus instead of judging us.

Many of us punish and condemn ourselves, wrestling with self-condemnation. What we're really doing is judging ourselves 'guilty'. Sometimes for something specific, sometimes for just not being good enough and sometimes for not being perfect. Either way, we've taken over the role of judge and decided to play God. And of course, when we do that, we can't approach His throne, because we're trying to sit on it!

Faith chooses to trust He's forgiven us and declared us 'not guilty.' Unbelief is continuing to treat ourselves as guilty when He says we're not. We receive His grace and mercy through faith, which means being thankful for it.

PUSH IN

- Do you ever condemn yourself or punish yourself when you feel guilty about something you've done or for who you are? How do you do that?

- How would your life change if you stopped doing that?

- How confident on a scale of 1-10 (where 1 = 'not at all' and 10 = 'very') are you that God wants to be gracious and merciful to you?

- Spend some time thanking Him that He's always merciful and that He has forgiven you. Be specific. 'Thank You for forgiving me for.....' 'Thank You that you don't judge me for...' Ask Him to show you anything He's forgiven you for that you haven't forgiven yourself for.

- If you need to say sorry for judging yourself, do so.

- Make a decision today to let go of any guilt you're carrying. Leave it at the cross.

READ: John 8:2-11

Read the passage slowly, and imagine yourself in the crowd, watching the scene unfold.

PUSH IN

– How do you think the woman must have felt, standing in front of all those people accusing her?

– What do you think she might have been expecting Jesus to say?

– Why didn't He judge her when she was guilty as charged?

– What's the difference between saying, 'I don't judge you' and 'Stop sinning'?

– Are you afraid of the judgement of others?

This woman was judged by others but not by Jesus. He didn't let her defend herself, but He did protect her from the impact of their judgement. She walked away in freedom, knowing she wasn't judged by the One whose judgement matters most.

– What implications does this have for you when you fear the judgement of others or feel they might be judging you?

Talk to Jesus about whatever this story raises for you.

READ: Deuteronomy 31:9-11
He shielded and cared for him; He guarded him as the apple of His eye.

As I open up my laptop this morning, I notice what I don't normally notice: the apple logo on its cover. It's a symbol of quality and value recognised the world over. You may not have thought of yourself in connection with an apple before, unless you've had some fun with that body shape stuff and you belong to the apple brigade! But God says to you today, 'You're the apple of My eye.'

What does that mean? A bit of background: the phrase 'apple of his eye' more literally translates as 'the little man or woman of his eye.' If you look carefully into someone's eyes, you can see a tiny reflection of yourself in their pupils. At some point, the 'little woman' became the 'apple' of the eye, maybe because pupils are round. The beautiful meaning of this phrase is that if you look into God's eyes, you will see your reflection. Why? Because He's always looking at you.

To be the apple of someone's eye is to be cherished and adored by them. To be looked at consistently with love and affection, as if you were their favourite. You may not have been the apple of your earthly father's eye, but you are the apple of your Heavenly Father's eye. He watches over you and takes care of you the way He'd take care of His own eye.

Many of us struggle to feel accepted by God and to believe this. It may be easier on our better days when we feel closer to Him. But on days when our faults and failings are staring us in the face, God's affection for us can seem harder to get our hearts round. The Father wants to write this truth more deeply on your heart this week. You're not just accepted, you're the apple of His eye. He loves you and He adores you.

PAUSE
Every time you see an apple today, let it remind you you're the apple of God's eye no matter how you feel. Each time, turn your heart to Him and thank Him that that's who He says you are.

PRAY
Put your hand on your heart now and ask God to write this truth more deeply on it. Ask Him to help you believe it. Hear Him saying to you 'I guard you (your name) as the apple of My eye.'

READ: John 4:4-26
The woman said, 'You must be a prophet!' (TPT)

The woman who met Jesus at the well concluded He must be a prophet. Jesus told her mid-chat that He knew she was living with a man who wasn't her husband. He also knew she'd been married five times. Not your average everyday small talk! If you're the apple of His eye, then He's looking at you. And if He's looking at you, He sees you. And if He sees you, He knows you. He knows you better than you know yourself.

Many of us are afraid of being seen and being known. The prospect of others discovering our darkest secrets is scary; we've no idea how they'll react. Will they judge us and reject us? Will they treat us differently or disadvantage us because of what they learn? Everyone knew this woman's failures and flaws. They managed to find out without Twitter! And they'd judged and rejected her, forcing her to go to the well in the midday heat so no one else would be seen with her. How typical of Jesus to pick that time. We're afraid of the judgement of others. But avoiding detection and trying to protect our hearts keeps us from the healing love of God.

The Father desires for us to live fully known and fully loved. We can't be fully loved without being fully known. No wonder this woman's life was turned upside down. No matter what you've done or what's been done to you, it doesn't change your value as the apple of His eye. A £20 note isn't any less valuable if it's dirty and dishevelled than the day it came off the printing press. And it's no more valuable if it's got glitter on! This woman discovered she *was* valuable, and she *was* loved. By Him. So are you. You're why He came. It takes courage to trust His love and to be honest with others. But you have that courage because you have Him.

PONDER
What do you do to earn affection or approval from others?

PRAY
Ask the Holy Spirit to show you where you're trying to make others think you're someone you're not. Ask Him to show you what step to take today to reveal more of your true self to someone.

READ: Zephaniah 3:14-17
He will rejoice over you...He will sing and be joyful over you. (NCV)

Have you ever thought about the fact that God sings? We may be used to hearing and seeing various singers and dancers in talent competitions and on the internet, but what if we could hear God sing? Have you ever wondered what His singing voice sounds like? Whether it's deep and has lots of vibrato or whether it's rich and mellow? One thing's for sure – He'd leave everyone else standing!

God sings, and it's not any old singing. It's not a gentle humming while He works or a quiet lullaby to calm us down when we're uptight, (although I'm sure He does that!). And He doesn't sing the blues because we don't measure up. He sings a full on, upbeat song of celebration. Because of you. What Zephaniah says here is that you delight the Father, and He's so excited about you, He can't help but sing.

We all have our own ideas about how God feels about us. For some of us, those ideas have been influenced by pictures we've seen of Jesus. Have you noticed how He so often seems to look like someone whose cat has just died? He certainly doesn't look like He'd ever be singing for joy. Some of our ideas about how God feels are shaped by how others have felt about us or by how we feel about ourselves. If I've disappointed others, I must disappoint God. If I feel ashamed of myself, God must disapprove of me not celebrate over me.

Friend, the Holy Spirit is always looking to replace your ideas about how God feels about you with the truth. He looks at you with joy, not judgement, and with delight, not disapproval. Let these verses reset your mindset. Hear Him say to you again, 'You're the apple of My eye'. You've chosen to trust what Jesus has done for you. He wants you to know you make Him sing. Believe Him, and be more confident of His love!

PONDER
Is there something about yourself or your life, or is there something you've done that makes it difficult to believe the Father is singing over you? Read these verses again, out loud.

PRAY
Talk to God about it. Ask Him what song you'd hear if you could hear Him singing over you.

READ: Luke 4:14-21
He has sent Me...to proclaim the year of the Lord's favour.

Some years ago, I flew back from Oman with a friend, having been there to speak at a conference. To our surprise, we were upgraded to business class at check-in. As we sat in the spacious seats, drinking champagne and staring at the gorgeous menu of food that was to come, we felt very spoilt as we hadn't paid for them. The treatment was so different to the treatment in economy!

There may be different classes of seats and standards of service on international airlines, but in the Kingdom, there aren't different classes of people. The world places more value and importance on some people than others, but the Father doesn't. If you're the apple of His eye, you're his favoured one. As Jesus arrived on the public stage, His first words to the crowd were essentially these: 'I've got good news everyone. God wants to bless you. The time of His favour has arrived.'

The word 'favour' is where we get our word 'favourite' from. It means 'excessive kindness or preferential treatment'. Or how you see a 'favourite' being treated. That's why it's such great news. Although the Bible says God doesn't have favourites (Rom 2:11), it's as if Jesus is saying to everyone who trusts Him, 'You're my favourite and I'm going to treat you like that.' His excessive kindness and preferential treatment are as real and available to you as the apple of His eye, as to anyone else.

There are different callings in the kingdom, but not different classes of believers. Some daughters (no matter who they are or what they do) aren't more favoured or special than others. But we can only enjoy His favour, we can't earn it. Like everything in the kingdom, it's experienced through trusting, not trying.

PONDER
Do you ever feel second class in any way, or envious of certain privileges that others are enjoying? Reject the lie that you're second rate and less favoured than others. Refuse to agree with it any longer. Hear Jesus declaring His words above over your life today. Decide to believe them.

READ: Mark 5:24-34
He asked 'Who touched my clothes?'

Have you ever been caught in a crowd? Perhaps you've battled the masses in a sale somewhere or been swept along in the human tide leaving a packed auditorium? It's cramped in a crowd. I love this story of a broken, heroic woman desperate to reach Jesus. And I love the question that Jesus asks in the middle of this intense situation. 'Who touched my clothes?' I bet the disciples had to bite their tongues not to come out with better banter. Let's face it, probably everyone had! Why did He ask such a ridiculous question?

Jesus had more for this beautiful woman, just like He always has more than we ask for. We want the answer to prayer, He wants to lead us into a deeper experience of His love. This woman got her healing. 12 years of poverty, loneliness and rejection caused by debilitating bleeding, over in a second. Amazing! She'd hoped to stay invisible, but Jesus wasn't playing ball. If you're the apple of His eye and His favourite, His eye is on you and His heart is for you. Even in the middle of a huge crowd.

No matter how invisible you feel, how much you're struggling, how much you've failed or how worthless you think you are, Jesus' eye is on you. He will meet your personal needs as you reach out to Him, like she did. He will do what isn't possible if you expect Him to, like she did. But He also wants you confident your identity isn't in your problem or your past, or in your circumstances or your sin. He didn't want this woman believing her past experience had anything to do with her identity. He wants you to be confident of the same. He calls you 'daughter' as He called her 'daughter.' He calls you out as the apple of His eye as He did to her. He calls you to come to Him every day, as you are. He wants to look you in the eye, affirm you and deal with your fears and your insecurities. Let Him do that today.

PRAY
Come to Him now just as you are. Trust His love and thank Jesus that He welcomes you as the apple of His eye. Hear Him say 'Daughter' as you come to Him. Listen for the love and affection in His voice and receive it. Ask Him to show you what fears or insecurities He wants to free you from.

RE-READ: Mark 5:24-34

PLAY the PART

Put yourself into the story. Imagine you're the one trying to get to Jesus that day, because you're longing for His power to break into your life in some way. Perhaps it's something you're embarrassed to share with other people.

– LISTEN to the noise of the crowd. Imagine what it feels like to try and get to Jesus. Push through until you manage to touch His cloak. Listen to His voice as you hear Him ask, 'Who touched Me?'

– RESPOND to His question and approach Him. Notice how you feel. What does He say to you? What do you say back to Him?

Write down anything that your heart needs to treasure.

READ: Psalm 17:6-8

David was bold enough to remind God that he was the apple of His eye. To do so is a declaration of trust in God's word about who He says you are. One of the obvious responses to being the apple of His eye is deep gratitude.

PRAY
Whether you feel like the apple of His eye or whether you're struggling to accept this truth about yourself, spend some time today thanking God that this IS who you are. Thanking Him for His truth helps bed it into your heart so that it begins to feel true as well as being true. Thank Him for all that He's said to you and reminded you of this week. Then ask Him for what you need, as David does here, and expect Him to respond (like David did)., because you are the apple of His eye.

READ: John 11:17-27

I am the Resurrection, and I am Life Eternal. Anyone who clings to Me in faith, even though he dies, will live forever. (TPT)

The coronavirus pandemic has shaken the world. One small virus, invisible to the human eye, moved nations indoors, cancelled events across the planet, rattled economies and put the global village on the back foot. It's been another reminder the world over, if we needed one, that life and death are beyond our control, no matter how advanced our science or how great our resources.

As Jesus arrived in Bethany, some of His closest friends were facing and feeling this reality. Their brother had died suddenly and prematurely. Family life had been turned on its head within a matter of days. As Jesus arrived, He was moved to tears by their pain. But before He brought Lazarus back to life, He wanted to make sure they understood something. He wanted to show them a new truth about Himself. He was desperate for them to know that there's a bigger reality than death. He needed to make sure they understood there is life beyond the grave. For those who believe and trust in Him. Life after we die is possible, but only through Him. Because He *is* the Resurrection.

Imagine you're holding a metre-long piece of string in your hands. Imagine the centimetre at one end covered by your thumb as you hold the string taut. That centimetre represents life here on earth relative to the future that eternity offers (the rest of the string). Friend, that eternal reality is our permanent destiny. Whatever we experience and live through here is temporary. What we experience there will be forever (2 Cor 4:17-18). Let's allow the horizon of Heaven to shape how we live today. Let it stir up hope, let it move you towards those who don't know Him and let it help you let go of whatever mindset is holding up your life.

PONDER

Read the verse over a few times, slowly. What does it stir up in you? Would you say you live this life with one eye on the horizon of Heaven? If you don't, how would it make a difference?

PRAY

Thank Jesus that He's turned the full stop of the grave into a comma for those who 'cling to Him in faith.' Ask Him to help you cling to Him and live today with Heaven on your horizon.

READ: John 20:11-18
'Don't cling to Me,' Jesus said, 'for I haven't yet ascended to the Father...' (NLT)

Sad fact that made my day: I found a packet of Easter eggs in the cupboard a couple of weeks ago that had fallen down behind some stuff and got missed. What an unexpected and welcome surprise on a rainy summer day with no known chocolate in the house! Do you like surprises? On this particular morning, Mary had the surprise of a lifetime. It didn't just brighten up her day, it changed her life. Forever. She went to the tomb to grieve her dead friend, and was greeted by Him outside the tomb, more alive than ever. That's a different league of surprise!

Resurrection happens after death. I know that's an obvious thing to say but it's a kingdom principle that a beginning comes after an ending. Jesus is the Resurrection. His nature is to bring new life from death. The only way for us to experience resurrection life, is to accept the death that precedes it. Mary had watched Him die on the cross, and watched His dead body get shut up in the tomb (Matt 27:61). She'd faced the fact and felt the grief that her precious Saviour had died. I cannot imagine the heaviness in her soul as she accepted that life with Him was over. But she did, and in that place of acceptance, Jesus met her and revealed His resurrection life to her.

Are you longing to see a resurrection in your own experience somewhere? Are you praying to see God bring new life? Are you living with disappointment? If so, have you embraced what isn't there or what hasn't happened? Have you accepted what's been taken away or what you've lost? Have you faced the fact and felt the grief? Whether that's a relationship, a dream, a plan, a season of life, a reputation or even your passion for Jesus, the way to resurrection life is always through death. Our losses in this life are real. But so is our resurrecting God.

PONDER
Are you tempted to overlook or underplay the losses, disappointments or endings in your life? If so, how do you do that? Do you expect resurrection to follow them in some way?

PRAY
Talk to Jesus about any areas in your life where you're longing for Him to bring about a resurrection. Be as honest as you can. Ask Him to help you face and feel whatever you need to.

READ: Matthew 26:36-43
My Father, if there is any way, get Me out of this. (MSG)

The Father is a miracle worker but He doesn't always work the way we'd like. Your own experiences tell you that. We pray certain prayers and don't get the answers we want. Maybe you have a story of a miracle you were longing for that didn't happen. Sometimes God demonstrates His power by turning a situation around dramatically. And He says we should expect that. But other times He has a deeper work and purpose in mind.

As its reality was looming, Jesus asked the Father to rescue Him from the cross if at all possible. That part of His prayer wasn't answered. The original plan they'd agreed on was one that would turn the future of the universe the right way up. So the Father allowed His precious boy to go through the agony of the cross. Instead of saving Him, He let Him die. Death was the tool God needed to use to fulfil His purposes. It was the only way to open the door to life for everyone else who would choose Him and accept His forgiveness.

Friend, your miracle may lie the other side of some difficult or painful circumstances. God doesn't prevent every trouble or save us from it immediately, as you already know. Instead of rescuing us as quickly as we'd like, and instead of saving us from setbacks or difficulty, He regularly saves us *through* them. Somehow they become tools in His hands to put to death some of the false identities, unhealthy attachments or old ways in us that stand between us and the life we long for. As we walk with Him, He's committed to dealing with those things that keep us from doing His will or walking in His love. But more always awaits us on the other side. Jesus *is* the Resurrection and He's always working to release resurrection life to us. Keep your heart open to Him and trust Him.

PONDER
Have you ever been through a difficult or painful experience with Jesus that in time, turned out to be a blessing?

PRAY
Talk to Jesus about any difficulties or trouble you are facing now. Invite Him to put to death in you whatever He needs to so you can walk more closely with Him.

READ: Ezekiel 37:1-10
He asked me, 'Son of man, can these bones live?'

When I ask someone a question, it's normally because I want to know the answer. When God asks someone a question, it's because He wants that person to know the answer! Ezekiel was looking out over a valley full of dead dry bones. Not your average picture postcard view. God asks him, 'Do you think these bones can live?' What was it that He wanted Ezekiel to know? How much faith he had. It's one thing to dream in our bedrooms, it's another to stare reality in the face and believe for a reversal of what we see. Ezekiel didn't answer 'no'. He passed the test.

The Holy Spirit continually needs to remind me that much of what I want to see God do in this world is hindered by my unbelief. It hampers His work in my life, and it handicaps my prayer life. They're connected. Jesus couldn't perform miracles when He came across unbelief. God wanted Ezekiel to admit whether he could believe for this miracle of resurrection before He told him how it was going to come about. He'd planned to involve Ezekiel but needed to know if he was bringing faith to the table. If we don't believe something will happen, we won't be willing to partner with the Holy Spirit to make it happen. What would be the point?

Is there a valley of dry bones in your life? A place of dryness or lifelessness that needs resurrecting? Is it in your relationship with God? Or in a relationship with someone else? Or in the place where you work? Or in the life of a loved one? Or in your community? Or beyond? God's command to Ezekiel was to speak out the word of God over the bones. To add his breath to God's words, so God could breathe out His power and bring the bones back to life. Dry bone situations need the word of God to see the life of God. When we face them, we're to speak God's word to them. We're to remind the Holy Spirit of what He's promised to do, and to proclaim God's word, in faith, over the situation as Ezekiel did. Don't just know God's word or learn it. Believe in its power and speak it out. Keep doing so until you hear those bones begin to rattle.

PAUSE
Hear the Father asking you the question above, about a situation in your life or that you know about. How do you answer? How do you think Ezekiel might have felt, speaking out God's word to a load of dead bones? Talk to Jesus about what this stirs in you today.

READ: 1 Corinthians 15:12-20
For if there is no resurrection of the dead, then Christ has not been raised either. (NLT)

A significant birthday is coming up for one of my sons. A big celebration with friends in our garden is one way we're marking the occasion. Not surprisingly, we've had to make plans and pencil in some time to prepare for it. We've also had to rearrange our diaries for that day. And of course, it will impact the bank balance for that month! It's a small event in the big scheme of things, but it *is* affecting us right now.

The physical resurrection of Jesus Christ is the most controversial but life-defining event in human history. Even our very calendar is based around it. Yet Paul is writing here to the believers in Corinth, feeling the need to drill the truth down into them that Jesus really did come back to life. He reminds them it was a fact, not a fantasy. And that it either changes everything, or it changes nothing. He says, 'If all we get out of Christ is a little inspiration for a few short years, we're a pretty sorry lot.' (v18 MSG). Why would he say such a thing? Because Jesus doesn't intend for us to live this life just appreciating His teaching or His help. He didn't plan for us to live for this world, but for the next one. Paul is urging the believers to let Jesus' resurrection impact them right now.

How does Jesus want His resurrection to change our today? He wants us to take eternity, and the future destiny of others, seriously. He wants to reach them through us, before it's too late, and rescue them to Heaven. He wants us to see what's going on in our world through the lens of His physical return, and be ready. He wants us free from the fear of death. He wants us confident that He'll reward us for sticking with Him through our struggles. And He wants us full of joy and full of praise. Because one day, weeping and pain, struggle and suffering will end. We will meet Him face to face and be with Him forever. In our own, new, resurrected bodies.

PONDER
Would you say the resurrection of Jesus impacts your every day? If so, how?

PRAY
Thank Jesus that He rose from the dead. Thank Him for all that the prospect of eternity with Him means. Ask Him to give you a new sense of urgency about living this life for Him.

READ: Ephesians 1:19-20, John 20:1-10

PLAY the PART

Read through the two verses in Ephesians. Then, as you read the verses in John, notice the details they describe about the shocking discovery that Jesus' dead body is no longer in the heavily guarded tomb.

– IMAGINE yourself outside the tomb with Simon Peter and John. Follow their example and walk in. Imagine Jesus' dead body lying there only a few hours earlier. Look at the strips of linen, now with no body inside them. Look at the separate piece of cloth that had been wrapped around Jesus' head.

– LET the impact of what you are looking at stir your heart.

– NOTICE how you feel. Do you have any questions? Do you notice anything else?

– INVITE God to speak to you about His power that raised Jesus from the dead, and what His power means for you. What response do you need to make?

READ: Revelation 21

The end of the book of Revelation gives us a glimpse of the end of the story and the resurrection life, fought for and paid for by Jesus. It's included in the Bible, because He wants us to be able to peek through the curtains, see what lies ahead and pin our hopes on it.

PUSH IN

– Read through the passage slowly, and note down anything that stands out to you, or that you have questions about.

– Spend some time thinking about and then praying about what you've read. Ask the Holy Spirit your questions. Notice any impressions that come to mind.

– Ask Him if there is something specific He wants you to do as a result of what you've read.

READ: Isaiah 61:1-6
You will be called priests of the Lord, ministers of our God. (NLT)

Please. Stay with me on this one! Minister is probably not a word you use every day and might have all kinds of connotations for you. Before I began to grasp my new identity, it was a word I associated with religious people in professional positions. And the associations weren't all good! But friend, we need to reclaim this word if we're to live the life He's called us to. Because Jesus calls you a minister.

What does Jesus expect His ministers to be? He expects them to be those who minister His hope and love to anyone they meet. In short, they are to be a blessing and bring life. You are His blessing to this world. Isaiah says in verse 4 that His ministers will rebuild, restore and renew. That could range from renewing someone's hope on a bad day, by listening to them and speaking life to them, to renewing the life chances of someone by rescuing them from slavery. It could range from helping restore someone's strength by looking after their kids so they can get some rest, to restoring the fortunes of an entire community.

You, friend, are a minister of God. You don't need special clothing, special training or special qualifications. You're qualified as His daughter and authorised to bring life. Those He calls ministers are those who've received the ministry of His Holy Spirit to their own hearts, rebuilding, restoring and renewing them. That's what the first three verses are describing. If you've known Jesus for more than a day, you're qualified because He's begun to minister to you! You're not perfect, but you're perfectly positioned and perfectly prepared. You have what you need because you have Who you need. Whatever your job, whatever your qualifications, whatever you spend your time doing, He's positioned you to bring His life to those around you.

PONDER
Who are the people God has positioned you to minister to?

PRAY
Let the truth of this verse sink in. Thank Jesus He's called you to be His minister and ask Him to help you walk more fully and freely in what this means for you.

READ: Luke 10:25-35
He went to him and bandaged his wounds, pouring on oil and wine.

Jesus was such a fantastic storyteller, don't you think? He tells a story here about a true minister. A Jewish chap's in trouble and he needs some help. That's all we're told. He could be a thief himself, a bad egg who's cheated on his wife or an innocent, lovely old man. That's clearly not the point. Ministers minister, no matter who's in front of them – enemies, strangers or friends. Everyone needs a touch from Heaven. That's what Jesus was about, and it's what He's called His daughters to, too.

Two men walked past, either too busy, too distracted or just reluctant to bless this guy. Ironically they were professional ministers. One was a priest, the other worked in the temple somewhere. But neither was a true minister of the Father's heart. The true minister noticed, interrupted his agenda, and did the bit he could. He couldn't fix the guy's wounds and he didn't have a house nearby to take the man to, but he had a donkey and a wallet. So he took him somewhere where others could do more.

Jesus doesn't ask us to do everything, He asks us to do something. But as in this story, it's often not convenient. Since being a minister is an identity not a profession, Jesus sends us to people at random times or in random places. Anytime, anywhere. You have something to offer those He brings to you. When He puts them in front of you it's because you have what they need, like this guy did. What gifts and abilities do you have? It may not be medical training but you do have a donkey, so to speak! You may not have a solution, but you do have ears to listen. You may not be able to give thousands but you can give something. You're a minister of the love and life of Jesus. How does He want you to minister that life and love today?

PONDER
Which one of the characters do you identify with most in this story? How interruptible are you?

PRAY
Since Jesus doesn't ask you to do everything or minister to everyone, ask the Holy Spirit to nudge you today when He puts someone across your path who He wants you to minister to.

READ: Matthew 25:35-40

I tell you the truth, when you did it to one of the least of these My brothers and sisters, you were doing it to Me! (NLT)

Once, when I was on an overseas trip, a friend invited one of my kids round to treat them. This particular child needed cheering up a bit and my friend wanted to bless them and spoil them while I was away. They weren't doing it for me, they were doing it for my child, but it *felt* like they were doing it as a gift for me. I was so touched and so grateful.

What we do for others we do for Him, Jesus says here. He's positioned and prepared us to minister His love to all sorts of people. That may be as small a thing as taking the time to notice and speak to the stranger on the till that everyone else ignored all day. My friend spotted a very sad looking teenager in a park this week, and ended up chatting to her. She needed a friend. Giving a stranger a drink, as Jesus describes here, doesn't require super powers and won't change the world in a day. But it might just change that person's day. And whether it does or doesn't, it changes Jesus' day, crazy as that may seem.

The enemy wants us to fall for the lie that unless what we're doing looks significant, it isn't. Serving a drink to an influential person may feel like a significant thing; social media might appreciate the selfie. It's not the same if that person is an 'unimportant' stranger who offers nothing back. Maybe that's why the people in this passage didn't realise their ministry had been so significant. But Jesus keeps a record of those we've ministered to on His behalf. Look for Him in others. When we're kind to someone in need because we love Jesus, we're blessing Him, not just the one in front of us. As this story shows, that's the kind of kindness that echoes in eternity and gets written on the walls of Heaven.

PONDER

What small things do you see as insignificant? When did you last do a small thing for someone who needed something? What about for a stranger?

PRAY

Talk to Jesus about what's on your heart today.

READ: Luke 19:1-10

Zacchaeus, hurry down. Today is My day to be a guest in your home. (MSG)

Not everyone's needs are obvious but let's be willing to make the first move. Jesus ministered the Father's love to the people He'd come for. He responded to those who came to Him, but also reached out to others. Zacchaeus was up a tree trying to get a good view of the good man in town. There's no evidence he was spiritually hungry and he wasn't calling out for help like others did. But people who are open to God don't always look like they're looking for God. Jesus made the first move towards Zacchaeus. And as He did, Zacchaeus moved towards Him; he ended up moving into eternity.

You're called and equipped to bring life to those around you, but sometimes you need to take the first step. Everybody has hidden hurts and hidden struggles. That first move might be praying and asking the Father to show you what's troubling your colleague, your friend, your relative or your hairdresser. He's promised to speak to you. Ask Him to bring what's hidden into the light so you can minister His life to them. Or ask Him to show you what's stopping them wanting a relationship with Jesus. You don't have to pray long prayers; pray specifically and regularly until He shows you. You're ministering to others even when you're asking the Father to minister His life to them.

That first move might be starting a conversation, like Jesus did, by showing an interest in the person He's put in your life. It might be crossing a street or a corridor to begin a connection with someone who's on the edge of your life. It might be starting an initiative that's been on your heart that brings life to others in some way. Friend, the Holy Spirit is at work around you in ways He wants to show you. He's setting you up to minister His life. As you do, you'll experience more of His life yourself. As Solomon said: 'The one who blesses others is abundantly blessed' (Prov 11:25).

PONDER
What is Jesus saying to you about making the first move today and with whom?

PRAY
Ask the Father to give you the eyes of Jesus to see the Zacchaeus that He's put near you today.

READ: Numbers 6:22-27

Whenever Aaron and his sons bless the people of Israel in My name, I will bless them. (NLT)

Do you realise how much power you have in your mouth? I'm sure you've experienced the impact of words spoken over you to build you up, and words spoken over you that have torn you down. Words are powerful because God made them so. He says, 'Words kill, words give life; they're either poison or fruit – you choose' (Prov 18:21 MSG). We don't get to decide what power they hold, only how we'll use them.

Aaron and his sons were ministers appointed by God. In the Old Testament, only certain, specially chosen people could be priests or ministers. One of their jobs was to bless people on God's behalf. Here, the Father tells them that He's given them authority to bless others with their words. He teaches them to declare His blessing and favour over His people (this isn't praying to God) and then adds, 'I'll back up what you say and bless them.' In other words, 'You say it and then I'll do it.' He says the same to you and me, as His New Testament ministers. The power to release God's blessing into someone's life lies on your lips.

This sounds arrogant to some, except it's God's idea. It's how He wants to partner with us. But it requires faith. To declare the Father's peace over someone when they're in turmoil demands faith that He'll move in response to your words. To declare His provision over someone in need requires your confidence that Jesus will back you up. I know someone whose wayward son became a father at a very young age. He had no desire or clue how to be a good dad. But each time she spoke to him, she declared in faith, 'You're a great dad.' She expected God to back her up, and He did, changing her son's life as he parented his kid. You're a minister of Jesus; He's put great power and authority in your mouth. Be bold, step out and use it to bring life and blessing today.

PONDER
Have you ever made a declaration over someone in faith, expecting God to back you up?

PRAY
Ask the Holy Spirit to lead you to someone today who needs His words of life spoken over them. Ask Him to give you the courage to go for it.

PUSH IN

Answer 'I agree' or 'I disagree' to the following statements:

1.   The Holy Spirit shows up in my life.
2.   I expect the Holy Spirit to show up in the lives of others.
3.   I'm called to minister to others in the same way that Jesus did.
4.   I have authority to release life and speak life to others.
5.   I have the same access to the same resources and the same power that Jesus had.
6.   I expect Jesus to answer my prayers when I pray for others.
7.   People who are spiritually lost are irresistible to the Father.
8.   He loves to use me to minister His love and life.
9.   I look for opportunities to live out my identity as a minister most days.
10.   I am interruptible.

Talk to Jesus about anything on your heart from this little exercise. Ask Him to speak to you about how He wants to grow you.

RE-READ: Isaiah 61:1-6

You will be called priests of the Lord, ministers of our God. (NLT)

PUSH IN

– Summarise what you sense Jesus has been saying to you this week.

– How is He wanting you to change the way you see yourself? How would it change how you approach your work and your home life if you lived out of your identity as minister?

– Ask Him any questions you have.

– Sit quietly in His presence for a few moments. Breathe deeply, relax and hear Him speak His words above over you. Thank Him for calling you to be His minister.

READ: Colossians 1:15-21
Everything was created through Him and for Him. (NLT)

Picture a stunning sunset you've stood and stared at, in awe of its beauty. Picture the waves you've stopped and watched on a stormy day, in awe of their power. Romans 1:20 tells us the Father speaks to us about what He's like through creation. It's as if nature is trying to get our attention to say, 'There is a Creator, a divine Designer, and He's behind all this. So look carefully because you can see what He's like from what He's made.'

What does nature tell us about the Father? It tells us He loves beauty, He's super powerful, He's a master designer with an off-the-scale imagination, He's recklessly extravagant and He loves variety. No two sunsets are even the same. God has also penned all kinds of messages about His love for us into His handiwork. The psalmist reminds us that, 'As high as the sky is above the earth, so great is His love for those who respect Him' (103:11). Wherever you live, whether in a city or by the sea, the Father planned for you to look up to the 'high sky' each day and be reminded of His huge heart for you.

Paul says God created 'everything', through Jesus and for Jesus. You're part of that word 'everything'. Whatever your human beginnings, the Father made you through Jesus and *for* Jesus. For His pleasure. For relationship with Him. I believe we need reminding of it every day of our lives. We're not here by chance and we weren't created just to do something for Him. He created us to receive and know His unchanging, unshakeable, extravagant love. To live loved and to love Him back. So He's penned it in a way we can read everyday. He's written it in the sky by making it so high! You were created for Jesus. Let Him speak to you about His heart for you through His creation today.

PONDER
What does it mean for you that the Father created you 'through Jesus and for Him'? Look out of your window and up at the sky. Ask the Holy Spirit to speak to you about Jesus' love for you.

PRAY
Spend a bit of time sitting in silence with your Creator. Then, thank Him for His deep love for you. Each time you're outside today, look up at the sky and let it remind you of His huge heart for you.

READ: Psalm 8
O Lord, our Lord, Your majestic name fills the earth!

Have you ever wondered why God made the world so beautiful? Why the trees are green, not black, why the fruit in your fruit bowl isn't grey, and why flowers aren't all white? God could have made the world in monochrome, but He created it in multicolour. He has even decorated the tropical fish (that so few see) with His heavenly paintbrush. Creation is beautiful because the Father loves beauty. And we need beauty. It inspires and strengthens our spirits. It lifts our mood. It heals us. And it draws us to Him. Because as this verse says, His name fills the earth.

Something I heard many say during the lockdown, was how much they loved going for a walk or run, to get outside. We're closer to nature outside than inside, wherever we live, and nature can help us feel closer to God. He designed us to live in a garden, remember? The beauty of creation inspires us, refreshes us and lowers our stress levels. Picture a river running through a meadow and a busy road running through a city. I know which one helps me relax more! Beauty makes us breathe more deeply and more slowly. It stirs our positive emotions. And it even heals our hearts in ways we didn't know we needed.

Creation is beautiful and it also brings perspective. As the psalmist stares up at the stars in the sky, he's reminded of the power and majesty of the Father and his own small place in the world. And he's impacted once again that God should care so personally for him. Friend, let me encourage you to get outside each day, even if it's only for a few moments. Even if it's for a quick walk down the street. Don't keep your head down or your earphones in but ask Him to speak to you through what you see. Talk to Him about what you notice like the psalmist did. Let the beauty of creation bless you, and let the Creator touch your heart.

PONDER
Think of a time when you were in a beautiful place. How did it make you feel? What impact did it have on your stress level or your mood?

PRAY
Look around the place you are in. Is there anything beautiful in it? Flowers, a piece of artwork, a photo? Look at it and as you do, ask the Holy Spirit to speak to you through it.

READ: Psalm 139:13-18

For You created my inmost being; You knit me together in my mother's womb.

Have you ever knitted anything? Knitting is a detailed and intricate business and even though He didn't use knitting needles, the Father formed you in a detailed and complex way. I love how The Passion Translation puts it: 'You formed my innermost being, shaping my delicate inside and my intricate outside, and wove them all together in my mother's womb.' The Father knows everything there is to know about you because He designed you.

Like everything else in God's creation, you are unique. Let me remind you today that He knows your unique set of needs, your unique wounds and how to heal your unique heart. He knows your unique struggles and secrets, and how to help you and how to grow you. And He knows your unique dreams and desires and how to lead you forward in this unique life He made you for. Do you believe that?

Are you comfortable being you? The reason trees can't swim, fish can't fly, and the moon doesn't produce heat is because the Designer didn't intend them to. But the world and the enemy try and persuade us we should do all kinds of things or be all kinds of things we weren't made for. One way that happens is when we get tempted to compare. How we parent, how we look, what we're achieving, how many followers we have, who we know, what we have... But the moment we start comparing, we begin to let go of who we are. We lose sight of our own uniqueness and our unique calling, and before long we're trying to be someone we weren't created to be.

Friend, don't doubt your unique value and your unique contribution to this world. Don't run from who you are. Instead, run to your Creator and let *Him* tell you again who you are and what He's made you for. Determine to be courageous and live the unique life only you can live.

PAUSE

Are you comfortable being you or do you feel pressure to be someone you're not? If so, where does that pressure come from? Thank the Father that He knows you completely. Ask Him to give you courage to live the unique life He's called you to and the strength to refuse to compare yourself.

READ: Mark 2:23-27
Then Jesus said to them, 'The Sabbath was made to meet the needs of people...' (NLT)

A few years ago, I wasn't concentrating as I stopped to put petrol in my car. As I drove off the forecourt, I realised I'd put diesel in instead of unleaded. My little car wasn't happy, and neither was my husband! We get the best from our vehicles when we run them according to the manufacturer's design, and we humans are no different.

The day after God created us, He created the Sabbath and rested. Rest was the first thing Adam and Eve did. Cars run on fuel, we're designed to live from rest. As Jesus pointed out to the Pharisees who were questioning Him about the Sabbath, God created it to meet our needs. We have a need for a Sabbath. We are the created ones, He is the Creator. We have a finite capacity, He doesn't. We need sleep, He doesn't. He has deliberately built limitation into our makeup. So when we neglect our need for the recharging and refuelling that rest gives, we are not just being disobedient, we're denying our design.

Friend, our Creator made rest one of His top 10 commands. That's how important it is. Even nature gets a season of rest every winter! Our bodies and minds need rest, our emotions need recharging, and our spirits needs refuelling. Regularly. Not just on holiday. Rest leads to re-creation and Jesus says we need that every week. Does your diary have a day off in it every seven days? Do you prioritise a day that looks different to the others, is free from work, and includes something to feed your soul and connect with the family of God, as well as the people you love? A rhythm of rest in our lives provides the antidote to hurry and stress. It also reminds us that the Father is the One on whom life depends. Not us!

PONDER
Do you have a regular Sabbath? If not, ask the Holy Spirit to show you what lie is preventing you from making one happen. What recharges your soul?

PRAY
Hand your heart and life back to your Creator today. Embrace your limitations again and invite Him to teach you how to live from a place of rest.

READ: Romans 8:26-30
And we know that God causes everything to work together for the good of those who love God. (NLT)

I have a friend who's a great cook. She has that amazing ability to take whatever's in her fridge and cupboards, often a combination of random ingredients that I wouldn't know what to do with, and turn it into something delicious. No matter what is or isn't there, she'll find a way of serving up a mouth-watering offering. She's a great friend to have!

This is a favourite verse of mine that I declare almost on a daily basis. The Father causes *everything* to work together for my good, not just the good things. It's true for you too. No matter what 'the thing' is, He can use and will use every circumstance and every event and non-event in your life and work it out for your good. Creators are unbelievably skilful with their raw materials, whether it's food, paint, a musical instrument or whatever. Our Creator is even more skilful with the raw material of circumstances, however desperate, dark or difficult they may be. There's nothing He isn't using. Everything. That word leaves nothing out.

Whether it's a mistake you've made, a choice you regret, a problem in your life caused by someone else, a situation you can't control, there's *no* ingredient about which God doesn't say 'Yep, I'll take that, I'll be creative with it, I'll use it and I'll bless you from it. Just trust Me.' Nothing is ever wasted if we love Him and believe this promise. Learn it and lean on it, friend. As you travel through your day, let it shape your response to whatever comes your way whether that thing throws you, scares you, upsets you or frustrates you. Be quick to tell Him you expect Him to use it for your good. It will protect your peace. He wants His daughters confident that 'everything' is an ingredient He can work wonders with.

PONDER
What do you see as the difference between God causing everything, and God causing everything to work together for good?

PRAY
Pick some of the challenges or regrets in your life at the moment and name them to Jesus. Thank Him in faith that He can use, and is using, each one to bring good to you because you love Him.

PUSH IN

If you can, find some time to go for a walk today with your Creator. Get outside where you live, even if it's for 10 minutes and walk at a leisurely pace. Chat to Jesus as you walk, and ask Him to speak to you through something in His creation. As you walk, look around, pay attention to the beauty you see, breathe it in and notice what catches your eye. When something does, ask Him what He wants to say to you through it.

RE-READ: Psalm 51:1-15
Create in me a clean heart, O God. (NLT)

David wrote these words after messing up big time. He'd committed adultery with Bathsheba and then had her husband murdered. The Holy Spirit convicted him of his wrongdoing through the prophet Nathan who went to talk to him. These are the humble words of a man, talking to his Creator, who knew that only the creative work of a loving Father could bring about the change in him that he wanted and needed.

PUSH IN

Pray your own prayer to God, inviting Him to 'create in you'. Tell Him what you'd love Him to do. Be as honest and real as David was and put your longings into words.

When you've finished, thank the Father that He's heard your prayer.

READ: Romans 12:3-13

Each of us finds our meaning and function as a part of His body. But as a chopped-off finger or cut-off toe we wouldn't amount to much, would we? (MSG)

Gross story alert! A distant relative of mine was in Africa many years ago and got bitten on the finger by a poisonous scorpion. He knew its venom was deadly and wouldn't take long to get into his system and kill him. So he made the brave decision to pull out a knife and chop off his finger. He did so and saved his own life.

Our spiritual health and wellbeing is connected to who we're connected to. And that doesn't just include being connected to Jesus. Although this isn't my favourite translation of these verses, it's a graphic image. Any body part, separated from the body, doesn't have a healthy future ahead of it. My relative used this fact to his advantage, and Paul encourages us to do the same. But in the opposite way. He's telling us *not* to get cut off from the body. If we do, our life will suffer.

We were created for connection. Connection first with Jesus, and then with His body. With His family of believers known as the church. What's your connection like? Is it an online connection or an in person one? Is it a strong one or a flimsy one? The kind of connection we have to His body is key to our wellbeing. This verse says its how we find our meaning and function. That's big. Jesus describes us a part. I know, a less glamorous dimension of our identity! He says you're a part of His body. And if we're a part of something, then we're only healthy to the extent we're healthily connected to that something. Friend, we can't grow properly on our own. We can't get healed on our own. We can't be restored on our own. We can't find freedom on our own. We can't thrive on our own. We can't get victory on our own, and crucially, we can't fulfil our assignments on our own. God doesn't intend for it to be just us and Him. As a finger needs the blood, muscles and nerves from the rest of the body to do what it's designed to do, so you need God's family of believers.

PONDER

Have you ever been disconnected from the body of Jesus for a season? How did it affect you?

PRAY

Re-read this verse and talk to Jesus about what it raises for you.

READ: 1 Corinthians 12:12-25
A diversity is required, for if the body consisted of one single part, there wouldn't be a body at all! (TPT)

Your human body is made up of lots of different parts, and I'm pretty sure you don't compare them! I'm convinced you don't look at your ears in the mirror and say to yourself, 'I don't like my ears nearly as much as I like my liver.' And I'm certain you don't look at your right foot and think, 'You're not nearly as useful as my left elbow.' You don't compare the parts of your body because you need them all; each one matters.

The enemy loves to get us comparing, and when we do, he pushes us towards one of two conclusions. Both damage our connection to God's body. The first conclusion is mentioned in verse 21: we feel bigged up because of our comparing. When we do, we think who we are and what we offer is better than what others offer. Our ego then says, 'I don't need you'. The other conclusion is identified in verse 14: we can feel beaten down. If so, we fall for the lie that who we are and what we offer is less significant than others. Envy chimes in with, 'I wish I was like you', or false humility says, 'You don't need me.'

The Father designed us each of us to play a key part in His family. You have your unique role to play because you're one of a kind. So am I. You have gifts and abilities and express them in unique ways that He wants His body of believers to benefit from, not just His world. Your role is as important as everyone else's even though each part looks different. Some parts are more visible than others. But visibility has nothing to do with value. My lung matters as much as my left hand. Resist the temptation to compare yourself and undermine your calling. Instead, rise up and remember how much you're needed. You're not a spare part, but don't be a missing part. You need His body to fulfil His purposes for you. And His body needs you.

PAUSE
How are you using your gifts to help your local body function more effectively? Offer yourself to Jesus again as a part in His body and ask Him if He wants you to use your gifts differently to how you're currently using them. Thank Him that He's made you with unique gifts for a unique purpose. Resolve not to compare yourself and ask Him to help you celebrate the gifts of others.

READ: Romans 12:4
Each part gets its meaning from the body as a whole, not the other way around.
(MSG)

As a part, the Father has designed you to need the other parts in His body to fulfil His purposes for you. Calling and connection go together. I have a friend who was working in a big bank. He was new to the job and knew God had put him there as a difference maker. But he also knew he was a part of the body. He knew he would make more of a difference if he was connected to those other parts. But he didn't know any other followers of Jesus in his workplace.

He began to pray with others in his local church body. They asked the Father to lead him to other believers at his work. They kept praying and a few weeks later, he met the first one by the coffee machine. The two of them agreed to meet to pray together during a lunch break each week. A few weeks later another dozen had somehow heard about it and joined them. They continued to pray and take the opportunities the Father gave them. A few months later, one of them was asked to write an article for the company magazine. That led to an opening to run a course for people in the company who were interested in exploring faith.

Fast forward some months and there were more than a hundred believers across three different sites nationally, connected by the company intranet. They prayed together and encouraged each other to bring God's life and kingdom to their workplace. My friend then moved on to run conferences across the nation. He wanted to help other parts of God's body get connected in the workplace for mutual encouragement and maximum kingdom impact. It's an incredible example of 'one part' knowing the power of being connected to the other parts.

PONDER
Spend a few moments dreaming with Jesus about what you'd like to see happen (and play a part in) where God has planted you.

PRAY
Talk to Him about it. Ask Him to show you who you might pray about it with if you're not doing that already.

READ: Hebrews 10:23-25

This is not the time to pull away and neglect meeting together, as some have formed the habit of doing, because we need each other! (MSG)

Have you ever watched a lion chasing its next meal on the plains of Africa? Some of the wildlife footage we have access to is not just amazing to watch, but a graphic picture of spiritual principles played out in the natural world. The lions seem to go after the animal that gets separated from the rest of the herd. Once a wildebeest lags behind, it's more vulnerable to attack than if it's protected in the middle of the pack.

In an age that celebrates individualism and independence, Jesus' plan for His daughters is radical. Each of us, as a part, needs the rest of the body for our own protection. Without it, we're vulnerable. Peter says the enemy prowls around like a roaring lion looking for someone to devour (1 Peter 5:8). He's looking for opportunities to weaken our faith, sabotage our confidence in God, cool down our love for Jesus and harden our hearts to the family of God and His purposes. We become vulnerable when we become separated from the church. The writer of Hebrews is blunt: 'We need each other, so don't stop meeting together.'

What kind of connection do you have with other parts of the body of Christ? Is it a consistent connection? Is it committed? And is it close? Do you need others in His body for strength and encouragement, for comfort and guidance, and for wisdom and healing in your life? And do you value those other parts? Or can you get by without them? Would your life not look much different if you were separated from His body? Friend, there are Facebook connections and face-to-face connections, and this verse is about the latter. They are sometimes more inconvenient, but they're what God wants for us. There are a pile of blessings Jesus will only give us through face-to-face relationships with other parts of His body.

PONDER
How have you experienced the protection of the body when you've been vulnerable to attack?

PRAY
Thank Jesus that His body is part of His design for your wellbeing. Thank Him for those He's used to bless your heart and life.

READ: Ephesians 4:14-16

As each part does its own special work, it helps the other parts grow, so that the whole body is healthy and growing and full of love. (NLT)

We can grow older and we can grow up. The first is unavoidable, the second is optional. To become all God has designed you to be, you need the 'special work' of others.

When you need comforting, He wants to throw His arms around you using the arms of another. When you're afraid, He wants to put courage into you through the words of another. When you're losing hope, He wants to remind you how He sees your future through the faith of another. When you've lost your way, He wants to bring you back through the wisdom of another. When you're in danger, He wants to warn you through the challenge of another and when you feel ashamed, He wants to lift that off you through the acceptance of another.

All kinds of good self-help books might tell us the right things to do. They promise that if we do what they say, we'll grow and our lives will change. But our Father who knows us, says we need more than that. He says we need His power in us, which we have through the Holy Spirit, and His presence at work for us through other parts of His body. We need others who will speak openly and honestly into our lives. People who know us so they can really love the real us. And that's only possible when we reveal what's really going on in our hearts and lives.

Do you have other parts of the body in your life who know about your fears, your hang-ups and your failures? People who God wants to use to help you grow? You don't need many, but you need a few. The risk of revealing our heart takes courage, but courage paves the way for life-changing connections.

PONDER
Do you have anybody in the body who knows about your fears, your hang-ups and your failures?

PRAY
If the answer is 'yes', thank the Father for them and for the blessing they are to you. If the answer is 'no', ask Him to show you whether that is to do with your fear of revealing your heart? Ask Him to give you courage to reveal something small of your heart to someone this week.

READ: Ephesians 4:31-32
Lay aside bitter words, temper tantrums, revenge, profanity, and insults. But instead be kind and affectionate toward one another. Has God graciously forgiven you? Then graciously forgive one another in the depths of Christ's love. (TPT)

So often the harsh words we speak are a result of pain we've experienced. Many people (myself included) have been deeply wounded by other parts of the family of God who were meant to be part of our healing and growth. The sense of betrayal can be huge. However, although the Father cares deeply about our pain and weeps with us, He doesn't throw up His hands and say, 'You know what, I don't blame you for not wanting to be a part of My weak, imperfect body. So say what you like and go it alone with your podcasts, worship music and closest friends and I'll bless you!'

He tenderly says what's written above to us. He says, 'Daughter, forgive them as I've graciously forgiven you.' That doesn't mean you have to trust those same people again with your heart. But it does mean you have to forgive them from your heart, so the words that come out of your mouth (the overflow of your heart) change.

PUSH IN

– Look at the five types of words listed in the first sentence. Are any of them relevant to you?

– Invite the Holy Spirit to show you if there is anybody from your past church experience that you need to forgive. Take note of anybody that pops into your mind.

– Tell Jesus how they've wounded you and why you feel so hurt. Ask Him to show you how He feels about what happened.

– Tell Him you want to give Him your pain and let go of any anger. Ask Him to help you forgive that person/those people. Imagine yourself with that person, walking towards Jesus. Hand them over to Him. Tell Jesus that you want to leave them with Him so you can be free. Walk away.

– Thank Him He has forgiven you. Ask Him to give you a new love for His body, despite all its imperfection.

READ: Romans 12:9-18
Don't just pretend to love others. Really love them. (MSG)

PUSH IN

Grab a pen. Paul is speaking to all parts of the body here, giving us a list of practical instructions as to how to make sure our connection to each other is one that honours the Father of the family and blesses others. Note down his main instructions, imagining he's writing to you.

– Circle any of them that surprise you.

– Circle any of them that seem unrealistic.

– Which one do you personally find most challenging?

– Why do you think this matters so much to Jesus?

Talk to Jesus. Be honest with Him about any struggles you have loving other members of His body. Ask Him if there is any stumbling block in your heart that's preventing His love flowing from you to others in His body in the way this passage describes.

Then, ask the Holy Spirit to speak to you, showing you if there's anything He wants you to do in response to what you've read. Spend a few moments waiting for Him to speak to you.

Pray about what He shows you and any decision you may need to make. Ask Him to give you a new, supernatural love for His body.

READ: John 1:9-18

No one has ever seen God but the one and only Son, who is Himself God and is in closest relationship with the Father, has made Him known.

God is a Father. He's powerful and He's Lord of all, but He's also a kind and loving Father who has always wanted to be known. We're made in His image, and the reason we want to be known is because He wants to be known. His desire from the beginning has always been relationship with the humans He's made. And relationship hinges on being known. God has always wanted to share His purposes and plans for the earth and work them out, but with people who know Him. Jesus came to give us back what Adam and Eve threw away – this privilege.

Friend, have you made knowing Him your highest goal? Look at what John says in the opening chapter of his book. Jesus came to make the Father known. Not to make His existence known, but to make His heart and nature known. We've dipped our toes in the water of His identity, of who He says He is and what He's like, but there is so much more. Just like in any friendship or relationship, the journey of knowing continues. But let's remember, it's never an automatic one, but an intentional one. There are some people who've known me for years and don't know me any better now than when we first met!

In Hosea 6:6 (NLT) God says to His people, 'I want you to know Me more than I want burnt offerings.' Hear His heart again today. He wants you to know Him as a Father more than He wants any other response from you. So when you read the Bible, look for His heart in what you read, not just His ways. Ask Him why He says what He says or does what He does. Pray and seek Him with all your heart and He says you'll find Him. And find people who know Him and hang out with them. Knowing Him changes everything, just as being known changes everything.

PONDER

Re-read Hosea 6:6 and the verse above and reflect on them. What do they mean for you?

PRAY

Thank Jesus for giving you the chance to know the Father and for making Him known to you. Ask Him to increase your hunger to know Him better. Ask Him to show you anything He wants you to do to allow that hunger to grow.

READ: Lamentations 3:22-23
His mercies begin afresh each morning. (NLT)

Mercy is a beautiful thing and mercy defines the heart of God. Without mercy, we couldn't experience the love of God and without mercy, we can't walk in freedom. Mercy means not getting the punishment we deserve. It doesn't mean not getting a pay packet when you deserve one after a month's work, it means not getting points on your license when you deserve them. It means not getting the treatment we deserve, because of Jesus.

The Father is merciful, but we experience His mercy when we become aware we need it. Any sense of entitlement or ignorance or blaming others prevents us from receiving mercy. The prodigal son was off doing his thing and enjoying how it was panning out. He didn't realise he needed mercy until he wanted to return home and benefit from the love of the father he'd publicly humiliated. Only then did he face the fact that what he deserved was to be rejected and punished.

The Father longs to be merciful to us each day. He doesn't want any of us living in fear of payback for anything we've done. His mercy never runs out; the cross is a fountain of mercy that will never dry up. There's no point at which He'll ever say to you, 'Sorry darling, I've shown you mercy for long enough, now you get what you deserve; you need to learn.' But to experience His mercy, we have to admit we need it. Which means facing up to our mistakes and accepting responsibility for the bad choices we make, whether they're deliberate or not.

The Father wants you to depend on His mercy for you, day in, day out. He wants you to come to Him, expecting Him to show you mercy because of who He is. He doesn't want us stewing on our sin or our struggles but to expect anything and everything from Him.

PONDER
Where is the Father showing you mercy in your life at the moment? Ask Him to show you if you're not sure.

PAUSE
Learn this short verse and turn it into prayer; keep reminding yourself of it during today.

READ: Luke 15:25-31
The older brother became angry and refused to go in.

Have you ever found yourself feeling disillusioned with the Father? I'll be honest and say I've wrestled with disillusionment at times. But I've realised it's part of my journey into more of His love. In those times the Holy Spirit has decided an illusion I've had about Him needs 'dissing'. As I look in my rear view mirror, no matter what the circumstances that provoked the disillusionment, I always find He never let me down or stopped loving me or providing for me in the way I needed, despite how it felt at the time.

The journey of learning to trust the Father more fully requires the Holy Spirit to 'diss' some of the illusions we have about Him. That's what Jesus was doing to those who were listening to Him tell this story. Who expected the father not to try to persuade his reckless son to stay? Who expected him to give the young man his inheritance so he could destroy it and himself? Who expected him to count the moments from then until his boy came back? Who expected him to run out to him to welcome him home? Who expected him not to make him pay and teach him a lesson? Who expected him to give him back his position and power in the family? And who expected him to throw a party to celebrate?

No one. Even the older brother. He became angry in his disillusion. Friend, the Father won't always do what we expect. Not because He's unpredictable and unstable but because our expectations of Him are limited by our human understanding and experiences. His heart for you is bigger than you imagine, His love for you is deeper than you know, His affection for you is stronger than you've experienced and His purposes for you are better than you think. But it doesn't always look that way.

If you're disillusioned with Him right now in any way, be honest with Him about it. He can take it, so let Him. But trust He's somehow leading you towards a deeper understanding of who He is as your perfect Father.

PAUSE

Do you need to be honest with the Father about anything you're disillusioned by? Talk to Him about it. Then spend a few moments in silence and ask Him to help you know His affection for you today.

READ: Psalm 145:8-13

The Lord is good to all; He has compassion on all He has made. (NLT)

Whether you're a fan of change or not, everything in this world changes, from the weather, to the elasticity of our skin and all things in between. The only thing that's unchanging is the Father's nature and His heart towards us. David wrote these words about God a thousand years before Jesus told His story about the Father. But they both describe His heart for us as being full of compassion.

Compassion isn't something we meet on an everyday basis. And yet it's something we all need, especially when we're hurting. So often, the world offers us indifference or judgement or advice or even sympathy. But compassion is something completely different. It's the feeling of being moved in your heart by someone's predicament, combined with a decision to help them at your own expense because you can't leave them the way they are. A compassionate heart doesn't distinguish between those who've brought their trouble on themselves and those who're struggling because of circumstances beyond their control.

The Father knows your weaknesses. He sees your past, your mistakes and He understands your struggles. He knows the wounds you've inflicted on yourself, the wounds you've inflicted on others as well as the wounds that others, and life, have inflicted on you. And He has compassion on you, friend. Today and every day. His love for us is a compassionate love rather than conditional on our accomplishments and achievements. Don't let the enemy lie to you that the Father is indifferent to your pain, your struggles or your stress or your sin. He feels your pain and runs towards you, like the father runs in this story, longing to embrace you, help you and restore you.

PAUSE

What particular wounds and weaknesses are you conscious of at the moment? Close your eyes and imagine yourself, His daughter, walking towards the Father. See Him running towards you. Feel His arms surround you and let His compassion touch your heart today. Thank Him that His love for you is based on His compassion, not conditional on anything you do or don't do.

READ: Luke 15:20-24

Quick. Bring a clean set of clothes and dress him. Put the family ring on his finger and sandals on his feet. (MSG)

The Father is not interested in keeping you small. He has a bigger life planned for you, no matter what your past.

This is possibly the most scandalous moment in this story. The son had been cruel to his dad. In asking for his inheritance he'd wished him dead, publicly humiliating him as well as privately sticking the knife in. The betrayal was off the charts. Social media would have had so much to say. Not only does the father welcome him home with open arms, he then gives him a makeover, and includes the family jewellery.

The significance of the outfit is huge. The father was demonstrating to everyone that he wasn't going to make his son pay with his future for what he'd done. He was going to treat him as if it had never happened and restore his authority. He was going to trust the one who'd proved untrustworthy, and give him a significant assignment in the family business. It's scandalous! Which is why it can be so hard for us to accept that the Father treats us in the same, scandalous way.

The Father doesn't have a problem with doing the things we think are impossible. He loves to stretch our limited thinking and smash through our assumptions about what He wants to do with us. Without the ring on your finger, you can't do much, whatever you think; you'll never be good enough. It's not about what you think you can do, or deserve or don't deserve to do. With that ring on your finger you can do whatever He wants you to do and calls you to do. Make sure the dreams you have are His dreams for you and not yours for you. If they're not, they're not big enough for a daughter of Heaven. Don't settle for small. He doesn't.

PONDER

What, if anything, do you believe may disqualify you from the Father's purposes for you? How do these verses speak in to that? Do you need to ask Him to enlarge your dreams with His?

PRAY

Confess any doubts you've had, thank God for His mercy and kindness towards you and for the ring He has put on your finger. Talk to Him about any dreams you have.

RE-READ: Luke 15:11-31

PUSH IN

Take some time to reflect again on this powerful story that Jesus tells to help us see the Father more clearly.

– Which of the two brothers do you find it easiest to identify with?

– Do you live with a sense that there are certain standards for you to live up to or certain things you must do to be more acceptable to God? What are they?

– Which aspect of the Father's behaviour surprises you most?

– Which aspect of the Father's nature would you most like to experience more of?

– How is He asking you to respond today?

Jot it down if it helps and talk to Him about it.

RE-READ: John 1:18
**No one has ever seen God, but the One and Only Son, who is Himself
God and is in closest relationship with the Father, has made Him known.**

PUSH IN

Look back at the contents page and remind yourself of the different dimensions of the Father's nature that we've looked at. He is beautiful, like a diamond, and there are many more facets of His identity to explore. Jesus has made Him known, but knowing Him is part of this journey of a lifetime. The more we know Him and His heart for us, the more confident we are as His daughters and the more effectively we partner with Him and reveal Him to His world.

– Repeat the word 'Father', or the word 'Abba', a few times and become aware of His presence with you.

– Spend some time reflecting on what you know of the Father.

– Praise Him for how He's revealed Himself to you. Praise Him for the different aspects of His heart that He's shown you. Thank Jesus for making the Father known to you and for the history you have with Him. Thank the Father for the dimensions of His identity that are particularly precious to you in this season of your life. Tell Him what they are.

– Let your longing to know Him better rise from the deepest place in your heart and put it into words.

READ: Matthew 17:1-6
This is My dearly loved Son, the constant focus of My delight. Listen to Him!
(TPT)

You are first and foremost, now and always, a daughter. So it deserves a second week! The more we're convinced that this is the core truth that defines us, the more secure, the less defensive and the more courageous we become. Jesus has many dimensions to His identity. He's the Bread of Life, Light of the World, Saviour, Redeemer, Healer, Deliverer, Resurrection and more. They all point to who He is. But when the Father spoke audibly about Jesus, which He did twice, He referred to Him in only one way: as His beloved Son. That was what mattered most.

We've explored a number of different aspects of our identity in this book. They are all the result of being His daughter and they point to how we've been remade by the power and life of the Holy Spirit. It's true on our worst days and our best days. It's true whether we're under the duvet or standing on a platform. It's true whether we're in the operating theatre or in prison. It's true whether we're awake or asleep. It's true whether we feel it or not, and whether we believe it or not.

The great news is, since you can't change the fact that you're a daughter, you can't fail at being a daughter. We can't become more of a daughter or less of a daughter. We can only become more confident that the Father will always love us and care for us because we're His. We grow our confidence when we spend time with Him, *and* as we intentionally turn to Him throughout the day. And we can do that in so many ways. Taking a moment to whisper His name. Turning aside to tell Him about our trouble. Pausing to thank Him that He's with us. Stopping to ask what He wants to say to us. Being still to tell Him we love Him. Calling a promise to mind. Looking to bless Him by loving the one in front of us. If walking as a son was the key to how Jesus lived and to what He did, walking as a daughter will always be the key to how we live and what we do.

PAUSE

Spend a few moments reflecting on the truth that you're *His* daughter. Let it sink in a bit deeper. Set an alarm on your phone to go off a number of times during the day today, and when it does, turn your gaze to Him in one of the ways mentioned above.

READ: John 5:16-23
I tell you the truth, the Son can do nothing by Himself. He does only what He sees the Father doing. (NLT)

The ultimate picture of what it looks like to live as a child of God is partnership. Separation and doing life independently from the Father was the tragedy of the Garden. Connection and doing life together is the dream of Heaven. The cross made that dream possible again. Jesus showed us how to live as God's child with a hand in His. And He sums it up here. He only ever did what He saw the Father doing.

Why did He say He couldn't do anything by Himself? Does that mean if He'd tried to walk on water and God didn't want Him to, He would have sunk? Does that mean God was pulling invisible strings and Jesus was just a puppet, with no thoughts or desires or feelings or opinions of His own? No – He was fully human like you and me. What He was saying was this: 'I can't be a true Son with every fibre of My being and also follow My own dreams and desires the way I want.'

The Father only wants to increase your influence in this world. He wants to release Heaven on earth through you, as He did through Jesus. He's empowered us to live ordinary lives with an extraordinary impact. The same power is in us that was in Jesus. That's the potential all His girls carry. The kingdom is *within* us. But His power is released in us when we swap our own desires and opinions for His. Verse 20 says, 'The Father loves the Son and shows Him everything He is doing.' That's what the Father wants to do with us. But that means me letting go of my methods and being willing to learn His. Yep, that's easier said than done. But it doesn't change the fact that He wants to walk through each day with us. Friend, He wants to show you what He's doing, and He wants to partner with you; in your home, in your workplace, in your gym, in the studio. Wherever you are. He needs your attention and your availability. Has He got it?

PAUSE

Picture what your day looks like today and imagine yourself walking through it with your hand in the Father's. This is how He wants to enjoy partnering with you today. Ask Him to open your eyes to what He's doing. Throughout the day, look for what He wants to show you, pray regularly for His kingdom to come through you. Be open to the promptings of His Spirit.

READ: Matthew 4:1-11
If you are the Son of God, jump off! (NLT)

Jesus didn't escape tough times, and neither do we. Being a precious daughter of the Almighty One doesn't give us a get-out-of-jail-free card. Testing times come. When they do, what really gets tested (as well as our patience, hope, strength and courage) is our confidence in who we are and whose we are. Am I really God's daughter? Am I really seen and known and loved by Him? Does He really hear me and is He really going to come through for me because I'm His?

Jesus was at breaking point. No food for forty days. In the desert. Alone. One of those elements would be more than enough to wipe me out, let alone all three. And when He was at rock bottom, the doubts came: 'Do something to prove you're the Son of God.' 'Take matters into your own hands and take the kingdoms, just in case the Father doesn't give them to you.' Who knows what other things He wrestled with in His wilderness. But His biggest battle was fighting to believe He was chosen, called, seen and heard. And that God would prove it by coming through for Him.

Friend, in the middle of some of your toughest times, don't be surprised when you face similar questions: 'Am I chosen?' 'Am I called?' 'Am I seen?' 'Am I heard?' 'Will the Father keep His promises to me?' 'Will He come through for me?' Heaven is sometimes silent – but only for a season. That's when we get to find out what we believe. When there's nothing else to show for it. The Father loves you, nothing's changed. He's close to you and He's preparing you, just as He was with Jesus. You have the same power in you as Jesus had. Pour out your heart to Him and cry out to Him. And expect Him to get you through it as He got Jesus through it.

PONDER
What questions are you wrestling with currently? What has the Father told you in the past that relates to your wrestle?

PRAY
Ask the Father what He's doing in your life at the moment. What's He asking you to do in response? Note down anything He says and pour out your heart to Him.

READ: Romans 8:12-17

Now we call Him, 'Abba, Father.' For his Spirit joins with our spirit to affirm that we are God's children. (NLT)

Life works when we personally know and experience God as a good Father who's passionate in His unconditional love for us. The desire in our heart to know and experience more of His love and affection for us is more than matched by His desire for us to know His heart for us. And for that very reason, He's given us His own Spirit to make it possible. The Holy Spirit is like the router in your home, which gives you access to the online world. He is in you to enable you to connect with Heaven.

'Abba' is the Aramaic word for 'Dad' that a child would use in its family set up. It's a personal term of trusting affection, not a cold, formal way of addressing a father. Without the Holy Spirit, we can't know the Father personally or intimately. And the less we know Him like that, the more likely we are to assume He'll reject us or judge us. But if we let the Holy Spirit have His way, He helps us to experience the Father's love. He loves to reassure us we're daughters who delight Him.

The Holy Spirit is the One who helps us call God 'Father'. The more we use that term, the more He reminds us we *are* His children, and the more convinced we become of His presence with us. But the Holy Spirit also releases this cry of 'Father' in us as a cry of longing. It's a way of telling God, 'I know you're my Father and I thank you that you are, but I need your love. I need to feel it today, not just know that it's there. I need to experience you as Father.'

The Father is so extraordinarily kind, that even our response to Him is empowered by Him. Why not invite the Holy Spirit to move in you today and release that cry of longing in you? To know Him better. And to know more of Him in more of you.

PRAY

Spend a few moments thanking the Holy Spirit that He is in you and wants to reveal more of the Father's love to you. Thank Him for all that He's already shown you and all that He's enabled you to experience. Then repeat the words 'Abba, Father' a number of times, slowly. Let the Holy Spirit stir up your desire and love for HIm.

READ: Psalm 131

I am humbled and quieted in Your presence. Like a contented child who rests on its mother's lap... (TPT)

However long we've been following Jesus and however much we know, we're still His children. No amount of experience under our belts or achievements to our name ever changes that. Life has a habit of growing us up, but growing down is the way of the kingdom. In this psalm, David (the mighty warrior and successful king of Israel) is describing his experience in God's presence. It was like being a contented child curled up in its mother's lap. Isn't that a beautiful picture?

There's a difference between being child-like and being childish. Despite being a powerful ruler of a nation, David says in the previous verse that he's chosen to let go of stuff. Stuff that's too much for his heart, too big for his brain or just beyond his pay grade! No wonder then that his soul is 'humbled' and his heart can be 'quiet' and still in the Father's presence. A child snuggled up on a parent's lap is a powerful picture of peace and simplicity. It seems to say, 'All is well in my world because my world is in the hands of the One who made the world.'

God welcomes you to His lap every day. He invites you to curl up, to snuggle in and to find peace and contentment in His strength and love. But like David, this only becomes our experience when we let go of our need to wrestle, to understand, to find answers or to remain in control. Child-like faith looks like this; a confidence in the Father's heart and a willingness to believe anything He says. A strong, responsible daughter has this child-like confidence. She knows she doesn't have to do anything to earn her place on her Dad's lap, or fight for her position in the world.

PONDER

Is your personal prayer time with God as simple as being able to curl up on His lap when you need to? How is the Father inviting you to become a bit more child-like today?

PAUSE

Re-read the verse above a few times, slowly, over yourself. Invite the Holy Spirit to speak to you about the Father's desire to draw you near and be your safe place. Is there anything you are wrestling with, trying to figure out, or wanting to control that He wants you to let go of today? Talk to Him.

READ: Romans 8:31-39

This passage is the last part of a chapter which talks about being children of God and life in His Spirit. It's His Spirit which marks us out as His daughters. These verses are like a magnifying glass, helping us to see more clearly and get in touch with the Father's love. A love so extra-ordinary that He gave up His own Son to have a personal relationship with us.

PUSH IN

– Read these verses slowly, as many times as you need to. Ask the Holy Spirit to give you a better revelation of the depth of the Father's love for you as you read them.

– Which words stand out to you? Note down any phrases that seem to have particular significance for you today.

– Ask the Holy Spirit to show you one thing you can do going forwards, to live more aware of His love for you.

– Spend some time delighting in the Father and His love for you. Open up your heart to Him again now and let His presence fill the dry and weary places. You are His treasured daughter, the apple of His eye. Receive His love and express yours back to Him.

PUSH IN

– Spend some time writing down what it means for you to be a daughter of God. Include what you find challenging and what you find comforting.

– Reflect on the way Jesus lived as a son. How would you like your life to be more like His? Talk to the Father about it.

– Ask the Holy Spirit to show you any mindset He wants to deal with today that's preventing you from growing in confidence as God's beloved daughter. Exchange it for the one He wants to give you.

READ: 1 Corinthians 13:13
Now I know in part; then I shall know fully, even as I am fully known.

The journey of becoming confident in who we are and whose we are is a journey of a lifetime. But like all journeys, the more steps we take, the further we go. You may still 'know in part', even though you are fully known by your Father, but you know much more about who you are than you did! The enemy will always try and attack our identity, like he did with Jesus. But the more confidently we hold firm to who God says we are, and who He says He is, the more we're able to live in freedom, with passion and purpose. I pray that is increasingly your experience.

PUSH IN

– Spend a few moments reflecting on who God says you are in His word. Write down as many 'I ams' as you can think of.

– Add to the list who you are according to any prophetic words you've had.

– Which truths about yourself does God want you to focus on in this season? How does He want you to continue to renew your mind so your confidence continues to grow?

– Create three declarations from what you've written about yourself that you can speak out over the coming days.

THANKS

Where do I start on a page like this? I'm not a fan of long Oscar speeches, but rarely is one piece of work due to one person. I'm thankful to those who encouraged me to write this, and to those who agreed to road-test it along the way. And a special thanks to Abi Lynch who, despite crossing the Atlantic during the process, has made it a bit tighter than it would have been without her!

The twists and turns of life have meant it's been a complicated journey to get this book into print, but a huge thanks to the friends who have kept cheering me on and believing in me. You have lent me your strength. And I'm always so grateful to those who pray. Thank you for continuing to hold me up from your knees.

Lastly, I want to thank my amazing family whose relentless encouragement and enthusiasm has been part of the wind beneath my wings. And my Father, for breathing His resurrection life on me, and enabling someone who's not a completer-finisher in the best of times, to cross the finishing line!

To order a copy for a friend, or to share your feedback with Hils, visit www.known.me.uk. She'd love to hear from you.